CONTEMPORARY ISSUES IN THE EARLY YEARS

CONTEMPORARY ISSUES IN THE EARLY YEARS

WORKING COLLABORATIVELY FOR CHILDREN

SECOND EDITION

Edited by
Gillian Pugh

Paul Chapman Publishing in association with
the National Children's Bureau

P·C·P
Paul Chapman
Publishing Ltd

**NATIONAL
CHILDREN'S
BUREAU**
Early Childhood Unit

Paul Chapman Publishing Ltd
144 Liverpool Road
London
N1 1LA

British Library Cataloguing in Publication Data

Contemporary issues in the early years: working
collaboratively for children – 2nd ed.
1. Education, Elementary 2. Education, Primary 3.
Early childhood education
I. Pugh, Gillian
372.1'9

ISBN 1 85396 323 2

Typeset by Anneset, Weston-super-Mare
Printed and bound in Great Britain

BCDEFGH 987

CONTENTS

LIST OF ABBREVIATIONS

AMA	Association of Metropolitan Authorities
BAECE	British Association for Early Childhood Education
CACHE	Council for Awards in Child Care and Education
CATE	Committee for the Accreditation of Teacher Education
CRE	Commission for Racial Equality
DFEE	Department for Education and Employment
DH	Department of Health
EC	European Commission
ECEF	Early Childhood Education Forum
EOC	Equal Opportunities Commission
ERA	Education Reform Act
ESAC	Education, Science and Arts Committee
EU	European Union
EYCG	Early Years Curriculum Group
HMI	Her Majesty's Inspectorate
IIU	Independent inspection unit
LA	Local authority
LEA	Local education authority
LMS	Local management of schools
MSC	Manpower Services Commission
NCB	National Children's Bureau

NCC	National Consumer Council
NCMA	National Childminding Association
NCVQ	National Council for Vocational Qualifications
NFER	National Foundation for Educational Research
NNEB	National Nursery Examination Board
NVQ	National Vocational Qualification
OFSTED	Office for Standards in Education
OMEP	World Organization for Early Childhood Education
PGCE	Postgraduate Certificate in Education
PLA	Preschool Learning Alliance
PPA	Preschool Playgroups Association
TEC	Training and Enterprise Council
TTA	Teacher Training Agency
SAT	Standard Assessment Task
SCAA	School Curriculum and Assessment Authority
VOLCUF	Voluntary Organizations Liaison Council for Under Fives

BIOGRAPHICAL DETAILS
OF CONTRIBUTORS

Gillian Pugh is Chief Executive of the Thomas Coram Foundation for Children. Until early in 1997, she was director of the Early Childhood Unit at the National Children's Bureau, a position she had held since the Unit was set up in 1986. She has worked extensively with central and local government on the development of a policy for young children, and has published books and training materials on policy development, on coordination of services, on curriculum, on parental involvement and on parent education. She was a member of the Rumbold Committee on the education of children aged three to five, of the RSA Start Right enquiry and of the Audit Commission study of early education. She set up and chaired the Early Childhood Education Forum and was a founder member of the Parenting Education and Support Forum.

Peter Moss is Senior Research Officer at the Thomas Coram Research Unit and Co-ordinator of the European Commission Childcare Network. He has worked at Thomas Coram for over twenty years, specializing in work on families with young children, services for them and work-family issues. He has co-ordinated the European Childcare Network since 1986.

Peter Elfer is Senior Development Officer at the Early Childhood Unit of the National Children's Bureau. He qualified as a field social worker in 1975 and since then has worked as a practitioner and manager in social services in the voluntary and statutory sectors. He joined the Early Childhood Unit in 1987 where he has been examining the implications of the Children Act for services for young children. He is currently working on a three year research and development project looking at the care and learning of children under three in early childhood centres.

Dorothy Wedge is County Adviser, Services to Under Fives for Cambridgeshire. Originally qualified as a social worker, she has worked with young children and their families in a number of capacities – nursery teaching and pre-school home visiting in London and social services under fives adviser in Norfolk. She has been the holder of her current post, jointly funded and managed by social services and education, since it was established in 1988.

Gerison Lansdown is currently director of the Children's Rights Office, and formerly of the Children's Rights Development Unit. She has published a number of articles and books on the subject of children's rights, and is currently on the management committees of Family Rights Group and Child Poverty Action Group.

Tricia David is Professor of Early Childhood Education at Canterbury Christ Church college. Prior to this she lectured at Warwick University for almost ten years; was a headteacher in both nursery and primary schools; worked as a researcher on one of the large-scale DES-funded projects in the 'seventies; and taught in schools, adult and community education. Tricia's experience with the non-governmental organisation, l'Organisation Mondiale pour l'Education Prescolaire, as a recent UK President, has involved her in links with early years colleagues in many other countries and some of her publications reflect this international dimension. She is currently looking forward to becoming a grandmother.

Mary Jane Drummond is Tutor in Primary Education at the Cambridge Institute of Education. She has taught in infant and primary schools in Hackney and Sheffield, and during the 1970s was a member of the Schools Council Communication Skills in Early Childhood Project led by Joan Tough. She joined the Cambridge Institute in 1985 where she works on in-service courses for teachers and early years educators in East Anglia. Her interests include personal, social and moral education, and the emotional dimensions of education, particularly assessment and staff relationships.

Cathy Nutbrown has considerable experience of teaching young children and working with parents, teachers, nursery nurses and other early childhood educators in a range of group care and education settings. Her research interests include children's early learning and development, early literacy and its assessment and work with parents. For four years Cathy has been Vice President of OMEP (UK) (1991–1995). She is an honorary lecturer at the University of Sheffield and Development Officer for the University-LEA, REAL (Raising Early Achievement in Literacy) Project.

Dr. Iram Siraj-Blatchford is Senior Lecturer in Early Childhood Education at the Institute of Education, University of London. Her research interests include quality and equality in ECE, she is currently researching children's learning through making and designing. Her most recent books include, *Praxis Makes Perfect: Critical Educational Research for Social Justice*, Education Now Books, 1994 and *Educating the Whole Child: Cross-curricular Skills, Themes and Dimensions*, Open University Press, 1995 with John Siraj-Blatchford. She is President of the National Association of Nursery Centres and has had the fortune of teaching and learning from children 0–7.

Professor Sheila Wolfendale has been a primary school and remedial reading teacher, an educational psychologist in several LEAs and is currently Director of a Doctorate in Educational Psychology training programme at the University of East London. She has authored and edited many books, booklets, chapters, articles and handbooks on aspects of special needs, early years, and parental involvement. She was recently awarded a PhD by published works.

Janine Wooster is Special Educational Services Manager for North West Kent Education. She has previously been a teacher for children with special needs and worked for seven years as co-ordinator of the Pre-school Home Visiting Team for pupils with special needs in the London Borough of Newham.

Sue Griffin is Training Officer for the National Childminding Association (NCMA). She was previously Development Officer for the NCMA in south-west England, during which time she was seconded to the Working with Under Sevens Project to develop standards for National Vocational Qualifications. She has also had a long involvement with the playgroup movement, going from parent helper to chair of the Pre-school Playgroups Association.

Dorothy Selleck is a Senior Development Officer in the Early Childhood Unit of the National Children's Bureau. She has worked **with** children in nursery and infant schools, and **for** children as a consultant and as tutor in training institutions. She has contributed to the teaching and learning programmes for educators in the private, voluntary and statutory sectors. Dorothy has a special interest in how children learn from birth to the primary school. Her recent work has focused on continuity and progression in the curriculum within the context of constant and close relationships in early childhood centres.

Margy Whalley is Head of Pen Green Centre for Under Fives and Families in Corby. She taught in primary schools in this country before spending seven years as an early years/community development worker in Brazil and

Papua New Guinea. She has an MA in Community Education. Her current research interests are Management in Early Childhood settings. She's recently completed an eighteen month secondment to the Open University writing for the parents and under 8's course team. Her 'spare time' is spent being an external examiner, a school governor (of a secondary and a primary school), working for the local Labour Party and spending time with her wonderful teenage daughter – who would still like her to stop working and cook some proper meals.

John Rennie has recently retired from the Community Education Development Centre, the National Agency based in Coventry. He was the Director of CEDC from it's establishment in 1980. Before that he was an adviser then senior adviser in Coventry's Department of Education from 1971–1980, having earlier taught in secondary schools in Manchester and at Nottingham University.

Dr. Denise Hevey is Director of the Vocational Qualifications Centre at the Open University. She was previously involved in the development of a variety of courses in Health & Social Welfare including 'Child Abuse and Neglect' and 'Working with Children and Young People'. During 1989 and 1990 she was seconded to the Local Government Management Board to develop national occupational standards for work with young children and their families in preparation for the introduction of National Vocational Qualifications in Child Care & Education. She is a Chartered Psychologist, Fellow of the Institute of Personnel & Development and former President of the National Childminding Association. Her current role involves supporting the development and implementation of higher level NVQs, Core Skills and GNVQs through the Open University's course materials and assessment strategies.

Audrey Curtis was formerly a senior lecturer at the Institute of Education, University of London where she taught on higher degree courses. She has been a playgroup worker, has taught early years and special needs, and trained teachers in initial and in-service courses. She has been a consultant to UNICEF and the British Council, and is currently European President of the World Organisation for Early Childhood Education (OMEP). Since retiring from the Institute of Education she is working as an External Verifier for the Council for Awards for Children's Care and Education (CACHE) on NVQ and STA programmes.

NATIONAL CHILDREN'S BUREAU

The National Children's Bureau was established as a registered charity in 1963. Our purpose is to identify and promote the interests of all children and young people and to improve their status in a diverse society.

We work closely with professionals and policy-makers to improve the lives of all children but especially those affected by family instability, young children, children with special needs or disabilities, and those suffering the effects of poverty and deprivation.

We collect and disseminate information about children and promote good practice in children's services through research, policy and practice development, publications, seminars, training and an extensive library and information service.

The Bureau works in partnership with Children in Wales and Children in Scotland.

The Early Childhood Unit was established in 1986 as a national centre for advice, consultancy, training and information on current practice, thinking and research in the early years field. It aims:

(1) to raise awareness of the needs of young children;
(2) to improve policy and service provision for children across social services, health, education and the independent sector;
(3) to support the raising of professional standards of practice.

INTRODUCTION

Gillian Pugh

A willingness to devote adequate resources to the care of children is the hallmark of a civilized society, as well as an investment in our future.

(Mia Kellmer Pringle, 1975, p. 148)

The best preparation for being a happy or useful man or woman is to live fully as a child.

(Plowden Report, CACE, 1967, para. 506)

This is a completely revised edition of a book first published in 1992, a book about meeting the needs of young children: children who are powerless and vulnerable, but children who are intensely curious, energetic, and instinctive and enthusiastic learners. And it is about the environment and the experiences that we offer to children: about equality of opportunity for all children, about respecting and valuing children, about carefully observing children and planning how to meet their needs as individuals now and in the future. It is also about the relationships between adults and children, about children's rights and how they can be met, and about relationships between the adults – parents and educators – who work with and care for children. It is about working across boundaries, boundaries between parents and professionals, and between 'carers' and 'educators', and finding time to care for each other as well as for our children.

1

But because how we view childhood and treat children is a reflection of the values of the society we live in, the book is also about the context and the systems within which we live and work in the last five years of the twentieth century.

The book is written at a time of considerable change in welfare services in the United Kingdom. Major legislation in health, education and social services has changed both professional practice and its impact on children and their parents. The Children Act, implemented in 1991, has had far-reaching implications for local authorities who must provide services for 'children in need' and whose responsibilities for registering, inspecting and reviewing child care services have been increased. The Education Reform Act, through the introduction of the National Curriculum and processes of assessment, and through the devolution of responsibility for the financial management of schools to school governors, has had a considerable impact on even the youngest children in the school system, and on the curriculum of private and voluntary sector day nurseries and playgroups outside the education system. The more recent proposals for a system of vouchers for the parents of four-year-olds will have an, as yet, unknown impact on the quality and quantity of early education. Changes in the management and funding of the National Health Service are leading to new relationships between purchasers and providers of health services, and an uncertain future for community child health services.

In all these areas the enterprise culture and a market-forces approach to service provision are leading to new roles for local authorities, as they become regulators, inspectors and enablers of private and voluntary sector provision as well as, and sometimes instead of, providers of services themselves. Issues of 'quality assurance', 'performance criteria', 'consumer rights' and 'value for money' are on many agendas, but there are different agendas, and the rights and needs of children are not always the first consid-eration. For this is also a decade in which an increasing number of families with children in the UK have been living in poverty, without access to a basic standard of living that most citizens have come to expect as of right (Bradshaw, 1990).

Since it was established in 1986, the Early Childhood Unit has been involved with many of these changes at central and local government level. Focusing as it does on the needs of children across the boundaries of health, care and education, and working at the interface between research, policy and practice, the Unit has been very busy during this period. The legislation has led to intense debate amongst politicians, managers and practitioners, and the increasing demand from employers for women to return to work has led to unprecedented interest in the national press about the shortage of child care. In the early 1990s the establishment of the committee of inquiry by the Department of Education into the education of three- to five-year-olds chaired by Angela Rumbold and the development of national guidelines on good practice in day care, play-groups, out-of-school clubs and childminding fed into the Department of Health's consultation process on the Guidance accompanying the Children Act.

More recently, the Unit has contributed to the deliberations of the National Commission on Education (1993), to the Royal Society of Arts Start Right enquiry (Ball, 1994), and to the Audit Commission's review of nursery education (1996). As national interest in early education has grown, the Unit has also been actively involved in setting up the Early Childhood Education Forum which brings together the thirty-five main national organisations – statutory, voluntary and independent – in this field to speak with one voice on policies for young children. The Forum has also been working on the development of a national curriculum framework for use in all settings which provide for children from a few months to eight years (Early Childhood Education Forum, forthcoming).

These national developments have taken place in a context of growing understanding of how early childhood services are developing in Europe, and how governments elsewhere are responding to the needs of families to be able to balance work and family responsibilities. The work of the Early Childhood Unit is underpinned by a number of basic principles that reflect the rights of all children to good quality services that support their overall development within the context of their family. Four of these principles formed the starting point for *A Policy for Young Children: A Framework for Action* subscribed to by all the main agencies – statutory and voluntary – who work with or are concerned about the health, welfare and education of young children in Britain, and it is perhaps fitting that a book that reflects so many current developments in the early years field should start with these principles:

- that young children are important in their own right, and as a resource for the future;

- that young children are valued and their full development is possible only if they live in an environment which reflects and respects their individual identity, culture and heritage;

- that parents are primarily responsible for nurturing and supporting the development of their children and that this important role should be more highly valued by society;

- that central and local government have a duty, working in partnership with parents, to ensure that services and support are available for families; services that encourage children's cognitive, social, emotional and physical development; and meet parents' needs for support for themselves and day care for their children.

(National Children's Bureau, 1990, p. 1)

Embedded in these statements are values and principles that are central to all the chapters in this book. The resurgence of interest in day care and early education brings challenges as well as opportunities for those who work with young children. The contributors to this volume have been invited to explore some of the key issues that face early childhood practitioners, managers and policy-makers in the 1990s, as they attempt to keep their sights clearly on the needs of our youngest children. Central to almost every chapter is a clear value position, and a call for establishing explicit principles to underpin our work.

Just as the Under Fives Unit changed its name to Early Childhood Unit during 1991 to reflect these changes, so the contributors have taken an overall 'early years' brief (usually seen as the years 0–8) whilst concentrating on the years 0–5. Contributors have also taken the view that care and education for young children should be inseparable, and most support the view of the Rumbold Committee that

> Education for the under fives can happen in a wide variety of settings and can be supplied by a wide range of people. Some will be professional teachers; many will not . . . we have therefore used the term 'educator' throughout to describe an adult working with the under fives, unless our meaning is more limited.

(DES, 1990a, Introduction)

The renewed emphasis on integration or co-ordination is welcome, but is not without its dangers. Within the education system, nursery education is seen as the first stage in a continuous process of learning, and nursery teachers in the UK – unlike almost anywhere else in the world – are accorded similar status to other teachers. One of the dilemmas reflected in this book is that of horizontal versus vertical co-ordination: if the pull towards co-ordination of all under-fives services becomes too great, is there a corresponding weakening of the continuity between education before five and education after five? In striving to 'upgrade' all non-education nursery provision, is there a danger that all non-statutory services – including nursery education – will instead be downgraded? This is thrown into relief most vividly in Chapter 12 on training.

The book is in three parts – Policy, Practice and Training – all three of which are informed by the implications of recent research. The first four chapters are concerned principally with policy. Gillian Pugh reviews early childhood care and education in the UK within the context of recent legislation and developments at local level and, despite some encouraging trends, finds a continuing lack of coherence, commitment and resources.

Peter Moss draws on his experience as co-ordinator of the European Childcare Network to examine policy and recent trends in Europe. Peter Elfer and Dorothy Wedge examine the concept of quality, looking at the importance of the values inherent in any definitions of quality and questioning whether the framework provided by the Children Act is adequate for monitoring and supporting quality services. In a new chapter, Gerison Lansdown examines the implications of the UN Convention on the Rights of the Child for those who live and work with young children, with particular reference to children's right to participate in decisions that affect them.

Part 2 on practice in the early years includes five chapters on the quality of the experiences that we offer young children. Tricia David asks what we mean by curriculum in the early years, looking at the context and process of learning, at breadth and balance, and at continuity and progression within early years settings and in relation to the National Curriculum. Mary Jane Drummond and Cathy Nutbrown identify and discuss the key questions that face educators as they observe and assess children, a process that should always be central to planning for children's learning.

Although the central tenet of each chapter is that of equality of opportunity and a quality service that meets individual needs, three chapters look at specific issues. Iram Siraj-Blatchford looks at the impact of racism on children's identity and attitudes, at the potential offered by the Children Act for combating racism, and concludes with some specific suggestions for promoting racial equality, arguing that understanding cultural differences is not enough on its own. Sheila Wolfendale and Janine Wooster review developments in relation to young children with special needs in the context of legislation, research and practice, including a case study of practice in one local authority, and conclude that special needs in the early years is currently in receipt of more attention, resources and provision than at any other time, albeit in a somewhat haphazard way. Dorothy Selleck and Sue Griffin look at the particular needs of children under three, concentrating on children's needs for relationships with significant responsive adults, and for developmentally appropriate learning experiences.

Two chapters focus on relationships between adults who work with children. Margy Whalley describes the process of developing and supporting a multi-professional staff team, working with parents, volunteers and workers from other agencies. John Rennie examines why working with parents should be an integral part of early years provision and argues for training to support the development of appropriate skills and attitudes.

In the final chapter, Denise Hevey and Audrey Curtis confront the complex issue of training to work in the early years, looking at the skills, knowledge and understanding that are required and at recent developments in teacher training and in developing National Vocational Qualifications, and conclude with a number of alternative scenarios to take training forward.

Early childhood care and education are indeed at the crossroads. New directions in research, in practice and in legislation offer early years educators the opportunity to build on their skills, their commitment and their enthusiasm and to ensure that all children have access to services that meet their individual needs. Young children, however, are not a national priority, and politicians may have other priorities and make other choices. Educators, too, have choices – about how they assess children and plan the curriculum, about how they exercise their power over children, about how they work with parents and other educators. If we are to seize the opportunities offered today, then surely we must work collaboratively, travel together and speak loudly and with one voice.

PART 1
POLICY

1

A POLICY FOR EARLY CHILDHOOD SERVICES?

Gillian Pugh

Within the context of developments outlined briefly in the Introduction, this chapter seeks to assess what progress, if any, has been made in the last ten years in developing a national policy on child care and early education to meet the needs of young children aged 0–8 and their families. It will outline eight areas that such a policy should address:

(1) an integrated national policy, ensuring equal access to services and supported by legislation and resources;
(2) an integrated policy at local level and the structures and systems to support such a policy;
(3) a range of flexible services to meet the needs of children and their parents;
(4) high quality services offering children an appropriate curriculum;
(5) information for parents;
(6) setting standards and monitoring quality;
(7) a rational system of training and support;
(8) adequate pay and conditions and improved status for early years educators.

The first three of these will be dealt with in most detail, as the rest are covered by other chapters in the book.

The Early Childhood Unit's initial review of services for under fives looked specifically at attempts to co-ordinate services traditionally provided by education, social services, health and the voluntary sector. The report reviewed the historical development of provision for under fives, and found a patchwork of fragmented and unco-ordinated services, showing wide variations between one part of the country and another, within the context of a 'low national commitment to developing and resourcing preschool services, and the absence of a national policy on what services should be provided, for whom and by whom' (Pugh, 1988, p. 80).

The Unit survey revealed a 'groundswell of interest amongst local authorities in rethinking provision, and in looking again at structures for planning and organizing services, but this in the face of low resourcing, seemingly intractable problems over vested interests between departments, and often no clear sense of direction as to the best way forward' (p. 81). The report concluded that 'The challenge now is for central government to provide an overall framework within which services can be developed flexibly at local level' (p. 81).

Some of the issues that such a policy should include formed the basis for the initial collaborative policy framework noted in the Introduction (National Children's Bureau, 1990), which in turn led to a study to assess what the costs of an integrated education and day care service might be and how these costs could be met (Holtermann, 1992). This study has just been revised in the light of recent changes (Holtermann, 1995), and the main findings are noted below.

The last three years have also seen the publication of a number of prestigious national reports and in mid-1995 the government's initiative to increase preschool education for four-year-olds. The two most notable national contributions to the call for a higher commitment to early childhood education have come from the National Commission on Education (1993), the first of whose seven goals was the development of a national strategy for early childhood education and child care, with specific targets for nursery education for all three- and four-year-olds; and the Royal Society of Arts whose *Start Right* report (Ball, 1994) called for high quality part-time nursery education for all children aged three to five, and for full time schooling to start at six. Although both these reports were strong in their support of nursery education, neither considered the need for an integrated approach to care and education.

The government's response to the growing demand for nursery education has been to announce some additional funding for the education of four-year-olds, but to make this funding available to parents through vouchers which can be redeemed in private, voluntary or local authority nurseries provided they reach nationally approved standards. Whilst the provision of some additional funding has been welcomed, the introduction of vouchers, which will largely be funded by removing money from local authorities who currently provide for some 85 per cent of four-year-olds, has been widely condemned. The value of the vouchers is insufficient to cover the existing costs of nursery education, and the scheme includes nothing for the setting up of new nurseries. It is feared it may reduce statutory provision particularly for three-year-olds, and that new provision will not be of adequate quality.

We now turn to the areas that should be addressed by a more coherent approach to early childhood services.

AN INTEGRATED NATIONAL POLICY

Whilst there is value in a diversity which can be sensitive to local needs, the current divisions between one form of service and another owe more to history and the professional jealousies of providers than to the needs of children and their families. It is now broadly accepted that in the early years in particular children's needs have to be seen as a whole and that services must respond to their social, emotional, physical and intellectual development. The starting point of a policy must therefore ensure that the underpinning principles, the aims and objectives, and the mechanisms for planning, delivering and managing services are developed in a co-ordinated way, drawing on the skills and expertise of parents and of all those who come to work with children from different professional backgrounds. If this were an easy challenge we would have made a great deal more progress than we have over the last thirty years. The obstacles have been well documented, and will be familiar to all early years practitioners who have tried to work across the traditional barriers. There will be different priorities between service providers, different ideologies, different boundaries – territorial and geographic, different training, different management and accounting systems, and even different vocabulary. We should not underestimate the difficulties of co-ordinating our approach, but in the interests of providing children with continuity and coherence and in making the most efficient use of scarce resources, then a co-ordinated policy, with mechanisms for joint planning, management and review, must surely be a first priority.

Trends in levels of provision

Services for children in the UK are variously described as a 'national disgrace' (Ball, 1994) or as offering parents a rich range and diversity from which to chose (Secretary of State for Education, 1994). The commitment in the 1972 White Paper to expand nursery education to accommodate 50 per cent of three-year-olds and 90 per cent of four-year-olds has never been implemented, although the new government initiative is intended to ensure that all four-year-olds have access to some form of education provision by 1997. Both this new initiative and the NCE and RSA reports, however, have neglected to address the crucial issue of day care. The number of mothers with children under five who are in employment is now approaching 50 per cent, and yet current statistics show how far short we still fall of a universal service. As can be seen from Table 1.1 showing current provision in England, there is still a very limited amount of full day care, particularly for children under three, and public investment in nursery education and day care remains limited. The figures show considerable increases in the percentage of children in private nurseries (numbers of places grew from 25,000 to 124,000 between 1985 and 1994) and with childminders; some increases in nursery education though all of this increase is part-time; and a slight decrease in playgroups. Comparisons with Europe show that we are still at the bottom of the league table in publicly funded day care and education (see Table 2.1, Chapter 2).

Table 1.1   Under fives in England: use of services 1975, 1985 and 1994

	1975	1985	1994
Places per 100 children 0–4:			
LA day nurseries	0.8	1.0	0.69
Private nurseries	0.8	0.8	3.83
Childminders	2.6	4.7	11.05
Places per 100 children 3–4			
Playgroups	23.3	33.8	31.33
Pupils as % of 3- and 4-year-olds			
Nursery schools and classes	10.0	22.5	26.40
Under fives in infant classes	18.9	20.7	24.98
Independent schools	2.1	2.5	3.69

Source: Early Childhood Unit statistics 1996, compiled from government sources.

These trends reflect both demographic changes and government policy. The number of children under five is likely to increase by about 7 per cent in the next ten years and considerable expansion will be required just to retain current levels of provision. The government response on day care and on nursery education has been to emphasize the role of the private and voluntary sectors:

> the government believe that in the first instance it is the responsibility of parents to make arrangements, including financial arrangements, for the day care of preschool children
> (Department of Health evidence to House of Commons, 1989)

and the role of employers in providing child care support for their workforce. The new education initiative was described by the Secretary of State as 'intended to increase the choices available to parents as well as to boost the number of private and voluntary sector preschool places... I fully expect that giving parents purchasing power through a voucher will stimulate the private and voluntary sectors to provide new places' (Hansard, 6 July 1995).

This emphasis on employers providing for the needs of working parents, on private and voluntary groups providing for the increase in nursery education, and an emphasis on public funding for day care only being for children in need (see below) is leading to a three-tier service: children of working parents in private sector provision; children in need in local authority nurseries; and children for whose parents part-time provision is convenient in nursery schools in some areas and in playgroups and private nurseries in others.

Equal access?

As the Rumbold Report acknowledged, 'access to services is still largely determined by where a child lives, when his or her birthday is, whether the parents have access to information about services, and whether they can afford fees where there is no public provision' (DES, 1990a, pp. 27–8). Clark's review of research (1988) pointed out that access to education has already become unequal for young children by the time they reach the statutory age for starting school.

For some children early education is particularly important. The House of Commons Select Committee report (1989) concluded that good quality preschool education is of benefit to all children but particularly those with special needs, from socially or economically deprived backgrounds, and for those whose first language is not English. Yet evidence shows that many of those most in need are those least likely to have had any preschool experience (Osborn and Milbank, 1987), and many children who would particularly benefit from nursery education are unable to take up places because the short hours do not suit the needs of working parents.

The Warnock Report (DES, 1978) estimated that one in five children of this age need some kind of support or additional help at some point, and it is at nursery that many such children are identified. For children with special needs, an early start to assessment, working in partnership with the child's parents in a nursery, can prevent the need for much more costly interventions at a later stage. Education legislation stipulates that children with special needs should be integrated into mainstream provision wherever possible, but in areas where there is little provision, nurseries and playgroups often have difficulty in meeting the needs of such children. The Code of Practice on SEN has been in force since 1994, but lack of resources impede its implementation and at present does not apply to non-statutory provision.

A policy that leaves service development to market forces tends to disadvantage those who are already disadvantaged, and is vulnerable to changes in the economy. The patchwork of provision also makes it difficult to ensure continuity between one service and another. Because of the paucity of services, some children may use two or three different services a day – perhaps starting with a childminder, going to a morning playgroup, then back to the childminder before going on to a nursery class, then back to the childminder before going home. Although parents are always the key figures in these transitions, for those who are working it is not easy to ensure that the needs of the child are met, and as Rumbold points out, the achievement of desirable educational continuity and progression may be at risk. Voucher systems such as that proposed for four-year-olds will do nothing to resolve this matter and will, if anything, make it harder for local authorities to plan and co-ordinate services, and to give priority to those children with the greatest needs.

In contrast to the rest of Europe, day care in the UK is seen as a private matter to be resolved by parents who are either expected to make their own arrangements with a relative or buy in services in the marketplace. The EC Childcare Network reports show that the UK has one of the fastest growing employment rates for women with a child under five (much of it part-time), but the poorest arrangements for maternity leave, and the lowest rates of publicly funded child care, though a substantial amount of private and voluntary sector provision (see also Chapter 2).

Legislation to support a co-ordinated policy?

The last ten years have seen a considerable amount of legislation affecting services for children, but none of it intended to create an integrated policy for young children and their families. The Children Act has perhaps had the most cohesive effect, through its requirement in Section 19 that local authorities should review their day care services for children every three years, and that this review must be undertaken jointly by social services and education and in association with the health authorities, voluntary organisations and others. The Act also introduced new standards for day care services, gave local authorities new responsibilities for registering and inspecting services, and required services to respect children's 'racial origin, religious persuasion and cultural and linguistic background'. The requirement to review services jointly has had a very positive effect in many authorities (Elfer and McQuail, 1996), but there have been two main problems in seeing the Children Act as the underpinning for a co-ordinated policy. One is that this is a piece of welfare legislation with a primary focus on 'children in need' rather than on making services available to all children. The other is the raft of education and health legislation that has led to the fragmentation rather than the cohesion of services.

Whilst the Children Act urges co-ordination, the 1988 Education Reform Act and subsequent education legislation reduces the role of the local education authority and in effect makes co-ordination more difficult. The introduction of the National Curriculum, with its subject-based programmes of study and assessment of all children from the age of seven, is not directly applicable to children before the age of five. However, it has had a considerable impact in nurseries and playgroups all over the country and has put pressure on some early years practitioners to alter the way in which they work in order to 'feed into' the National Curriculum and prepare children for base-line assessment at five. We return to this issue under the section on curriculum below.

With regard to local management of schools (LMS) and delegated budgets, as governors take over many of the responsibilities of the LEA in relation to the running of a school, it is becoming increasingly difficult for local authorities to implement policies in relation to nursery provision in general and co-ordinated provision in particular. Because nursery education is discretionary, it is perfectly feasible for governors to create their own policies on under fives, and, for example, to decide to employ a nursery nurse rather than a nursery teacher, or to employ teachers in reception and nursery classes with no early years experience, or to create very large reception classes. Centres jointly funded by education and social services present particular problems, unless the governors are willing to pass funding over to a separate management committee.

The Children Act, the Education Acts and indeed the NHS and Community Care Act all have a clear focus on monitoring, regulating and reviewing services, on quality control and on making information available to consumers/parents. But as the Cornish have it, you can't fatten a pig for market by continually weighing it. Inspection on its own will neither create new services, nor produce quality in those that exist. The legislation fails to provide a lead in creating a co-ordinated framework for the development of services, and the resources to take that development forward.

What about resources?

In the last five years, the government has funded a £45 million initiative to develop out-of-school care, and has announced an additional £165 million to introduce a voucher system for education for four-year-olds. But despite this limited expansion, it is clear that in terms of a national policy there is no overall commitment to resourcing services for young children. The question of what it would cost to expand services to the point where they met demand, and how such an expansion would be costed and paid for, has been the focus of two National Children's Bureau studies (Holtermann, 1992, 1995). The costs were estimated on the basis of an entitlement to a free 'nugget' of early education for all three- and four-year-olds, either in nursery schools and classes or in infant school classes and playgroups of comparable quality, integrated with a system of day care which parents would use according to their needs and pay for according to their means. Holtermann estimated that about a third of parents would pay for this in full, a third would be partly subsidized, and a third fully subsidized. The report concludes that this package would require additional public spending of £2.7 billion, and that this amount would be more than covered by the income tax and national insurance contributions of the women who could return to employment.

A national policy

There has, then, been no shortage of government initiatives and new legislation, but can they, taken together, be seen as a co-ordinated approach to child care and early child education within a clear policy framework? The evidence suggests that the answer has to be no. There are many issues that have not been addressed, and the education and health legislation are in fact moving towards fragmentation rather than co-ordination. A national policy should:

- provide the necessary legislative support;
- require a lead department at national and local level to take responsibility for implementation;
- identify clear targets for expansion;
- allocate sufficient financial support to ensure the achievement of these targets;
- provide a national database of information on service provision;
- ensure that criteria for adequate quality are agreed across all services, and can be readily identified by parents and providers;
- ensure the availability of appropriate initial training and opportunities for continuing training and development;
- create a national framework for adequate pay and conditions of service.

This policy must be developed in the context of a wider debate about the interrelationship between work, family responsibilities and child care.

As to which government department should take the lead, the view of most working party reports and of Labour and Liberal Democrat party policy is that this should be the Department for Education and Employment (Equal Opportunities Commission, 1990; Association of Metropolitan Authorities, 1991; National Consumer Council, 1991; Labour Party, 1994). This would reflect developments in countries such as Spain and New Zealand, although care would need to be taken that the needs of children under three were properly acknowledged.

AN INTEGRATED POLICY AT LOCAL LEVEL

Despite legislative change and a reduction in the power and role of local authorities over the last ten years, local authorities do still play a key role in both providing and supporting others to provide for young children and their families. This role can be summarized as:

- identifying levels of need and types of services required, through consultation with parents;

- providing early childhood care and education, and support services for families, planned in association with parents;

- assessing and providing for children with special educational needs (as required by the Code of Practice);

- administering grant-aid to voluntary organizations, and purchasing services in voluntary and private sector provision;

- registering and inspecting services against nationally agreed criteria;

- providing on-going support and training to staff working in all sectors;

- providing information on all services available to parents, employers and others.

Structures at local level

If local authorities are to develop a coherent and corporate approach to planning and supporting early childhood services, it is important that they should have management structures to support such an approach. The Early Childhood Unit's work with the majority of local authorities over the last eight years has shown how difficult it is to develop effective policies and structures without a clear lead from central government. However, the impetus of the Children Act, with the requirement that the review of services should be undertaken jointly, and within the context of a development plan and a co-ordinated structure, has led local authorities to review their collaborative procedures. Three main strategies have evolved:

(1) The most common is to establish an under-eights subcommittee of education and social services committees. In order to ensure collaboration with other agencies, this committee co-opts representatives from the health authority/ies, from other authority departments such as leisure services, housing and planning, and from the voluntary and private sectors.

(2) An alternative approach is to establish a committee (with the same co-options) as a subcommittee of the policy and resources committee, with delegation of general duties as above from education and social services. Officer support, sometimes in the form of a separate under-eights or early years unit, may well be based in the chief executive's department.

(3) A third alternative, which begins to move from co-ordination to integration, has been to delegate responsibility for all under-eights services to the education committee, and to delegate management responsibility to the education department. Strathclyde was the first authority to do this, since when some fourteen other authorities (although none of them counties) have followed suit.

A recent study of eleven local authorities (McQuail and Pugh, 1995) to assess the extent to which integration, co-ordination or collaboration led to improvements in services, found that the advantages of a more co-ordinated approach could be summarized as:

- for children, and particularly children in need, an increasing emphasis on a quality curriculum in all settings but particularly in day nurseries;

- for parents, better information, more involvement in services, greater flexibility in the services that are offered, less stigma and more choice;

- for providers, better information, more formal involvement in service development, and greater access to training, particularly to accreditation through NVQ;

- for the local authority, a better use of resources, the provision of a wider range of services, a clearer sense of purpose and direction, and early years services moving higher up the local agenda.

(Ibid., pp. 8–9)

With regard to structures, the report concluded that

> Structures are important, but so too are relationships between key individuals who must be able to transcend the barriers of professional jealousies and vested interests and work openly together in the best interests of children and their parents.
>
> The key is to develop strategies for planning, resourcing and reviewing high quality services that are 'owned' by all elected members and senior officers. These strategies need to be supported by the capacity to make executive decisions, which requires some control over budgets. An overall vision, shared by all the 'stakeholders' and which takes account of local circumstances and traditions, together with the means of implementing it, is as important as the type of political or management structure.
>
> (Ibid., p. 9)

Drawing on this study, on the evaluation of the first of the Children Act reviews (Elfer and McQuail, 1996) and on the Unit's work with local authorities, we can conclude that effective co-ordination or integration depends on:

- A clear policy agreed by all the main providers, setting out the principles upon which services should be based, the aims and objectives for the service, a development plan, and a clear process for implementation and review.

- A committee structure and departmental/administrative structure which supports an integrated approach to planning.

- A committee or subcommittee with delegated powers for policy development and resource deployment.

- Clear support from senior elected members and chief officers. This is particularly important in an area of discretionary expenditure.

- Clarity about roles, and about management responsibility, and clear lines of communication both within departments (between senior management, middle management and practitioners) and between departments.

- Clarity about relationships with health authorities and trusts. This has proved particularly difficult over the years, largely due to the frequent reforms to which the NHS has been subjected, but the potential for joint commissioning/purchasing now offers important opportunities.

- Involvement of the voluntary and private sectors. Local authorities have not traditionally involved these sectors in planning services, and yet in many authorities families are almost entirely dependent on playgroups and childminders, and increasingly employers and private nurseries are meeting the needs of working parents. In relation to the process of planning and review, it is important to establish systems whereby all voluntary groups can be represented, and not just well-established organizations such as the Preschool Learning Alliance. This may be most effectively managed through a voluntary sector forum, which can provide a mandate for a representative to the under-eights committee (see Ball and Stone, 1991).

- The establishment of local early years liaison groups or forums. This model is now being widely adopted, and provides both a forum for multi-disciplinary co-operation and training, and a means of consulting on and implementing policy.

- A dedicated post to support a co-ordinated approach to service delivery.

FLEXIBLE SERVICES TO MEET THE NEEDS OF CHILDREN AND THEIR PARENTS

If we look at what parents are asking for, we find that demand greatly outstrips supply and that surveys over many years show a continuing preference for nursery education over playgroups and for more day care and after-school and holiday provision (Meltzer, 1994). A review of parental preferences obtained by local authorities during the Children Act review concluded that parents wanted:

- more provision,

- provision that would promote the education and social development of children,

- reliable standards (or high quality in terms of curriculum and well-trained staff),

- low cost (but not necessarily free day care),

- facilities located near to where they live or work,

- provision flexible enough to meet changing needs, and

- better information about services. (Elfer and McQuail, 1996.)

However, there is considerable variation between surveys, reflecting different local circumstances and expectations. For example, the tight-knit community in Sunderland, with high levels of nursery education and where most young families have access to the extended family, brought a lower than usual demand for further day care (Statham, 1991). A recent project to develop 'wrap-around care' in Birmingham discovered that many parents in fact wanted somewhere to meet and access to training, rather than day care facilities (Birmingham Social Services, 1996). Where parents are given the option of new and extended provision, they have shown a preference for multi-purpose centres, offering both nursery education and day care (see Scott, 1989). In consulting parents, as with involving voluntary groups in planning, it is important to ensure that the mechanisms are in place to support that consultation, if it is not to be just a token gesture. Finding out parents' views and involving them in the process of planning and reviewing services requires resources, particularly staff time.

The need for flexibility in the provision of services in order to meet the needs of children and their parents has been well documented, and the value of combined nursery centres and community nurseries offering day care and nursery education, and often drop-in facilities, health surveillance and a range of support services for parents as well, was reinforced by the Rumbold Committee (DES, 1990a) and the RSA report (Ball, 1994). For parents who are working, two and a half hours of nursery education or three mornings a week at a playgroup is hardly likely to be suitable, and the importance of linking existing services to each other, or of running a range of services from one base, is slowly becoming better understood. A number of local authorities have continued to support the development of combined nursery centres, and some primary schools are beginning to see their role extending to encompass support for families, but shortage of funding and the pressures of continuous legislative change have meant that these developments are still not widespread. Other multi-purpose centres are being established through partnerships between the local authority and employers, TECs and voluntary childcare organisations such as Barnardo's or the National Children's Home. Figure 1.1, taken from Pugh and McQuail (1995) illustrates the range of services that could be linked into a primary or nursery school or family centre. This report also includes a 'vision' for what a centre in the year 2010 might look like, and a similar vision is developed by Moss and Penn (1996).

In rural areas, the emphasis may need to be more on networks than on centres. A network of childminders, playgroups linked to schools, mobile groups in playbuses or vans, and peripatetic nursery teachers (Hanney, 1993; Cameron and Statham, 1994) all have an important part to play in a rural development strategy.

In looking at a balanced local service, which gives both diversity and choice, two issues are emerging. The first is to ask how, if most parents want nursery education for their children and many also want longer hours than nursery education provides, this is to fit into the patchwork of private and voluntary sector provision. The second issue, which will perhaps ultimately help to resolve the first, is to point to the new role that many authorities

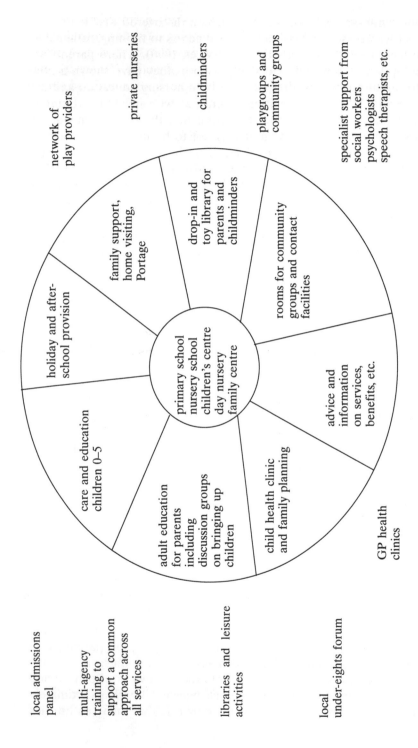

The outer circle indicates additional services which might be based in schools, nurseries and centres. Beyond the outer circle are community-based services with which the centres can develop links.

Figure 1.1 Services for children under eight: a centre and community network model.

Inner circle:
primary school
nursery school
children's centre
day nursery
family centre

Middle circle segments:
holiday and after-school provision
family support, home visiting, Portage
drop-in and toy library for parents and childminders
rooms for community groups and contact facilities
advice and information on services, benefits, etc.
child health clinic and family planning
adult education for parents including discussion groups on bringing up children
care and education children 0-5

Outer labels:
local admissions panel
multi-agency training to support a common approach across all services
network of play providers
private nurseries
childminders
playgroups and community groups
specialist support from social workers psychologists speech therapists, etc.
libraries and leisure activities
local under-eights forum
GP health clinics

are taking on as development agencies, establishing partnerships with the voluntary sector and with employers in developing nurseries, consultancies and consortia in tandem with their own role as providers of services. A proactive approach to partnership within an integrated policy framework may well help to prevent the two-tier or even three-tier system outlined above.

A HIGH QUALITY SERVICE

The issue of quality has been discussed in almost every book on early childhood services published during the past decade, and must be seen as a complex process rather than a set of tidy outcomes. As Moss and Pence (1994, p. 5) argue,

> quality is never an objective reality, to be finally discovered and pinned down by experts. It is inherently subjective and relative, based on values and beliefs, that may not only vary among and within societies, but will undoubtedly vary over time . . . It is also a political process. It involves interplay, negotiation and possible conflict between, and sometimes among, those stakeholder groups who are included and who may have different perspectives about objectives and priorities arising from different values and beliefs, interests and needs.

A policy on early childhood services must, however, develop a number of 'quality indicators' that are applied to all services across the board and it is possible to summarize such a set of indicators drawing on the Rumbold Report (DES, 1990a), the guidance to the Children Act (Department of Health, 1991) and guidelines on day care published by the National Children's Bureau (Cowley, 1991). Other national guidelines have been published by the Preschool Playgroups Association (1990a, 1990b), by Kids Club Network (1989) and by the National Childminding Association (1991).

- The need for clearly defined aims and objectives.

- An effective management structure.

- A policy on equal opportunities encompassing gender, ethnicity and disability which promotes an understanding of cultural and physical diversity and challenges stereotypes.

- Close relationships between staff and parents, and the involvement of parents in the running of the nursery.

- An atmosphere in which every child and adult feels secure, valued and confident.

- Good relationships between adults and children, between children and children and between adults and adults.

- A broad, balanced and relevant curriculum, appropriate to the physical, emotional, spiritual and intellectual development of children, informed by observation and assessment of children.

- Evidence of children being actively involved in their learning, with a strong emphasis on play and talking.

- A system of record-keeping which monitors children's learning and is shared with parents.

- Well-trained staff who can understand and respond to the needs of individual children and structure and support their learning.

- Warm, sensitive and responsive care-givers, able to provide continuity of care through a key worker system.

- A staff development plan, which ensures access to regular support, supervision and training of all staff.

- A good ratio of staff to children, and small groups.

- A well-organized physical environment, with access to appropriate resources both inside and outside and due attention to health and safety.

- Liaison with others involved in the child's health, care and education in the local community.

- A system for monitoring and reviewing provision.

The three key issues here are the provision of an appropriate curriculum, well-trained staff and good relationships between staff and parents, all of which are covered in later chapters. The central focus of the Early Childhood Unit's work – and indeed of this book – is the need to ensure that all children have access to high quality learning experiences, which respond to their individual needs, in whatever setting they find themselves. This is as important for children from black and minority ethnic families who may find the curriculum does not value and reflect their own culture, as for disabled children who may not have access to mainstream services; as important for children of eighteen months old who may be in day care for the first time, as for children who are just four and find themselves in a group of thirty-five children in a primary school. It calls for skilled educators whose understanding of child development, and ability to observe and assess the progress of individual children, enables them to structure and support children in their learning. As Sylva (1994) has pointed out, unless the curriculum is of a high quality, building on children's disposition to learn and giving them a sense of 'mastery' over their learning, then it is not worth the additional investment. These issues are taken up in more detail in Chapters 4–8.

There have been concerns that the introduction of the National Curriculum would lead to pressure to formalize education at the earliest opportunity and follow a narrow and more rigid curriculum which would not be in the child's best interests. This is of particular concern for the substantial and growing number of four-year-olds who are now going early into primary school, often into classes where teachers are inappropriately trained and the curriculum is not well suited to the needs of such young children. There is now very clear evidence that there are no educational or behavioural advantages in entering school early, and a growing body of research (Clark, 1988; DES, 1989a; Pascal, 1990; Cleave and Brown, 1989; OFSTED, 1993a) which shows the adverse effects of introducing children too early to an inappropriately formal curriculum.

The Rumbold Committee was able to resist the suggestion that there should be a national subject-based curriculum for under fives, and focused instead on the principles upon which early education should be built. These words have been frequently quoted in the years since that report was published:

> The educator working with under fives must pay careful attention, not just to the content of the child's learning, but also to the way in which that learning is offered to and experienced by the child, and the role of all those involved in the process. Children are affected by the context in which learning takes place, the people involved in it, and the values and beliefs which are embedded in it. For the early years educator, therefore, the *process* of education – how children are encouraged to learn – is as important as, and inseparable from, the *content* – what they learn. We believe that this principle must underlie all curriculum planning for the under fives.
>
> (DES, 1990a, paras. 67–8, original emphasis)

The publication of reports and guidelines that point to the needs of our youngest children are helpful, but we should not underestimate the pressure that early years educators are under from some parents and from teachers of older children to subscribe to other principles and other approaches. A recent illustration of this point is the SCAA paper (1996) on 'desirable outcomes', discussed in Chapter 5. It is perhaps particularly important that parents understand how young children learn, for, as Watt (1990, p. 130) argues, 'if the child-centred curriculum is to survive within National Curriculum guidelines, then not only must teachers be seen to be committed to it, but parents must identify with it'. The development of a curriculum framework for use with children from birth to eight, being devised by the Early Childhood Education Forum in its Quality in

Diversity project, includes parents as well as early years workers such as nursery teachers, playgroup leaders and childminders.

CONSULTING WITH AND INFORMING PARENTS

It is often easier for professionals to provide services that they think parents and children ought to have, than to take time to talk to and listen to parents. The concept of partnership that is central to the Children Act is to be welcomed, but partnership is an elusive concept (see Pugh and De'Ath, 1989) and the increased emphasis on consultation will require new skills and a change of attitude on the part of many managers and practitioners (see also Chapters 9 and 10). In their evaluation of the first Children Act review, Elfer and McQuail (1996) found that most authorities had made some attempt to consult with parents, but that the consultation process had usually been very broad and unrealistically ambitious. Open meetings had been of limited value, although smaller meetings with specific groups had been more useful. Some nineteen authorities had done surveys of parental preferences, but even these were limited by parents' lack of clarity on what the options were.

As noted above, the involvement of parents in their children's preschool provision is a key to the quality of that provision. Although parents are often described as their children's first educators, and the rhetoric of partnership is constantly quoted, the research that points to the gains to children if parents are involved in their learning still presents a challenge to many practitioners. This is discussed more fully in Chapter 11.

Both the Children Act and the education legislation oblige local authorities and schools respectively to provide parents with information which will inform their decisions when choosing child care or education, a requirement that is long overdue. In addition to the published information which is now widely available, over the last five years there has been a steady growth in the establishment of computerized children's information services. Some forty are either in operation or being developed across the country, usually with funding from the local authority, the TEC and local employers (Choices in Childcare, 1995).

SETTING STANDARDS AND MONITORING QUALITY

One of the main concerns in an unco-ordinated system which depends so heavily for service provision on the voluntary and private sectors, is how quality is to be established and maintained. The Rumbold Report commented on the 'need to raise the quality of a good deal of existing provision' and referred back to concerns raised by the Education Select

Committee on the educational component of playgroups and day nurseries. Clark (1988, p. 268) had expressed particular concern at failure to meet the needs of many children in day nurseries who she felt needed to have access to stimulating and varied experiences if 'their own characteristics and home circumstances are [not] to lead to very early failure in the educational system'.

The Children Act and its accompanying Guidance (Department of Health, 1991) responded to both these issues, in providing a baseline below which standards must not fall, and a structure for registration, inspection and review. The Guidance sets standards on ratios, room size and space, record-keeping, health and safety and discipline, and, drawing on the Rumbold Report, goes further than previous government guidance in looking at curriculum issues and equal opportunities as well as the number of toilets and amount of floor space. The list of 'quality criteria' above derived from these and other 'quality guidelines' can provide the base for national standards to be applied across all services.

In addition to these guidelines there are, of course, the quite separate requirements of the education system as articulated, in relation to inspection, by the OFSTED inspection framework. The two inspection systems have operated quite separately, with nursery and primary schools being inspected against this framework every four years (although in reality this timetable is proving unworkable), whilst all other services are inspected every year by social services inspectors using the Children Act criteria.

Bringing these two systems together is a high priority, and the problem has not been solved by the proposed introduction of a third 'light touch' system of inspection for the new 'voucher redeeming institutions.'

TRAINING AND SUPPORT

High-quality work in early childhood education is only possible with sufficient staff of high calibre and with appropriate training. In the UK, as indeed in many other countries, those who teach the youngest children are lowest in the pecking order, although Britain is one of the few countries in the world where nursery teachers are qualified to teach throughout the primary years. It is often assumed that anyone can teach young children, and yet as many primary heads will argue, four-year-olds are the pupils who demand the greatest skill, the most organization and the most energy. A recent national survey found that two-thirds of teachers working with children under five had no specific training to work with this age group (Blenkin and Yue, 1994). There is also a growing concern about the appropriateness of teacher training, with its continuing emphasis on subject specialism and its neglect of child development. As a result of a working party meeting over a number of years (Early Childhood Unit, 1992) a number of universities are now responding to the inappropriateness of many initial training courses by pioneering integrated early childhood studies degrees, but it is still not clear whether these will be acceptable as the basis for teacher training.

In the private and voluntary sectors, well over half of all workers are not formally qualified. The introduction of National Vocational Qualifications, although offering the promise of accreditation to many, has not been fully implemented and, indeed, the initial development work at level 3 is still unfinished and work at level 4 has not even begun. It is also not clear how NVQs will relate to the new Specialist Teacher Assistants. These issues and a consideration of the links between professional and vocational training are discussed in more detail in Chapter 12.

Initial training is important, but continuous in-service training and the development of a culture of reflection and self-appraisal in all early childhood settings is crucial. If regular training and development were an integral part of all services, then formal inspection would be far less important as a tool in measuring and improving quality. But such development requires the support of advisory teachers within each local authority who can support staff teams, and almost all local authorities have had to make drastic reductions in their early years support staff in recent years, with grave consequences for the professional development of workers in all settings.

A national early years policy should require all staff working with young children to be trained to at least level 3 NVQ or equivalent, and would create opportunities for access to training to ensure that this was implemented. Heads of all preschool institutions should be at graduate level or NVQ level 4, and the teams who work in nurseries and playgroups should include or have regular access to early years teachers.

PAY AND CONDITIONS

Whilst the status and pay of nursery and infant teachers may not match that of teachers of older children, it is considerably better than that of all other early years workers. The experience of combined nursery centres (see, for example, Chapter 9) shows just how difficult it is to agree a common scale of pay and conditions for staff from different backgrounds. This is an issue which can only be resolved nationally, and yet the recommendation in the AMA report (1991) for a national working party to resolve this issue has never been implemented. New discussions are currently under way.

CONCLUSION

Developments over the last decade have created a number of building blocks in an early years policy, and the chapters in this book celebrate many of them. The concern for quality and for quality assurance is to be welcomed, as is the emphasis that the Children Act places on co-ordination and review, and on responding to children's cultural and linguistic background. The demand for day care is forging some imaginative partnerships, and the need for further expansion is generally more widely understood. But the introduction of a system of vouchers for the parents of four-year-olds is a diversion that fails to confront the need for a national policy that reflects the areas outlined in this chapter, or the broader issues of work and family responsibility. Fragmentation, lack of resources and lack of vision persist in preventing all children having access to the start in life they so richly deserve.

Further reading

Writing at the end of 1995 it is not possible to predict how the current proposals for an expansion of provision for four-year-olds will develop, nor how the proposed 'activities and outcomes' devised by SCAA or discussions about the new quality assurance arrangements will be resolved. In addition to the issues raised in this chapter, further discussion can be found in *Effective Organisation of Early Childhood Services* (both the full report and the summary and strategic framework, McQuail and Pugh, 1995; Pugh and McQuail, 1995); in *Transforming Nursery Education* (Moss and Penn, 1996); and in the *Start Right* report (Ball, 1994).

2

PERSPECTIVES FROM EUROPE

Peter Moss

INTRODUCTION

This chapter is an attempt to put a quart into a pint pot. In the space of a few pages, I shall try to give an overview of early childhood services, and related policies, in the fifteen member states of the European Union (EU); to discuss some general problem areas; to introduce some innovative developments; and to consider the content and significance of a growing 'European dimension' in services and policies. The process of condensation is inevitably at the expense of nuance and qualification, and several important issues are entirely omitted. For example, any attempt to discuss quality has been defeated by shortage of space, compounded by the lack of information available about quality in services and more conceptual problems about defining 'quality' which would require a substantial preamble.

Having acknowledged the problems in the task set, I am encouraged to proceed for a number of reasons. Readers can get lost in long and detailed accounts comparing different countries; a brief overview, presenting a few broad features, may be a better way in (readers whose appetites are whetted may like to consult EC Childcare Network (1990 and 1996) for more detailed accounts of services and policies in EU countries). Above all, it is important that those interested in issues to do with children and their welfare and with women and gender equality (or both) should understand both the potential and the limitations of the EU with respect to early childhood services, and the possibilities for influencing the direction of European policy and initiatives in this area. A democratic Europe cries out for the participation of concerned individuals and organizations, rather than leaving developments to politicians and bureaucrats however well intentioned.

Finally, I refer in this chapter to 'early childhood services'. By this, I mean services often referred to in the UK under the headings of 'day care', 'child care' and 'preschool or nursery education'. I have used the term 'early childhood services' as a convenient umbrella, but also because, as I shall discuss later, the more specific and common terms seem to me to be problematic, reflecting and encouraging a fragmented way of thinking about provision for young children and their carers.

EARLY CHILDHOOD SERVICES IN EUROPE: A BRIEF OVERVIEW

The infrastructure of early childhood services

By making some broad generalizations and ignoring some important exceptions, it is possible to describe a pattern of early childhood services found in most countries in the European Union (see Table 2.1 for a league table of levels of publicly funded provision). The upper age limit, if 'early childhood' is defined as ending when compulsory schooling begins, is normally six or over. Preceding this, countries provide nursery education or kindergarten for most children from three upwards. In some cases (France, Italy, Belgium) provision is already almost universal, while in others (Denmark, Finland, Germany, Spain, Sweden), there is a political commitment to achieve services for all 3–6-year-old children whose parents want them to attend. In most cases, too, this provision is available for at least the equivalent of the British school day.

For children under three, the picture is rather different. Most children in this youngest age group attend services because parents are at work, and the extent of this (or rather maternal employment) varies considerably (see Table 2.2). Use of services for children under one is also influenced by leave provision, first maternity leave (universally available, on average for about three months after birth), then parental leave. Maternity leave protects and promotes the health and well-being of the mother and her new-born child and is, by definition, only for women. By contrast, parental leave provides parents with an opportunity to care for a very

Table 2.1 Provision of publicly funded services in member states

	A	B	C	D	Children 0–3	Children 3–6	Children 6–10
BE	27	**	6	93	30%	95%+	??
DK	30	**	7	94	45%	82%	62%+ all 6-year-olds in pre-primary education
GE	36	*	6	90	2% (W) 50% (E)	78% (W) 100% (E)	5% (W) 88% (E)
GR	9	**	6	93	#3%	#70% (a)	?<5%
SP	36	*	6	93	?2%	84%	??%
FR	36	**	6	93	23%	99%	?30%
IR	3		6	93	2%	55%	?<5%
IT	9		6	91	6%	91%	??
NE	15	**	5	93	#8% (a)	#71% (a)	?<5%
AU	24		6	94	3%	75%	6%
PO	27		6	93	12%	48%	10%
FI	36		7	94	21%	53%	5%
SW	36		7	94	33%	72%	64%+ some 6-year-olds in welfare and education services
UK	7	*	5	93	2%	#60% (a)	??<5%

Key: **Column A** gives the length of Maternity Leave + Parental Leave in months available per family after the birth of each child. **Column B** indicates whether subsidies are available to parents (in addition to subsidies paid direct to services) to cover part of their costs for using services for young children. * = subsidy available to lower income parents only; ** = subsidy available to some/all parents, irrespective of income. **Column C** shows the age at which compulsory schooling begins. **Column D** shows to what year the figures in the next three columns refer.

(a) = figure includes some children in compulsory schooling (ie. where compulsory schooling begins before 6).
?? = no information.
?<5% = no information but under 5%.
? = approximate figure.
= important qualification, see 'Notes'.

Notes: The age of compulsory schooling affects the figures given for services for children aged 3–6. This group of services includes: pre-primary schooling; early admission to primary school; *and children attending compulsory schooling* (in the case of countries where compulsory schooling begins before 6). However, the column for services for children aged 6–10 *does not include children in compulsory schooling*; it is confined to services providing care and recreation to school-aged children.

Countries (or even different systems within the same country) vary in whether they collect data on 'places available' or 'children attending'. The Table reflects this mix of data, giving information on:

places available for Belgium and France (0–3, except for 2-year-olds in pre-primary schooling); Germany, Italy (0–3), Netherlands, Portugal and UK;
and information on:

children attending for Belgium and France (2-year-olds in pre-primary schooling and 3–6), Denmark, Greece, Spain, Ireland, Italy (3–6), Austria, Finland and Sweden.

The two measures will not differ significantly when all or nearly all 'places available' are used full-time and if there are few or no vacancies. However, in some services in some countries a significant number of places are used on a part-time basis and, in effect, shared by two children; in these cases, data on 'children' attending will significantly over-state the 'places available' and the volume of services supplied. The difference between 'places available' and 'children attending' is significant in services in the welfare system in Ireland, the Netherlands and the UK and in pre-primary schooling in the UK. In these cases, estimated 'places available' data rather than 'children attending' data have been used where available (ie. for the UK and Netherlands).

Greece, the Netherlands and the UK do not produce statistics for children aged 0–3 and 3–6 in welfare system services; in Greece, statistics are for children aged 0–2 $^1/_2$–5 $^1/_2$ years, in the Netherlands for children aged 0–4 years and in the UK for children aged 0–5 years. The figures in the Table for children aged 0–3 and 3–6 for these countries are therefore estimates.

In nearly all cases, 'publicly funded' means that more than half of the total costs of a service are paid from public sources, and usually between 75% and 100%. The main exception to this is the Netherlands, where public funding usually covers less than half the costs of services in the welfare system. These services in the Netherlands are included, except playgroups; although most playgroups receive some public funds, average hours of opening and attendance are so much shorter than for other services that it would be potentially misleading to include information on them either for 'children attending' or 'places available'.

Source: EC Childcare Network, 1996.

Table 2.2 Employment status of women and men with child aged 0–9 years: 1993, EU member states, excluding Austria, Finland, Sweden

Country	% of mothers employed		% of fathers employed	
	Total employed	(FT/PT)	Total employed	(FT/PT)
Belgium	62	(38/24)	92	(91/1)
Denmark	74	(49/25)	88	(86/2)
France	59	(40/19)	90	(88/2)
Germany	51	(26/25)	92	(91/1)
Greece	44	(40/3)	95	(93/1)
Ireland	35	(24/10)	81	(78/2)
Italy	43	(37/6)	93	(91/1)
Luxembourg	42	(29/12)	93	(93/–)
Netherlands	46	(6/41)	92	(85/7)
Portugal	70	(63/7)	95	(93/1)
Spain	35	(29/6)	85	(84/1)
UK	53	(18/35)	84	(82/2)
EU12	50	(30/20)	90	(88/2)

Source: EC Childcare Network (1996), from special analysis of 1993 Labour Force Survey undertaken by EUROSTAT.

young child and should be equally available to mothers and fathers (hence employer-provided 'career break' schemes are not the same as parental leave, being only available to one parent unless both parents happen to work for the same employer).

Every country in mainland Europe (except Luxembourg) now offers some form of parental leave, lasting from six months to nearly three years. A well-developed system of parental leave can have a substantial impact on the demand for and use of early childhood services. The clearest example of this is Sweden, which offers twelve months' leave at 80–90 per cent of earnings, with a further three months at a low flat rate; parents have the right to take their leave full time or part time, and in one continuous leave period or as several shorter periods of leave. The development of this leave provision means that few children under twelve months in Sweden are now found in any form of early childhood service. In 1994, there were only 155 children under twelve months in public nurseries, compared to 3,000 twenty years earlier; yet during the same twenty-year period, the number of children in early childhood services increased five-fold (Möller, 1995). Another distinctive feature of Sweden is the relatively high take-up of parental leave by fathers; nearly half of all fathers now take some period of leave (EC Childcare Network, 1994).

However, in non-Nordic countries, parental leave (unlike maternity leave) is unpaid or paid only at a low flat rate, and is taken almost entirely by mothers. It many cases, it is also rather inflexible, not giving parents the right to decide how they will take it; for example, part time or full time, in one block or several. In these cases, leave has far less impact on early childhood services (for more details of parental leave in the EU, see EC Childcare Network, 1994).

Most children under three receiving non-parental care are provided for privately (that is, both the provision and its funding are private), mainly by relatives (grannies remain a vast and publicly neglected source of care), family day carers or 'babysitters'; family day carers are rare in Spain, Italy and Greece, where individual care is more commonly provided by 'babysitters' looking after children in the children's own home. Some form of publicly funded service is also available for this age group, mostly in centres, though some countries (notably the Nordic countries, Belgium, France and Portugal) also have extensive or growing systems of 'organized family day care', where family day carers are recruited, paid and supported by local authorities or publicly funded private organizations (for more information on organized and private family day care in the EU, see EC Childcare Network, 1995a).

Levels of publicly funded provision are low in most member states – available for 12 per cent or less of the 0–3 age group (see Table 2.1). There are five countries with higher levels of provision. France and Finland provide for nearly 1 in 4 children under three, Belgium and Sweden for 30–40 per cent. The relatively high rates in France and Belgium are partly because they have more extensive provision specifically for this youngest age group, but also because they have adopted the practice of admitting two-year-olds into a nursery school system which mainly caters for children over three. Indeed in France, nearly half of all two-year-olds are in nursery schools.

The country with the highest level of provision is Denmark. Employment rates for women with children are among the highest in Europe; nearly 90 per cent are in the labour force. Compulsory school (as in the rest of Scandinavia) begins at seven, prior to which the great majority of children over three attend some form of publicly funded service. Most three- to six-year-olds go to kindergartens or similar services offering full-time provision, while nearly all six-year-olds attend part-time preschool classes in primary school (which they mostly combine with services providing care and recreation for school-age children).

About half of all children under three attend publicly funded services. This figure has to be seen in the context of a recently extended parental leave system, which has substantially reduced the number of children under twelve months in services – in other words, attendance by one- and two-year-olds is probably well over 50 per cent. Some children are in centres (increasingly, age-integrated centres which take children under and over three), but most (nearly two-thirds) are in organized family day care. This high level of public provision means that in Denmark (and also in Sweden) most children receiving non-parental care do so in publicly funded services, rather than in private arrangements; care by relatives is now relatively uncommon.

The Danish Government has made a political commitment to provide publicly funded services for all employed parents who want a place for a child aged one to six years. Sweden and Finland have introduced legal entitlements to publicly funded provision – for children from one to twelve in the case of Sweden, and for children from birth to seven, from 1996, in the case of Finland. In Denmark and Sweden, the policy is based on an assumption that parents should be in the labour force, except for a substantial period of paid leave, and should be supported in combining employment with family responsibilities. In Finland, the explicit aim of policy is to support choice for parents with children under three between employment and caring for their children at home, and again to do so through active policy interventions; since 1990, every child under three has the right to a place in a publicly funded service while families are entitled to receive financial support to care for their children either at home or in private services. However, in all three countries, the concept of a right of access to publicly funded early childhood services is well on the way to being put into practice.

Three exceptions

This is the broad pattern in most countries in the EU. Three countries, however, are significantly different. Ireland, the Netherlands and the UK have had low levels of maternal employment (although all three have shown significant increases in recent years, with the UK rates now around the EU average); moreover, employed mothers in the Netherlands and the UK have high levels of part-time jobs, with part-timers working on average shorter hours than in other member states (see Table 2.2). The UK and Ireland have no statutory parental leave, publicly funded services for children under three are at a low level and parental employment is not one of the criteria for admission to what services there are (as is the case in other member states). The role of public provision is limited to providing support services to children and families deemed to be at risk or in need.

The Netherlands does provide statutory parental leave, but only since 1990 and only in the form of part-time leave, with no full-time option; every other member state offers full-time leave, sometimes with a part-time option. Provision of publicly funded services for children under three has increased substantially since 1990, due to a special government programme.

The most striking differences between these three countries and the rest of the EU concerns children over three. Compulsory schooling begins at five in both the UK and the Netherlands, and at six in Ireland, but these countries have limited (in the case of the UK and Ireland) or no nursery education. All three countries have responded to this gap in provision in a similar manner; many children are admitted to primary school before compulsory school age and extensive playgroup provision has developed.

There are many similarities between the playgroup movements in these three countries (which are the only ones in Europe where playgroups have a significant presence); for example, children attend playgroup on average for only five or six hours a week, far less than even part-time nursery education. There are also some important differences. For example, playgroups in the Netherlands provide for two- and three-year-olds, while nearly all four-year-olds are in primary school (on a non-compulsory basis); moreover, most playgroups in the Netherlands receive some public funds. By contrast, playgroups in the UK and Ireland have fewer two-year-olds and more four-year-olds, and only a minority get any public funds (for a fuller comparison of playgroups in the three countries, see Statham, Lloyd and Moss, 1989.)

The UK and the rest of Europe

This brief overview highlights a number of broad and widespread features of early childhood services in the European Union, including the introduction of parental leave as a universal entitlement; a recognition of some public responsibility for the children of employed parents (though in most cases, with a large shortfall in the supply of publicly funded services); and a recognition of the need to develop nursery education or kindergarten for children over three, offering three years attendance usually for at least what we would consider a full school day (and here, the shortfall in supply is generally far less).

In all three respects, Britain differs. There is no statutory parental leave. Public policy explicitly rejects any public responsibility for supporting working parents and their children; parents should be free to choose whether or not they work, and government should remain neutral. Underpinning this is an ideological position that the care and upbringing of young children is essentially a private parental responsibility, except in those cases where child, parent or family are deemed to be at risk in some respect.

The UK is the only member state in the EU to provide nursery education on a part-time, shift system as a matter of deliberate policy. The recent government commitment on early childhood services is to provide one year's 'preschool education' for four-year-olds by 1997 (e.g. about 500 hours of nursery education compared to nearly 5,000 hours that a child in France would receive through three years' attendance at nursery school). Whereas most children aged three to six in the EU can expect a three-year period of nursery education or kindergarten, many children of the same age in the UK face a period of great discontinuity, moving from home to playgroup to nursery class, then on to reception class – and all before the age of five. Indeed, the long tradition of starting compulsory schooling at five, with the associated trend to take children into primary school at four, can be seen as having a profound and adverse effect on early childhood services in the UK – but like so many aspects of policy in the UK, has been the subject of no serious debate or review.

Some specific features

The overview above outlines the basic infrastructure of early childhood provision. Some other, more specific common features should also be noted. First, there is considerable diversity in how publicly funded services are delivered. In some countries (for example, Italy), publicly funded services for children under three are almost entirely provided directly by local authorities (though nursery education, while publicly funded, is delivered by a mixture of central government, local authorities and church and lay organizations). In other countries (for example, Ireland or the Netherlands), publicly funded services are provided almost entirely by private, non-profit organizations. In other cases, there is a mix. Denmark, for example, has very extensive publicly funded services which may be provided by local authorities or private organizations; however provided, there is a high level of autonomy for individual centres.

Second, most European countries operate some form of regulation of private sector nurseries, but no country regulates 'babysitters' and there is considerable variation in the extent to which family day care is regulated. Moreover, even where registration of family day carers is required, there is considerable variation in actual coverage achieved. For example, while most family day carers are probably registered in the UK, in Germany the opposite is true (for more information on regulation of family day care, see EC Childcare Network, 1995a).

Third, while all countries in the EU fund services directly (to a greater or lesser extent), nine – Belgium, Denmark, France, Germany, Greece, Luxembourg, the Netherlands, Spain and the UK – at present also subsidize parents' costs directly in one form or another; tax relief, available in four countries, is the most common method of subsidy. In each case, however, tax relief or other forms of subsidy are a supplement to, rather than a substitute for, the direct funding of services. The most comprehensive system of subsidies paid directly to parents is found in France, in addition to a relatively high level of publicly funded services. French parents may claim tax relief on what they pay out for services (whether private or publicly funded) and in addition, parents using a private family day carer get a financial grant and their social security payment as employers is paid for them from public funds (for further information on the costs and funding of services, see EC Childcare Network, 1995b).

Finally, the pay, conditions and training of many workers with young children is poor. The worst conditions occur among those working with the youngest age group, children under three, and particularly among those who provide services privately (family day carers, relatives, babysitters). In general, the situation is better for workers in nursery education and kindergarten, although often their position remains inferior to teachers working with older children in the compulsory school system (for further information on pay and training of workers, see EC Childcare Network, 1995b and 1996).

SOME COMMON PROBLEMS IN
EARLY CHILDHOOD SERVICES

As well as common features, we can identify a number of common problems in the systems of early childhood services in the European Union. In this section, I want to pay attention to certain 'problem areas' which seem particularly important.

Local inequalities in provision

Considerable variations exist in levels of publicly funded provision between member states (see Table 2.1). However, variations also exist within every country. In France, for example, nearly half the places in nurseries are in the Ile-de-France area, although this area accounts for less than a fifth of the population. In Italy, there are large regional variations for children under three; regions in the north provide for over 8 per cent of children (with nearly 20 per cent coverage in the Emilia-Romagna region centred on Bologna) compared to 1 per cent in the south. In Denmark, the highest levels of provision are found in the two largest cities (Copenhagen and Arhus), the lowest levels in small urban and rural local authorities. Overall, levels of services are highest in large urban areas, lowest in rural areas and smaller towns, though even within these broad groupings there are large differences. Variations are also most common for children under three; nursery education is more evenly spread, especially where overall levels of provision are high.

Some of these variations may be put down to differences in need or demand, but most can only be fully accounted for in terms of the priorities of local or regional authorities and the commitment of politicians in these authorities to the needs of young children and their families. The underlying problem, however, arises from the provision of many services, especially those for children under three, being left the subject of local discretion. No member state sets targets, at national level, for services. The inevitable consequence is that access to services becomes a lottery, depending on where children live rather than what their needs are.

One very particular example of regional variation should be noted. Prior to reunification, West Germany had publicly funded provision for about 2 per cent of children under three and about two-thirds of three- to six-year-olds; in East Germany, there was almost universal coverage for children over twelve months. Since unification, the coverage rate for children under three in the East has dropped, but is still far higher than in the West. Kindergarten provision in the East, for three- to six-year-olds, remains almost universal, and is mostly available on a full day basis. In the West, kindergarten provision is mostly part day and not yet generally available – although as a result of reunification, a legal right to a place for all children will be implemented during the next few years.

Costs and funding

While an increasing number of member states fund virtually universal nursery education, none have yet managed to fund services for under threes that meet demand (the Nordic countries, however, are close) or parental leave that provides a high level of compensation for lost earnings (with the exception of Sweden). The consequences include parental leave that is structured in such a way as to ensure that it is unlikely to be taken by fathers; major inconsistencies in the cost of services to parents (parents paying far more for services for children under three than over three); and the continuing poor pay, conditions and training of many workers in early childhood services, an inevitable consequence of being dependent on what parents can pay.

All EU countries face a similar and profound problem. As long as women have provided care and education for young children on an unpaid basis (as mothers or relatives) or a low-paid basis (as family day carers or babysitters), the costs of providing this service have been carried by women, particularly in the form of foregone earnings and lost benefits (such as pension rights). The costs have been real and heavy but also invisible, in the sense that politicians have either not recognized them or felt able to ignore them, taking it for granted that women would and should continue to carry them. However, as the labour market demand and employment opportunities for these women carers increase, the question of cost becomes visible and pressing. Children need more non-parental care and education; traditional non-parental carers prove harder to recruit on the previous low-cost basis; there is likely to be a growing concern with quality of children's experience, and evidence suggests that quality requires certain material conditions (for example, in terms of pay and training for workers, staff/child ratios and so on) (Clarke-Stewart, 1991).

Add to this a similar set of issues concerning other types of care (for example, for elderly people) and it is clear that the cost of caring and how that cost is to be allocated represents a central political, social and economic issue. However, it is also clear that no EU state has really confronted the issue. Instead, there have been a series of *ad hoc* responses: small increases in public expenditure here, an interest in employers paying for services there, small-scale support for parents' costs through tax relief in some countries, unpaid or low-paid leave measures, and so on.

Within this broad failure to confront and consider a fundamental issue, we can discern several possible future strategies. Denmark (along with Finland and Sweden) has tackled the issue head on, through funding services directly from taxation, together with a substantial parental contribution. In 1994, public expenditure on services for children under six came to nearly 11 billion Danish kroner or about 1.2 per cent of GDP; overall, parents paid just over a fifth of all costs.

France has sought to fund services through general taxes (including the whole cost of three years' nursery education), but supplemented by an employer levy; all French employers contribute to regional funds, from which are paid cash benefits to families and subsidies to local authorities to support and develop services for young children. The Netherlands also seeks to involve employers in the provision of services, but on a very different basis. Under a special funding programme introduced by the government in 1990 and due to finish at the end of 1995, central government funds contribute to the costs of new places, but at a low level (less than half); the remaining costs are paid partly by parents and partly by either local authorities (for children in need) or individual employers. Central government funding is therefore being used as an inducement to individual employers to subsidize places for their employees. Dutch employers contribute if they consider it in their interests to do so, and then subsidize places specifically for their own employees. By contrast, all French employers must contribute, and their money goes into a general fund used to support a wide range of services, not only for children with employed parents, let alone only for their employees.

In the UK, the strategy is for costs of services outside the education system to be mainly borne by parents: 'the Government believe that in the first instance it is the responsibility of the parents to make arrangements, including financial arrangements, for the day care of preschool children' (Department of Health, 1989, para.1). The main exception is public funding for a small number of families deemed to be 'in need' and a limited subsidy of low income families using services through the child care disregard. Employers are not required to contribute to costs, nor are there inducements for them to do so.

Fragmentation and incoherence

Early childhood services are, in most cases, conceptually fragmented and incoherent in practice. The division between 'care' and 'education' continues to be widespread, in particular between services for children under and over three. In some countries (e.g. the UK, Ireland, Portugal and Greece) this division is also apparent in a split between different services for children over three. Services for the under threes continue to be seen primarily as meeting the needs of children of working parents for care while parents are at work (with the additional function of providing a preventive and support service to children or families with major problems). For the over threes, services are primarily seen as part of a general education system, which often takes little note of the care needs of children and parents.

Lack of coherence in practice is pervasive, and flows in large measure from the conceptual fragmentation of services. The availability of services varies (more shortfall for under threes), as do hours of opening (under-threes services have longer hours and are open for more weeks in the year); administrative responsibility differs, involving not only different depart-ments (health, welfare, education) but also often different levels of gov-ernment (local, regional, national); funding arrangements and the cost to parents are quite different (thus nursery education is free of charge, while parents pay for publicly funded nurseries); and the pay, conditions and training of workers are related to children's ages and the responsible sys-tem, rather than to the actual needs of children and the value of the work undertaken.

Responding to ethnic diversity

Many European countries have substantial minority ethnic populations, and most have begun to respond to this in their thinking about early child-hood services. The main response, however, has been either assimilationist or multi-cultural. In this respect, the UK is unique in the relative promi-nence given to anti-racism as a basis for service development.

TOWARDS A NEW APPROACH TO SERVICES

In recent years, and since the publication of the EC Childcare Network's reports on child care in Europe (European Commission, 1988, 1990), the 'league table' approach to Europe has become particularly influential in the UK, by which I mean the constant emphasis on quantitative aspects of services and, in particular, levels of publicly funded services. This approach may have served some purpose, in raising awareness in the UK about the relatively low priority given in public expenditure to early childhood ser-vices. To the extent that this level of expenditure has reflected a govern-ment view about the boundaries between public and private responsibility for the care and education of young children, it has revealed an important difference in orientation between the UK and many other European coun-tries.

However, the 'league table' approach may have helped to conceal some other important parts of the overall picture. The situation in the UK con-tains some real strengths: there are many individual centres of excellence; nursery education, where it exists, is of a high standard, with nursery teach-ers enjoying the same training and pay as primary school teachers; the Children Act promises important improvements in the regulation and review of services; and important and often innovative work has been undertaken in areas such as curriculum for preschool education, quality and anti-racism. Standards in some European services are lower than many people in the UK would consider adequate. But above all, the 'league table' approach has led people to ignore some important developments emerging in parts of Europe and the ideas behind them. I want in this section to highlight three innovations which seem to me to be of particular significance.

Towards coherent early childhood services

There is an increasing questioning in parts of Europe of the fragmentation and incoherence that often underlies early childhood services. Since the 1970s, there has been a strong movement in parts of northern Italy to emphasize the educative role of nurseries, and nursery and nursery school provision is integrated into education departments in many northern local authorities. A number of local authorities in the UK have also made significant moves to integrate responsibility for early childhood services (see Chapter 1).

The process of integration has been taken furthest in Spain and the Nordic countries. In Spain, the whole education system has recently been reformed through a major law, passed in 1990 (Ley de Ordenación General del Sistemo Educativo – LOGSE), and preceded by several years of public debate and widespread experimentation. LOGSE recognizes the 0–6 age range as the first stage of the education system and has brought all services within the education system. At the same time, a new basic qualification has been introduced – the early childhood teacher – covering work with all children under six and involving a three-year, post-18 university course.

Spain has therefore created an integrated framework, within which all services for children from birth to six have the possibility of developing in a coherent manner; however, there is a long way to go before this reform is fully implemented and Spain has, in practice, a coherent and integrated early childhood service. Such a service, however, already exists in the three Nordic member states. The Danish, Finnish and Swedish systems for children under seven are totally integrated. Services are recognized as having a dual care and pedagogical function. The pay, conditions and training of workers is the same, whether working with children under or over three.

In general, responsibility for services rests with one department at local and national level, in this case with social welfare rather than education. The main exception is in Sweden, where since 1993 responsibility for early childhood services and schools has been integrated within one department in many local authorities; at national level, however, responsibility for early childhood services still lies with the Ministry of Social Affairs. In Denmark

and Finland, care and education services for children under seven (and outside school hours provision for children over seven, which is part of the
same system) dominate the work of local welfare departments, while there
is a strong pedagogical tradition (reflected in high standards of training)
in this area of work.

Finnish and Swedish early childhood services are generally age integrated, taking children under and over three. In Denmark, the integrated
system has enabled them to question and revise their approach to the age
grouping of children in services. Originally, services were strongly age segregated: nurseries for under threes, kindergartens from three to school, and
centres providing outside school hours care for schoolage children from
three to seven. In recent years, there has been an increasing concern to
provide wider age groupings, in the interests of children's relationships and
experience. Most services developed in recent years have been 'age integrated institutions', providing for children from babies up to seven and, in
some cases, up to ten or older (Jensen, 1993). Examples of similar
approaches, combining services for children under and over three, are also
to be found in some other non-Nordic countries, although age segregation
remains the norm (the problem of developing an integrated approach when
under threes are a local welfare responsibility and over threes a national
educational responsibility should again be emphasized).

The questioning of old divisions, especially between care and education,
has also been reflected in the language used to describe services. The Danes
refer to pedagogical services (with workers called pedagogues). In Spain,
the word for nurseries (guaderia) is being replaced by the term escuela
infantile (infant schools), to reflect the educational orientation of all services for children aged 0–6 years. The earlier French term for care (garde)
has generally been replaced by the word acceuil, which means literally 'welcoming', while the term acceuil educatif introduces an educative orientation. In English, however, terms such as 'day care', 'child care' and 'nursery
education' remain common, without an adequate alternative ('educare'
may carry the meaning, but is a clumsy term; the generic term 'educator'
used in the Rumbold Report (DES, 1990a) for workers in early childhood
services provides another contribution to the search for a new English-lan-
guage terminology); in this case, terminology both reflects divisions and
reinforces them.

Towards multi-functional early childhood services

Northern Italy has early childhood services that are both extensive in quantity and widely recognized to be of high quality. However, this area of
Europe has undergone a series of important developments in thinking

about the purpose of these services. Following the passing of a law in the late 1960s, which transferred responsibility for nursery services for children under three to local and regional government, a number of more vigorous and committed local and regional authorities in the north took the opportunity to develop the number of places available. From the beginning, these services were seen as providing care for young children while parents were at work. However, in the early 1980s there was a period of re-assessment leading to a new emphasis on the educative as well as caring role of nurseries, with measures (for example, in training and support) taken to develop this broader role. Most recently, there has been a further process of evaluation. A diversification of services has begun, to enable them to meet the needs of a wider range of children and their carers. This means, for example, providing part-time services for parents with part-time jobs, drop-in sessions, playgroups and playgrounds and so on.

This process of diversification is not at the expense of the original function of nurseries; good quality provision for children with full-time working parents remains a central task. Diversification means extending nurseries to become multi-functional centres for all children and carers in their area, as well as opening new services that complement nurseries. This approach breaks down not only the care-education divide, but the tendency to fragment services, conceptually and in practice, so that one service provides 'child care for working parents', another 'day care for children in need', a third support for mothers at home and so on.

Examples of multi-functional services are also emerging in other countries (Pen Green Centre in Corby is an exemplary case in the UK – see Chapter 10). However, unlike some family centres in the UK, most of these multi-functional services do not have a 'therapeutic' or 'community work' orientation. They develop from a perspective which regards early childhood services as a need and right of all communities and families, and as an expression of social solidarity with children and parents which recognizes the needs of both employed and non-employed parents and their children.

Parental involvement

There are a number of examples of service systems which place emphasis on parental involvement in management, for example in the nursery services in many parts of northern Italy where parents play an active part in the system of social management, and in Danish services where services managed by local authorities must have a management board with a parent majority. An example of a service actually run by parents is the system of crèches parentales in France. The number of these parent-run nurseries has increased from 30 in 1982 to 700 in 1991, providing for 12,000 children (many in rural areas and small towns). They provide services for children under three, including all-day care; parents set up and run the service, and there is a national organization (ACEP) with regional branches. Parents who use the service have to commit themselves to working with the children (for example, half a day a week) and to participating in management.

An important feature about this service (and one of several ways in which the crèches parentales differ from 'community playgroups' in the UK, another example of a parent-run service) is that it is publicly and substantially funded and employs full-time workers who receive the same pay and conditions as workers in more traditional nurseries. Finally, it should be noted that crèches parentales are one of a range of publicly funded services; most provision for children under three is provided in ordinary nurseries or 'organized family day care'. This means that parents who want to run the service attended by their children can have the opportunity to do so, but that playing such an active role is not an expectation of all parents wanting services.

THE 'EUROPEAN DIMENSION' IN EARLY CHILDHOOD SERVICES

This chapter has dealt mainly at the level of individual European countries. In conclusion, though, I want to consider developments at a European (or more specifically European Union) level. The EU's interest in aspects of early childhood services goes back to the Treaty of Rome and Article 119 which commits the Community to seek equal treatment for men and women in the labour market. The European Commission, in its attempt to promote such equal treatment, has identified the 'reconciliation of employment and family responsibilities' as one of the conditions required – and this in turn has led the Commission to take an increasing interest in issues concerning the care of children as an essential part of the solution to this reconciliation condition.

In 1983, as part of the Community's First Equal Opportunity Programme, the Commission proposed a Directive on Parental Leave and Leave for Family Reasons. A Directive is legally enforceable in member states, and the Commission's proposal envisaged setting minimum standards for these two types of leave throughout the Community, including each worker having an entitlement to at least three months of parental leave, with the entitlement to be non-transferable (in other words, if fathers did not take leave, their entitlement could not be transferred to their partners). To come into force, Directives must be adopted by the Council of

Ministers, representing the governments of each member state (the Commission initiates Directives, the Council decides whether to adopt them). Unfortunately, mainly because of opposition from the British Government, the proposed Directive was not adopted, and was withdrawn by the Commission in 1994 (although by this time, most member states had introduced statutory parental leave offering an entitlement to leave of at least six months per family) (EC Childcare Network, 1994).

Subsequently, the Commission has used the procedure laid down in the Social Protocol of the Maastricht Treaty for the adoption of measures in the area of social policy. As the first stage, the Commission drafted a consultation text for the social partners (representatives of employers and organized labour), and in February 1995 invited them to give their views on parental leave and other measures to support reconciliation of employment and family life. At the time of writing, it seems likely that this procedure will lead to agreement on minimum standards for parental leave in the EU – with the exception of the UK, whose government has opted out of the Social Protocol.

In 1986, as part of its Second Equal Opportunities Programme, the Commission established a Childcare Network, consisting of an expert from each member state. During the remaining four years of the Programme, this Network undertook a range of work, publishing a number of reports, reviewing policies and services in general, and analysing a number of specific issues (for example, rural families, workers in services and men as carers). The Network was continued under the Third Equal Opportunities Programme, which runs from 1991 to the end of 1995, and was renamed the European Commission Network on Childcare and Other Measures to Reconcile Employment and Family Responsibilities. The Programme defined the Network's role as 'to monitor developments, evaluate policy options, collect and disseminate information and establish criteria for the definition of quality in childcare services'. Its work has focused on leave arrangements for parents, measures to support increased participation by men in the care and upbringing of children and services for children under ten, where apart from reports on specific issues (for example, family day care and school-age child care) and a new review of services in the expanded EU, it has developed a unique body of work on quality.

In 1990 the Community Charter of Basic Social Rights for Workers, under the heading of 'the Right of Men and Women to Equal Treatment', called for 'the development of amenities enabling those concerned to reconcile their occupational and family obligations more easily' (Eurospeak for services and other measures to support employed parents). The Action Programme for Implementing the Charter, and the Community's Third Equal Opportunities Programme which began in 1991, called for the Commission to prepare a Recommendation on Childcare.

A Recommendation, like a Directive, is a Community measure. Unlike a Directive it is not legally binding, being confined to recommending action to member states (both the Childcare Network and the European Parliament in a Resolution on Childcare and Equality of Opportunity (April 1991) have argued for a Directive). A Recommendation can take two forms – a Commission Recommendation (as originally proposed) or a Council of Ministers Recommendation, which carries far more political weight since it is adopted by all member state governments, rather than simply being issued by the Commission.

The Recommendation on Childcare was adopted in March 1992 – as a Council Recommendation. Despite being diluted and heavily qualified, an inevitable consequence of a document that has to secure the approval of a wide range of governments, the Recommendation is the clearest statement yet of European policy on reconciliation. It offers a framework of objectives and principles which can form the basis for future development.

The objective of the Recommendation is 'to encourage initiatives to enable women and men to reconcile their occupational, family and upbringing responsibilities arising from the care of children' (Article 1). It identifies four areas where measures need to be taken: services for children; leave arrangements for employed parents; making the environment, structure and organization of the workplace responsive to the needs of workers with children; and the encouragement of increased participation by men in the care of children to ensure a more equal sharing of family responsibilities between men and women. By implication, each area is considered necessary, but not sufficient by itself.

The section on services is confined to provision for children with 'parents who are working, following a course of education or training in order to obtain employment or are seeking employment or a course of education or training in order to obtain employment'. It does not therefore support the concept of multi-functional early childhood services, available to all children and carers. This is because, at present, the EU has no legal authority to take measures concerned primarily with child welfare; indeed, in many ways children are invisible in the EU, which remains essentially an economic institution. The Recommendation, it should be stressed, is primarily an equal opportunities measure, since the EU has legal authority to pursue gender equality in the labour market as a policy objective.

Despite this omission, the Recommendation proposes, in Article 3, a number of important principles, of relevance to all early childhood services. These principles include: affordability; combining reliable care with a pedagogical approach; availability in urban and rural areas and accessibility to children with special needs; flexibility and diversity, combined with 'coherence between different services'; working closely with local communities and being responsive to parental needs and local circumstances; and staff training, both basic and continuous, that is 'appropriate to the importance and the social and educative value of their work'.

The Council Recommendation should be seen both as a tool and as part of a process. As a tool, it provides one means to support the development of national policies on early childhood services and reconciliation of employment and family responsibilities. The principles and objectives contained in the Recommendation, together with its framework of four areas requiring measures, can provide a useful starting point for such development – assuming, of course, a political will to undertake this work.

The Recommendation is also one stage in an evolving European perspective on early childhood services and reconciliation. In 1995, member state governments were required to inform the Commission on what measures they have taken to give effect to the Recommendation, on the basis of which the European Commission will prepare a report on implementation. The Commission is also preparing a Guide to supplement the Recommendation, which will elaborate the principles and objectives it contains. The Childcare Network has prepared a document setting out 40 Quality Targets, which it believes could be attained throughout the EU within ten years. Both documents should be published in 1996.

The Recommendation, despite its omissions, ambiguities and qualifications, marks an important milestone in the development of a European policy in the area of early childhood services. Ultimately, this means a convergence of principles and objectives, rather than the imposition of some standard system of services. That process of convergence will be gradual and incremental, and the pace and extent of convergence will depend on a number of factors, not least the ability of organizations concerned with children and early childhood services to develop a co-ordinated and effective lobbying capability aimed at the European political process. Unfortunately, the Recommendation did not have the benefit of such a lobby to press for a strong and effective measure; indeed, combined with media disinterest and a general ignorance of the workings of the EU, the Recommendation (like many other social measures) received little attention in the UK.

The development of formal policy and other initiatives at EU level is not, however, the only 'European dimension' in the development of services and policies. Perhaps as important in the long run is the framework provided by the European Union for the exchange of ideas, experience and knowledge between member states, regional and local authorities, organizations, projects and individual workers. What this exchange can do is contribute to the spread of good practice and ideas, a raising of expectations and greater understanding of the assumptions and context which have influenced the developments in each member state.

This chapter is written in expectation and with a certain degree of wishful thinking. There are risks. Dragging back advanced services to a lowest common denominator might occur rather than a process of levelling up to the best. Cheap and dubious practices in one country may attract the attention of the government in another country. Perhaps, above all, balancing the interests of economies with those of women and children may not be achieved. The need to extend the EU's legal authority to include citizens outside the labour force, including children, and to develop a Community that has strong social objectives, as well as economic ones, is essential if this balance is to be attained. Finally, all organizations with interests in children and their carers must inform themselves of European Community processes, initiatives and structures, to fit themselves to play an active role at a European as well as a national level.

3

DEFINING, MEASURING AND SUPPORTING QUALITY

Peter Elfer and Dorothy Wedge

INTRODUCTION

It is important to define quality in relation to care and education provision for young children for at least two reasons.

First, although we have in the UK a wide range of types of service, offering very different experiences to children (including childminding, day nurseries, playgroups and nursery schools), they are sometimes grouped together under a single heading such as nursery education (Angela Rumbold, Hansard, 4 February 1991) as if they were one coherent service. When we are discussing the quality of a particular service, we need to be sure we do so on the basis of a common understanding of the objectives and underpinning philosophy and values of that service.

The importance of this has been reinforced by the government's voucher initiative, in which the parents of 'every four-year-old will receive a voucher which they can exchange for education in the maintained, private or voluntary sectors' (DFEE, 1995). In order to be able to redeem vouchers, providers of services will need to be able to demonstrate that the education they offer is 'appropriate to desirable learning outcomes'.

© Copyright, 1996 Peter Elfer and Dorothy Wedge.

Second, the last decade has seen an emphasis on the economic value of commodities or services, particularly in the public sector. This too has reinforced the need to be able to define and describe clearly the objectives any service has for young children and the conditions and circumstances in which it will be possible (or difficult) to achieve those objectives.

There have been a number of recent reports and initiatives aiming to describe the characteristics of high quality provision for children (Williams, 1995). These have sometimes been in the form of principles of good practice and sometimes entailed more detailed standards. We refer to these different ways of defining and describing quality collectively as quality frameworks.

Whilst quality frameworks and clear standards are important, it is also important to remember that the care and education of any child happen primarily through a set of unique relationships. The younger the child, the more important these relationships are. One danger of the use of quality frameworks is that they focus attention on the framework itself and easily measurable standards such as ratios or space requirement, rather than the quality of interactions with children.

The early years workers' task, therefore, is not only to apply the quality frameworks that their service works within but to remember that the most important aspects of quality are the relationships with and between children and how these relationships support each child's overall care and education. It is for this reason that the role of keyworkers and the importance of reflective practice have been twin themes in many reports on the quality of early years services. We therefore believe the key to the effectiveness of quality frameworks is the extent to which they help focus, rather than distract, workers' attention on their relationships with children.

The chapter is in two parts:

(1) issues in defining and describing quality;

(2) the role of inspection, practice development and service reviews in assuring quality.

In the second part, we give three examples of initiatives to develop quality on the basis of experience in a large county council.

ISSUES IN DEFINING AND DESCRIBING QUALITY

The pressure to define quality

At the time the Children Bill was making its passage through Parliament, the Early Childhood Unit at the National Children's Bureau received a large number of requests, particularly from private, voluntary and social services settings, for a statement of quality and standards in work with young children.

The pressure for externally produced statements of standards mainly arises because of:

- the wish to have the 'local view' of what are appropriate standards endorsed by an external 'authority';

- the need for consistency between one locality and another.

However, some of the pressure may also be because agreeing standards at the local level (the local authority and each local service), is hard work if different stakeholders are to be involved and the process can be a painful one. As individuals and teams consider how a standard should be implemented in practice, for example providing 'warm and close relationships' with children, different workers will have different views. These views may be passionately held and will touch on workers' own childhood experiences. What one worker regards as a 'warm and close relationship', another may consider to be too intense or protective. Turning to external experts and research findings is one way of avoiding these difficult discussions.

Limitations of research

External 'experts' and researchers do of course have an important part to play in defining quality and are likely to agree in general terms on what it should look like:

> There is broad agreement about what children need in order to develop properly, and that first consideration should be given to the welfare of the child, whilst not interfering unnecessarily with the rights and wishes of the parents.
>
> (Thoburn, 1986, p. 546)

> Assumptions about what children need and how adults might provide it have varied widely even this century. Very generally, however, there is consensus in much of the current child development literature that children need to feel loved, respected and listened to.
>
> (European Commission Childcare Network, 1991, p. 5)

But this consensus is limited as these writers are quick to point out:

> When it comes to individual cases, however, there may be disagreement about whether the care given in a child's own home is 'good enough', or about the respective weight to be given to different needs, especially if not all can be met.
>
> (Thoburn, 1986, p. 546)

We can therefore make informed guesses about what young children need. But our understanding is relative and is coloured by our wider social perceptions and values. We recognize that in stating the needs of children we are also making a statement about our own beliefs.

(European Commission Childcare Network, 1991, p. 5)

It is striking that much recent work on approaches to quality emphasizes that it is a more complex notion than one that can be addressed by research alone. Four common ideas emerge as important to a fuller understanding of quality:

(1) The notion of quality is meaningless unless there is clarity about the values and beliefs that underpin a service.

(2) In the provision of any service there may be a number of 'stakeholders' who could be considered as users and other groups who may have a key interest in the way the service is provided.

(3) Review of quality needs to entail more than a review of the individual service and must include the policy and organizational framework within which a service operates.

(4) Assessing quality must go beyond the application of checklists and frameworks.

Values and beliefs

Reference has already been made to the way values and beliefs underpin any discussion about the needs of children. Other writers concur:

This raises the question of whether governments have any responsibility in this area and if so, whether the responsibility is primarily to protect children from possible harm through enforcing minimum standards for all services or to ensure good quality services for all children. In either case terms need defining. What harm do we wish to prevent? What do we mean by good quality? The answers to either question are bound to be value based.

(Moss and Melhuish, 1991, p. 11)

I am interested in not only the small 'r' ruler we use in attempting to measure quality, but also the capital 'R' Ruler who defines what it is that will be measured . . . 'Who is the Ruler?' appears to be the question one must address before the questions of 'What is the ruler and what is to be measured?' can be considered.

(Pence 1992 in Moss and Pence, 1994, p. 4)

Any approach to assessing quality must be preceded by a working through of what we believe matters, what we are trying to achieve and how we will reconcile competing or conflicting goals. Within this process, research has a role to play but it has a supporting rather than a leading part. Our values and beliefs should be more openly informing our choices about the research areas we consider important rather than the other way round. Farquhar summarizes this well:

> In order for the definition and assessment of quality in early childhood centres to be appropriate and acceptable it is important that the way quality is defined and the methodological approach taken is developed from our knowledge and understanding of empirical research in the area, the philosophical base of the individual programme, and our current social and cultural values for early childhood education.
>
> (Farquhar, 1990, p. 73)

This has two implications. First, the appeal for an 'off the shelf', authoritative statement of quality and standards in child care needs to be responded to with caution. It is extremely important that there should be national statements of good practice, that is, statements which are government led, for example *Starting with Quality* (DES, 1990a) or official guidance (DH, 1991), as well as statements or codes of good practice which are based on widespread consultation (for example Cowley, 1991; PPA, 1990a, 1990b; Kids Club Network, 1989; National Childminding Association, 1991).

However, it is difficult for these documents to be explicit and detailed in the values, beliefs and standards laid down as they need to be acceptable to a very wide range of organizations and constituencies. Their main function is primarily as source documents to assist direct service providers in the process of determining their own specific value commitments and priorities:

> Our discussion of quality acknowledges a diversity of circumstances and a diversity of perspectives or values. . . Indeed, we believe that the process involved in defining quality – with the opportunity it provides to explore and discuss values, objectives and priorities – is of the utmost importance, and can be lost where people simply adopt existing measures.
>
> (European Commission Childcare Network, 1991, p. 8)

In this sense national frameworks are an essential and valuable tool but their contribution is more to the process of defining quality than prescribing it directly.

Stakeholders in quality

The second idea in much recent writing on quality is that a focus on values and beliefs prompts recognition of the existence of other groups (parents, other carers, staff, local communities) who also have a legitimate interest in quality:

> Issues of who are the users of a service underlie the concept of quality in public services . . . Who are the users of child care? The child, the parents or society at large? Whose interests may be damaged by this service or the way we provide it?
>
> (Stewart and Walsh, 1989, p. 8)

Farquhar identifies four groups of 'user': 'In the social, educational and political context of New Zealand pre-compulsory education, there are four different ways of viewing how to ensure and promote quality' (Farquhar, 1990, p. 79), and she goes on to refer to the perspectives of parents, staff, cultural and child development, whilst Moss in the UK speaks of 'what we want or do not want for children, parents, workers and local communities' (Moss and Melhuish, 1991, p. 11).

The perspectives of local communities and differing cultures is perhaps one of the most important and neglected areas in considerations of quality. We live in a multi-cultural, multiracial society in which variations in patterns of parenting and the differing priorities held by parents for their children's development have largely been ignored (Maximé, 1986).

The Children Act 1989 should help to change this through its general requirement that needs arising from race, culture, religion and language must be taken into account by service providers. There is also the more specific power to cancel the registration of providers of childminding and day care where care is 'seriously inadequate' having regard to the child's religious persuasion, racial origin and cultural and linguistic background (S.74(6) Children Act 1989). However, an approach is also needed which will enable judgements to be made about quality in relation to the extent to which the needs of children are positively identified and met rather than only when minimum standards are breached. The Department of Health has funded the development of training materials specifically to help registration and inspection staff in local authorities address this with providers (Elfer, 1995).

The policy and organizational context

Not only do we have to consider different interest groups but also whether judgements about quality are made at the individual service level or in relation to the policy and organizational framework within which services are provided.

Farquhar seems to suggest that these two levels are alternatives:

Definitions of quality may focus on the whole childhood service ...
Alternatively, definitions of quality may be specific to individual early
childhood programmes.

(Farquhar, 1990, p. 75)

The implication is clear that any approach to assessing quality needs to be
centred on the specific aims, objectives and operating conditions of an individual service although the assessment will be made in the context of the
policy of the overall organization, for example the local authority.

The key point here would seem to be the need to establish an approach
to evaluation that does not become too biased towards either the policy-
making level or the local service level of the organization.

Moss emphasizes the relationship between policy and service levels more
strongly than Farquhar:

As a society we have yet to draw up the full policy agenda which recognizes the profundity and inter-connectedness of the issues facing us
concerning childhood and the upbringing of children, the relationship
between employment, parenthood and gender equity and the allocation of work and cost across the whole field of caring work.

(Moss and Melhuish, 1991, p. 18)

Yet even within the limited scope of policy options at local authority level,
the complexity of applying broad values set nationally to local areas
and individual services has perhaps not been sufficiently recognized.
The values that underpin parts of official guidance, for example that
the *fact* of need rather than its cause is to be a prime feature of local
service philosophy (DH, 1991, para. 1.9), will conflict with the values held
by some local elected members. In addition, parents of children with disabilities may not wish their support services to be merged with those
for children whose need arises because of family, emotional and social difficulties.

Beyond checklists and frameworks

A fourth idea in recent writing on defining and measuring quality is the
extent to which the application of checklists and frameworks can offer an
adequate approach to quality assurance. Two writers in particular refer to
this:

Some elements of quality proposed in the literature are easily articulated and enumerated ... However, if the only indexes of quality used
during centre inspection and review are those that are measurable and

required of every centre then this will limit the promotion of high
quality education and care.

(Farquhar, 1990, p. 77)

Any system of quality control which tries to rely too heavily or exclusively on rules, flow charts and checklists of warning signs and to reduce
the part played by the individual family, child, residential or field social
worker in decision-making may be of limited relevance and value.

(Thoburn, 1986, p. 550)

The view of both these writers is that measurables (ratios, qualifications,
group size, training, etc. in the case of early years care and education and
procedures, documentation and decision-making in the case of child protection) cannot alone provide an adequate analysis of quality. This appears
to be in marked contrast to guidance from the Department of Health on
the use of independent inspection units (IIUs): 'The inspection process
should be rooted in explicit values and measurable standards' (DH, SSI,
1991, para. 4.6).

In relation to monitoring and evaluating the curriculum, the Rumbold
Committee considered that: 'it should take place at three levels: within the
individual class or group; within the institution (school, unit, day nursery,
playgroup, etc.) and across all the services for under fives within a local
authority' (DES, 1990a, para. 134) and the committee called for educators
to build into the planning cycle a broad review of the effectiveness and
value of the provision they make, extending beyond the immediate setting
to include parent and community links and other factors (para. 95).

We cannot stress enough how important this three-level monitoring and
evaluation is, not just in relation to the quality of curriculum or activities
offered to children but in relation to wider issues of quality concerning the
availability of provision, how well it meets the needs of families and its
cost. This approach also allows the concern of Farquhar and Moss to be
addressed that the perspective of all 'stakeholders' should be taken into
account in thinking about quality.

The opportunity for monitoring and evaluating quality across all services
for young children within a local authority is provided through the review
duty (S.19 Children Act 1989) and we refer to this in the second part of
the chapter.

THE ROLE OF INSPECTION, PRACTICE
DEVELOPMENT AND STRATEGIC REVIEW

Any effective approach to assuring quality in early years services must
involve powers (through legislation) to inspect services and ensure at least

minimum standards are being maintained (note in this context 'minimum' does not necessarily mean low but the bottom line below which standards must not fall), *and* a strategy for supporting the implementation of the standards into practice.

Historical divisions in the organization and funding of early years services have led to divisions in inspection arrangments too. Daycare services for children under eight, located in the private and voluntary sectors, are inspected under the Children Act 1989 whilst nursery schools and classes are inspected through OFSTED under the Education (Schools) Act 1992.

Legislation and inspection

Part X of the Children Act, implemented in October 1991, gives powers and duties to local authorities in England and Wales to inspect and develop standards of day care. Services for children under five have been registered and inspected since 1948, under the Nurseries and Child-Minders Regulation Act, but the Children Act increases the age range and strengthens the powers of authorities, including new powers to cancel registration.

The central concept of both the 1948 and 1989 Acts in relation to registration and inspection is that of a 'fit person'. New powers and duties and detailed guidance (DH, 1991) on standards and assessing fitness were broadly welcomed by local authorities and providers as implementation of the Act approached in October 1991 although there was some disappointment that the difficult concept of 'fit person' remained. However, the previous regulatory framework under the 1948 Act had become almost unusable because of wide variations between local authorities in the standards they expected providers in their area to comply with. Very few local authorities used their powers to refuse or cancel the registration of a provider. Even where they did, if the provider appealed against the decision through the Magistrates Court, in most cases the Court overturned the decision of the local authority (Elfer and Beasley, 1991).

At the time of its implementation, it looked as if the Children Act would lead to a more effective framework to support quality because of:

* greater powers to inspect and cancel the registration of providers not meeting minimum standards, including the specific power to consider how well each child's needs are met with regard to their religious persuasion, racial origin and cultural and linguisitic background;

* powers to collaborate with education departments in developing standards and inspection and a new duty (S.19) to review the development of provision overall;

- the production of detailed national guidance on standards;

- funding to develop training materials specifically for registration and inspection staff, on implemenation of Part X of the Act.

However, if there was optimism as the Children Act was implemented, one year later, the picture was looking very different. There were said to be many complaints from service providers to MPs about local authorities being over-zealous in the implementation of standards. Whilst no doubt unreasonable requirements were made from time to time, a survey of providers found that all types of providers were overwhelmingly in favour of the principle of registration and inspecting services, most providers thought standards were 'about right' and half to two-thirds of providers who had been inspected had found it to be a positive experience (Moss *et al.*, 1995).

In January 1993, the Department of Health issued a further circular calling on local authorities to assess the overall quality of care likely to be avialable to children, and in relation to any requirements imposed on providers, apply the standards reasonably, influenced by their perception of local conditions and needs:

> local authorities will wish to use the Volume 2 guidance (standards of care and education provision for young children) constructively and not overly rigidly . . . safeguarding standards remains a key objective but all local authorities are invited to review the balance of their registration process and work to encourage the expansion of local services.
>
> (LAC 93(1))

Later that year Mrs Davies won her appeal in the High Court against a decision by the London Borough of Sutton to refuse her registration as a childminder because of her insistence on the right to smack children in her care if their parents wished her to do so (although the Judge was careful to point out that his ruling concerned how binding the standards set out in government guidance should be considered rather than any comment on the rights or wrongs of corporal punishment of children).

As we learned from experience under the 1948 Act, an effective regulatory framework that really does guarantee minimum standards, depends as much on confidence in the framework by those who use it and are subject to it as it does on the powers of the framework itself. LAC 93(1)) and the High Court decision will have inevitably affected confidence in the regulatory framework of the Children Act. The Department of Health has now commissioned the Early Childhood Unit at the National Children's Bureau to undertake a second 'trawl' of cases where local authorities have decided to refuse or cancel a provider's registration and appeals against these decisions. This trawl will provide evidence of the effectiveness of the Children Act as a guarantee of minimum standards compared to the preceding legislation.

Whilst day care provision is registered and must be inspected at least once a year under the Children Act, nursery schools and classes are inspected, at most once very four years, under the Education (Schools) Act 1992 through OFSTED.

This system of inspection has been operating for a much shorter time than inspections under the Children Act. However, it is already clear that a shortage of inspectors trained in early years curriculum and the long intervals between inspections are seriously undermining the effectiveness of this system and its ability to secure reliable standards of care and education for three- and four-year-olds.

Developing practice from minimum standards

Whatever legislative framework is adopted to ensure minimum standards can be guaranteed, we have emphasized that adults are best helped to reflect on and develop their practice when they feel supported and valued in that process rather than feeling 'regulated'.

Many local authorities have held to this principle in providing support for carers and educators in the past. In this section we use two experiences of a large county council which set its principles into policy. The first example describes the way in which it implemented its own policy and the second sets out its attempts to provide access to the National Vocational Qualification in Childcare and Education through a multidisciplinary assessment centre. While both examples demonstrate the effectiveness of outside support and the value of quality frameworks, they also point to the fragility of such initiatives if they have to survive without subsidy in a market environment.

Example 1. Working for quality in reception classes   It is the county council's policy to admit children at the beginning of the school year in which they will become five years old and schools have been partly funded to enable reception classes to make 'near nursery' provision for them. A team of six advisory teachers was appointed to support the policy.

The under-fives team was very successful in working alongside others to improve the quality and continuity of provision. Travelling around their different areas they demonstrated good practice, taking ideas, equipment and an extra pair of hands to encourage appropriate activity-based learning for young children. Their practical play workshops demonstrating mathematics, science, creativity, emergent reading and writing in imaginative ways inspired parents, playgroup leaders, headteachers and governors. Their enthusiasm was catching and many support groups developed. Examples of work they helped to develop formed the main part of curriculum guidelines as a quality framework for four-year-olds in schools and these were issued as policy throughout the county.

However, at the time of the Education Reform Act, it was decided to move curriculum support into an agency and the services of the team, which had been highly valued when they were free, were not bought sufficiently to retain them. Schools were too concerned with the National Curriculum to attend to its foundations. Although Community Education took half the team to build up family education with young families (which was also successful), they too are threatened with redundancy in 1996 because of cuts which have been imposed on the non-statutory service so that school budgets will be protected.

So despite a recent evaluation of reception class practice which has shown the long-term effects of their work, and the fact that the team is working with colleagues on a new foundation curriculum document, it is very likely that when the nursery voucher scheme is introduced, the team will no longer be available to ensure that the proper foundation is laid.

Example 2.   Making National Vocational Qualifications (NVQs) happen
It was clear from taking part in the pilot study that the NVQ would be able to have as great an impact on quality of provision as the Children Act – if it could be made to happen. What follows is not a success story, but it may be typical of the experience of many groups who have struggled to set up an assessment centre which could offer the qualification at reasonable cost to low-paid established workers.

A multi-disciplinary consortium, including the private sector, was set up in 1993 to work together for the new NVQ and make it available to the large numbers of people who were already working with young children but had never had the opportunity to gain a qualification. A feasibility study had been done, potential numbers of candidates identified in all sectors and a commitment obtained from members. Commitment, but no money.

Both education and social services were able to make contributions of worker time and operational support, but neither could fund a co-ordinator post. A bid was prepared for the European Social Fund (ESF) but by the time the money was available it was obvious that meeting the deadline for the criteria would be difficult. Nevertheless, an application was made to the Council for Early Years Awards (now the Council for Awards in Childcare and Education) to become an assessment centre and funding accessed from the Training and Enterprise Council to train assessors and make a skills check of numbers of people working in playgroups, nurseries and family centres and an application was made for a second year to the ESF.

This time the target candidates had to be people working fewer than ten hours a week and they were harder to find than was anticipated. Workers in family support projects had enough to do without thinking about port-folios, and eventually playgroup workers from the Diploma course agreed to be candidates.

Perhaps it was too ambitious a project – a multi-disciplinary centre try-ing to change the status quo but having to concentrate on twenty candi-dates to stay in business. One of the consortium members from the health service told of the hospital with forty assessors trained with government money with only one candidate who was paying her own expenses. By com-parison the consortium was doing well but had still not found a way to offer the qualification at a price which people could afford.

In 1995 there were candidates and assessors working together at last. The positive effects of NVQ competencies on standards have been immediate, and the verifying body is very positive about the achievements so far. It has been hard work and everyone involved has given long hours of their own time and commitment. Moreover, yet more effort has to be put in to iden-tifying potential government initiatives into which some candidates can fit in 1996/7. Nevertheless, the consortium is determined to succeed.

Towards an integrated approach to quality assurance

We have outlined the two legislative frameworks for inspection of care and education services for young children and the importance of regulation and practice development operating hand in hand in any quality assurance approach.

As day care services in the private and voluntary sectors increasingly attend to the quality of educational experiences offered to children and nursery schools and classes take a greater role in the care of children and family support, the need to integrate inspection arrangements becomes greater. As part of the government's nursery voucher initiative, the Department of Health and the Department for Education and Employment have issued a consultation paper which proposes to introduce a new educational inspection regime to apply to all institutions registered to exchange vouchers.

Whilst there are serious reasons (see Chapter 1) to doubt that the voucher inititative will contribute to the quality and availability of an inte-grated early years service, the need to integrate the two current separate inspection and quality assurance systems is at least addressed by both gov-ernment lead departments.

The initiative does present an opportunity to move towards an integrated approach which could provide quality assurance, if it:

- is related to an effective framework of standards drawing on research and experience from both the 'care' and 'education' traditions

- ensures inspection arrangements have teeth so that if minimum standards are not being reached, remedial action can be taken quickly;

- involves providers and users (including children) in the inspection process;

- has a clear strategy for service development based on the inspection and including a development plan, in-service training, staff supervision, and external advice and support.

There is, however, little point in integrating inspection if financial cutbacks continue to mean the gradual disappearance of early years advisers in education departments, the inadequate funding of support workers in national organizations such as the National Childminding Association and the Preschool Learning Alliance and the impossibility for social services departments of funding training and support beyond the minimal statutory annual inspection.

In our third example below, we illustrate how regulatory powers can be used to ensure minimum standards are being maintained whilst a practice development approach can be used to support providers as they move beyond this minimum.

Example 3.   Evaluation of the quality of care and education of babies and toddlers in independent day nurseries   The authority's approach to annual inspection is that it is a joint evaluation process, checking that minimum registration standards are still in place but also looking at the quality of care and education together. This has been found to be successful with the reports of advisers regarded as helpful by providers and improvements in standards achieved each year.

However, it is generally acknowledged that the annual inspection is not the best means of assessing the care provided on a daily basis because the date of the inspection is known in advance. For this reason, and because anxieties were raised by seeing the inadequate care given to small children in two nurseries filmed in a *Panorama* programme (BBC, 1994), the social services department decided to undertake spot-check visits to all nurseries providing for babies and toddlers and produce a report which would inform nurseries, parents and the public of the standard of care provided across the county.

The evaluation would also be valuable in checking the consistency of the registration process and provide a means of working closely with nurseries to consider ways in which quality can be continually reflected upon and improved. Day nurseries were told of the exercise in a letter which enclosed the evaluation schedule and assured them that no nursery would be named in the report. It was agreed that they would receive a copy of the report, together with a summary to be given to parents. Both the report and copies of the summary would be available in public libraries.

A working group of advisers devised an evaluation framework, using national guidelines (DH, 1991; Cowley, 1991) and a recent and authoritative statement of good practice in work with under threes (Goldschmied and Jackson, 1994). It was agreed that the focus of the evaluation would be interaction between staff and the children in their care, in the context of staffing, play, safety and health and hygiene.

The advisers visited 54 nurseries, spending two hours in each room providing for babies and toddlers, and observing the way in which staff acknowledged children's need for individual attention by giving them approval, praise and encouragement, by offering them stimulating experiences and by respecting their wishes and preferences and those of their parents.

The evaluation report includes examples of best practice and that which falls below standards. Following a rating scale adapted from McCail (Smith and Vernon, 1994), the report shows the proportion of nurseries assessed as 'inadequate', 'minimal', 'good' or 'excellent' on each aspect of provision. This rating scale will also be included in the leaflet to parents to support them in evaluating the quality of care.

Open meetings are being held with day nursery proprietors and managers after publication of the report and it is hoped that a series of workshops can be arranged which will follow up the recommendations of the evaluation.

Strategic review

One of the most promising features of the Children Act 1989 in relation to young children is that the call in previous guidance (LASSL(76)5 and LASSL(78)5) for co-ordination and collaboration is developed into a specific duty (S. 19). The review must be conducted with the education authority and includes all registered provision for under eights, holiday and out-of-school provision for older children 'in need' and arrangements for the provision of advice and support. Review of provision for children in need does not apply in Scotland. The review must have regard to provision that is not registered; for example, education facilities for young children.

In introducing the review, the Guidance says that 'The review duty gives legislative support to government policy that the level, pattern and range of daycare and related services for young children should be worked out at local level' (DH, 1991, para. 9.1). Whilst the words 'level, pattern and range' indicate the main function of the review is to co-ordinate the development of services overall, the *quantity* of services cannot be divorced from their *quality*. The review therefore presents an important opportunity to consider strategically issues closely related to quality such as:

- collaboration across departments and sectors on the development of standards against which quality should be assessed;

- strengths and weaknesses in services evident in an overview of inspection reports;

- the quality of the inspection process and the extent to which children, parents and early years workers are involved in the inspection; and

- the development of a training strategy and the extent to which training resources are shared.

The first reviews have now been completed with over 90 per cent of authorities publishing a report of the review in their area and the second round of reviews was due for completion in October 1995. It is too early to assess what impact the first reviews have had on the quality of services as experienced by children and their families. However (Elfer and McQuail, 1996) a detailed evaluation, found that the reviews were valued by those who participated in them from all sectors for four reasons:

- Despite weaknesses in their process, they had established the discipline of a regular dialogue in each authority between different providers and taking account of the views of service users.

- They had begun in many authorities the establishment of the first systematic data base of what provision existed in that area.

- They had been an important opportunity for learning about early years services for many groups of officers or elected members who may have known little about this area of service provision overall or only about one part of it.

- They had helped keep the importance of services in the minds of officers and members at a time of stringent expenditure constraints.

CONCLUSION

Quality frameworks are an essential part of developing quality provision. However, quality itself may be a misleading concept if it encourages the idea that we are all agreed on what we are looking for and want for children before we have actually gone through a process to ensure that. The translation of frameworks into practice is complex and demands time and resources. That is because working with children is primarily a matter of reflective and carefully managed relationships which take time to understand and change.

In the past, training has implied that experts hold the right messages which have to be passed down to other people. This is no longer an appropriate way to develop quality frameworks for individual services. Service users and front line staff need to feel that they understand and agree with standards they are expected to implement, and that they have had some opportunity to influence these rather than simply receiving them from an ivory tower. Surely we can look forward to a dynamic process in each setting that is based on mutual respect and understanding of skills and experiences across disciplines, that draws on the concerns and expertise of parents and that supports a quality framework that has a shared sense of ownership.

Topics for discussion

In completing this review of approaches to defining, measuring and assessing quality in the mid-1990s, it seems to us that the questions below are ones it would be helpful for those working with young children and those managing services to consider. We would very much encourage you to think about them as part of your own reflective practice and, if you work with other adults, to put them on the agenda of staff or team meetings.

(1) Which aspects of your own upbringing gave you most pleasure, security and satisfaction? Do you think the adults responsible for your care as a young child were aware of these aspects? Have you made a conscious effort to ensure these aspects underpin your own practice or that of your team?

(2) How do you judge the quality of your work with young children, either individually or as a team of workers? What opportunities do you get or make to reflect on your practice, either alone or with a colleague or line manager?

(3) Who are the big 'R' and small 'r' rulers for your service (see page 54) and how do they influence the way the quality of your work with children is judged?

(4) What would be the advantages and disadvantages of giving the children you work with a greater say in how the quality of the service they use is defined and assessed (as has been done in some Danish nurseries)?

4

RESPECTING THE RIGHT OF CHILDREN TO BE HEARD

Gerison Lansdown

AN INTERNATIONAL CONTEXT
FOR CHILDREN'S RIGHTS

Debates over the rights of children have had a high profile in recent years, with growing acceptance in both national and international law that children are people entitled to basic human rights. Arguably the most significant contribution to this profile was the adoption by the UN General Assembly in 1989 of the UN Convention on the Rights of the Child and its subsequent ratification by the UK Government in December 1991 which represented an explicit commitment to respecting and promoting the principles and standards it embodies. The Convention has been ratified by 186 countries (March 1996), a level of support unprecedented in the history of the United Nations. No other international treaty has achieved a comparable level of commitment. This near universal acceptance of the importance of respect for children's rights lends considerable international authority to the need to review our attitudes towards children. Ratification by countries representing almost every culture, religion and language in the world also demonstrates powerfully that the rights it embodies are universal rights applicable to all children and not subject to grounds of cultural traditions or history. As such it establishes tional law a unique challenge to the traditional assumptions ab status of children in society, and recognition of children's right only to survival, development and protection but also to basic civil right – the right to freedom of expression, religion, conscience, association, information, physical integrity, and to participation in matters of concern to them.

In the preamble to the Convention it is stated that children should be 'fully prepared to live an individual life in society and brought up in the spirit of the ideals proclaimed in the Charter of the United Nations and in particular in the spirit of peace, dignity, tolerance, freedom, equality and solidarity'. In other words, children should be brought up in an environment in which they learn to value and respect themselves as well as others. Central to the process of learning a sense of personal value and respect is the recognition that children have the right to express their views and have them taken seriously. This right is clearly defined in Article 12 of the Convention which states that:

1. States Parties shall assure to the child who is capable of forming his or her own views the right to express those views freely in all matters affecting the child, the views of the child being given due weight in accordance with the age and maturity of the child.

2. For this purpose, the child shall in particular be provided the opportunity to be heard in any judicial and administrative proceedings affecting the child, either directly, or through a representative or an appropriate body, in a manner consistent with the procedural rules of national law.

This Article stresses that all children who are able to express their views must be provided with opportunities to participate in decisions that affect them. The right extends from decisions that are made within the private sphere of the family to those made, for example, in the public arena of health, education and local authority care. It encompasses decisions affecting the individual child as well as those affecting children as a body. It is therefore a powerful assertion of children's right to be actors in their own lives and not merely passive recipients of adults' decision-making.

However, an explicit commitment to respect for the voice of the child does represent a significant shift away from a more traditional understanding of children's status in society and indeed within the family, and it can therefore provoke concerns about its implications for adult/child relations. The language of children's rights can become synonymous with a fear of children acting as autonomous individuals without discipline, control or responsibility. It is important therefore to clarify the nature of children's

Convention on the Rights of the Child and in
mplications of Article 12.

S TO CHILDREN'S RIGHTS

69

out question a range of fundamental rights for
little disagreement, for example, that children
have the best possible health, to free education on the
basis of equality, ortunity, to play and recreation, to freedom from
discrimination, to a standard of living adequate for their proper development. In other words children's rights to survival and development are not
contentious. There might be disagreement over the level of provision necessary to fulfil the obligations to children associated with those rights, or
indeed, over where responsibility for such provision lies, but the principles
are not in question. Similarly, in the field of children's rights to protection,
there would be general agreement that children have the right to protection from sexual exploitation, from abduction and from violence and abuse.
Again there might be considerable dispute over the nature of protection
necessary and, indeed, what constitutes violence in respect of children, but
the principle that children are entitled to protection from a range of experiences that could be harmful to them is not challenged.

Acceptance of the legitimacy of these rights derives from a view of childhood in which the child is constructed as the recipient of the adults' protective care and responsibility. It constructs parenthood as a set of
obligations which at the same time confers on them certain rights and from
which the child is intended to benefit. And whilst the fulfilment of those
obligations imposed by recognition of the child's rights might at times be
demanding, difficult or onerous, the obligations themselves do not in any
way threaten the status of the parent. The right of the parent to consent
to treatment of a child, to change their name, to determine where they live,
which school they go to, to punish them, all derive from implicit assumptions about the child's right to care, protection and guidance. In other
words, these rights to not undermine the rights of the parent. On the contrary, they are the very source of the parent's authority in relation to the
child, and will, in the vast majority of families, be used to promote and
ensure the child's well-being.

It is when one moves into the field of children's civil rights which require
that adults' role in relation to children becomes not only that of protec-
tor, provider or advocate but also negotiator, facilitator or observer, that
the willingness to accept the legitimacy of the rights is less widespread. If
children not only have a right to express a view on matters of concern to
them but also to have those views taken seriously, then parents have obligations to consult with and negotiate with children. Whilst the right of the

child to participate does not remove from the parent the ultimat[e] [author]ity to make decisions in relation to the child, it does significantly aff[ect the] process by which those decisions are made. 'The change seems to be [that] parents no longer have rights "over" children but have rights which the[y] hold on behalf of children' (Open University, forthcoming).

However, it could also be argued that it is in this arena of social relations that there is most to gain for both adults and children by recognition of children as active participants in their own lives. Participation is a fundamental right of citizenship. The creation of a society which combines a commitment to respect for the rights of individuals with an equal commitment to the exercise of social responsibility, must promote the capacity of individuals, from the earliest possible age, to participate in decisions and issues that affect their lives. But whilst some welcome progress has been made in recognizing children's right to participate in decisions that affect them, further changes in legislation, policy and practice as well as social attitudes towards children are necessary if we are to respect the fundamental human right to participation embodied in the UN Convention on the Rights of the Child, and the consequences that these changes will make for improved emotional and psychological health for children, better decisions, and a more democratic and participative society.

THE CHANGING STATUS OF CHILDREN

Both the status of children and the role of the family have undergone significant changes over the course of this century. The family is no longer considered without question as a secure, safe and stable environment for all children. The past thirty years have been characterized by growing recognition first that physical abuse and neglect and more recently that sexual abuse of children exist quite widely within families. These discoveries have led to greater questioning of the rights of parents and increased powers on the part of the state to intervene to protect children. In addition, we have been forced to confront the painful reality that children are equally vulnerable when removed into the supposedly protective arena of the child care system. A series of scandals in the field of residential care have exposed the powerlessness of children living in local authority accommodation in the face of abuse and exploitation by adults with responsibility for caring for them (Levy and Kahan, 1991; Kirkwood, 1993).

We have witnessed massive changes in the nature of family life. Many children can expect to live through periods of marriage, divorce, single parenthood, and possible remarriage. Over 150,000 children are affected by divorce each year. Substantial numbers of children are likely to live in several different configurations of the family and their experience of family

stant. The needs, interests and rights of children
⸱t always coincide. It is no longer possible there-
⸱subsume children within the family, for children
within the family.

ave challenged the view that children 'belong' to
⸱ents, within the privacy of the family, have unlim-
ak on their behalf. They have challenged the view
that the state and induced parents are invariably benign towards children. This awareness, arising as it has in the context of the broader debate around the rights of the individual within the welfare system, has lent some urgency to the need to ensure that children themselves are guaranteed avenues through which they can articulate their concerns with confidence that they will be taken seriously.

It is in this context that the growing debate about the status of children and their rights to participation has been taking place. A model of parents as holders of all rights and responsibilities in respect of children is no longer accepted as either possible or desirable. Children are beginning to be acknowledged as individuals both separate from as well as part of the family unit. This shift in thinking has resulted in the reconsideration of traditional approaches to child care, legal protection, and service provision. But the effect of these changes has largely been to transfer responsibility from the exclusive domain of the family into a wider public sphere. It is still other adults with positions of statutory responsibility – the police, the courts, teachers, social workers, doctors – who have powers to contribute to or impose decision-making in children's lives, and not the children themselves. Despite some changes in the legislation affecting children, they remain largely locked into paternalistic structures in which adults, not children, are the actors. Public policy as well as family life continues to restrict the rights of children to effective participation.

THE LEGAL FRAMEWORK

The Children Act 1989 in England and Wales does require that courts and local authorities take account of the wishes and feelings of children when making decisions affecting them, but this Act, although significant, only relates to a very limited number of children in very limited aspects of their lives. In particular, it contains no duty on parents to take account of their children's wishes and feelings, and no right for children to participate in broader matters of concern to them. What this means is that there is no general presumption in legislation that children have a right to participate in decision-making or that they should be encouraged to articulate their views. Such a presumption only comes into play once the child is in a situation of conflict. But real movement beyond the rhetoric of participation will not happen until there is both a legal responsibility and cultural expectation on adults to consult with children on matters of concern to them in the normal day-to-day living of their lives – within the family, at school, in the wider public arena – and not only at a point of conflict necessitating state intervention. Without this, how can we expect children who are not used to being listened to, suddenly to acquire the skills and the confidence to articulate their experiences at a point of crisis in their lives? At the point of parental separation or divorce, for example? Or when seriously ill and needing to make decisions about treatment? And how can we expect adults to listen effectively when to do so is not part of the normal expectation of relationships with children?

The Children (Scotland) Act 1995 introduces a far broader principle of the right of children to be consulted on matters of concern to them. It contains a specific provision which states that

A person shall, in reaching any major decision which involves his fulfilling a parental responsibility ... or his exercising a parental right ... have regard so far as practicable to the views (if he wishes to express them) of the child concerned, taking account of the child's age and maturity ... and without prejudice to the generality of this subsection a child twelve years of age or more shall be presumed to be of sufficient age and maturity to form a view.

(Section 6)

In other words the obligation to take account of the views of children extends into the family in line with the right contained in Article 12.

In addition to the rights embodied in the Children Act, there is also a highly significant House of Lords ruling from 1986 which goes beyond the right to participation and clarifies the extent of a parent's authority in relation to decision-making on behalf of a child. The case concerned the right of a child under the age of 16 years to seek contraceptive advice without the parents' prior consent. Known as the 'Gillick' judgement, the Lords' ruling concluded that

parental rights to control a child do not exist for the benefit of the parent. They exist for the benefit of the child and they are justified only in so far as they enable the parent to perform his duties towards the child, and towards other children in the family.

It went on to state that

parental rights yield to the child's right to make his own decisions when he reaches a sufficient understanding and intelligence to be capable of making up his own mind on the matter requiring a decision.

In other words, parental rights are not universal – they exist only in so far as they are necessary to promote the interests and rights of the child and as soon as children are capable of meeting those needs or exercising those rights themselves, then the parental rights recede. They are therefore time limited and highly restricted. Parental rights, as defined by Lord Scarman in the Gillick judgement, derive from their responsibilities to promote the child's welfare and are limited by that responsibility. This ruling asserts that children who are competent to make a decision affecting their lives are entitled to do so. It therefore extends the right embodied in Article 12 for all children capable of expressing a view to participate in decision-making to the right of 'competent' children to make decisions for themselves. The judgement does not apply any age limits in determining a child's competence, allowing a flexible interpretation in respect of each individual child and every individual situation. Clearly the older the child the greater the breadth of competence that will be achieved. But some competencies can be attained by very young children. For example, the work done at Great Ormond Street Hospital with children and pain has demonstrated that children as young as five years old can understand and take responsibility for control of their own pain relief. Similarly, Alderson's work reveals that young children, given the appropriate support and encouragement from adults, can make profound decisions about their treatment and health care needs (Alderson, 1993).

However, the Gillick judgement has not been incorporated into primary legislation and has subsequently been undermined by a ruling in the Appeal Court in 1992 which distinguished between the right of the child to consent to medical treatment and to refuse it. In this judgement, it was asserted that the Gillick decision only extended to the child's right to give consent, and not to refuse treatment. Until the child reached 18 years of age, a parallel right of consent continued to be vested in the parent and if the child refused to give consent, the parent could give consent on their behalf, irrespective of the competence of the child. Despite the fact that this judgement was made in a lower court than the Gillick decision, it is being widely used as a redefinition of the Gillick judgement and as such significantly sets back the rights of young people to participate in decisions affecting them.

Children have no formal rights to participation in matters concerning their education. The focus of politicians in addressing rights of access to information or choice of school has been exclusively on the parents. It is parents and not children who are defined as the 'consumers' of education; the child is seen as the 'product'. Children do not have the right to participate in individual matters such as school choice, curriculum, or appeals over exclusions nor in school policy or administration. There is no requirement to involve children in decisions on, for example, school uniform,

arrangements for school meals, supervision in
lying or discipline. Schools are not required t(
cedures and comparatively few have school
structure within which to consult children and e\
reflected in the development of policy. Pupils und\
representation on school governing bodies. Jeffs a\
meaningful pupil representation means that even on
school councils have been established, they will often \   ...ed
enthusiasm from pupils, the reasons being that school   ...ack access
to the next tier of decision-making and they only exist ⌐y the goodwill of
the headteacher or governors. This means that headteachers can close them
down without being held accountable for the decision, thus seriously con-
straining the ability of pupils to speak freely on controversial issues (Jeffs,
1995). If, for example, children in a school are asked to participate in the
development of school behaviour policy, it is far more likely that they will
take the exercise seriously and act responsibly if they know that what they
produce is actually going to be implemented.

HOW FAR WE RESPECT CHILDREN'S VIEWS

Children's views are still, for a substantial proportion of the adult population, often treated as ill-informed, irrational, irresponsible, amusing or cute.
It is much more unusual for them to be given serious recognition and, then,
primarily when their views coincide with those of adults. There are also
differences between cultures about how children should behave and attitudes towards growing independence. Whereas generally speaking, independence in Western culture is likely to mean leaving home and
establishing a separate life, African, Asian and Oriental traditions measure
maturity in terms of being old enough to take on the mantle of responsibilities for parents and other family members (Lindon, 1996). Inevitably,
the expectations parents have of their children will inform the way in which
they wish to bring them up. The ways in which families begin to evolve
more participative relationships with their children will necessarily be influenced by and will reflect their culture and traditions. There is no blueprint
for the development of parent/child relationships. However, whatever the
culture or background of the family, the Convention, including Article 12,
does provide a universal principle demanding respect for the views of the
child. And the view that children have a right to participate in decisions
affecting their lives provokes a number of responses from families in all
cultures which merit some analysis. These responses range from the concern that children cannot have rights without responsibilities, that they are
not competent to be involved in decision-making, that they already have

reedom, that participation conflicts with the rights of parents
stability of family life, to fears that giving children greater involve-
in decision-making takes away their opportunities for childhood.

In assessing these concerns, it is important first to distinguish between
participation on the one hand and *autonomy* or self-determination on the
other. Participation is based on a recognition that children are players in
their own lives, that they have views and experiences which can contribute
to effective decision-making, and that they must be involved in such decisions. Article 12 clearly insists on respect for this right for all children capable of expressing a view. However, it qualifies the *exercise of choice* for
children by stating that 'the views of the child shall be given due weight
in accordance with the age and maturity of the child'. In other words, it
does not grant the child autonomy. Respect for the child's right to participate is not the same as granting the child autonomy. Autonomy which
allows the child the right to determine decision-making, must necessarily
be bounded by assessments of the child's competence and understanding
of the choices available to them and the implications of those decisions.

However, respect for the child's wishes has to take place within the context of the needs, wishes and rights of others, as well as the need to promote the best interests of the child. The child's competence to make an
informed choice cannot always be the sole determinant of the fulfilment
of that choice. Children live within families in which there will be a range
of different needs to be met and rights to be respected amongst the members of those families. Factors other than competence inevitably must come
into play in determining children's freedom to act, in the same way that
they do for adults.

In order to analyse those processes, it is useful to distinguish between
different types of decisions or choices in which children might seek to
express a view or to exercise a choice. It is possible to identify three broad
categories of issues in which a child might be involved:

- Issues which only directly affect the child, e.g. what clothes to wear, what
  activities to participate in at school, whom they play with at school or
  nursery, consent to treatment.

- Issues where the exercise of choice imposes obligations on others or
  relies on implementation by others, e.g. moving house, choosing which
  parent to live with following divorce, certain social activities, payment
  for clothes.

- Issues where the exercise of choice has the potential to interfere with
  the exercise of rights of others, e.g. choice of TV programme, noise levels, use of space at home.

Issues directly affecting the child

If the decision is one which is exclusively about the child and is one which does not rely for its implementation on the agreement or goodwill of others, then the only justification for overriding the child's expressed wish should be that the child is not competent to understand the implications of their choice *and* that to exercise that choice would not be in that child's best interests. Such an approach is consistent with the Gillick judgement and is also consistent with Article 5 of the Convention which states that parents have rights and responsibilities to provide direction and guidance to their children but that this must reflect the 'evolving capacities of the child'. Parents are under a clear duty to help the child develop the potential and the confidence for effective decision-making in their own lives.

For example, many children from a very young age wish to choose what they wear when they get up in the morning and are capable of making realistic decisions. Basic information from the parent about the weather and the likely activity of the child that day can encourage the child to make appropriate choices. If a child refuses to put on her coat prior to going out, it is possible to allow her to make that choice, take the coat and allow her to choose whether or not to put it on once she is outside and more likely to understand the need for it. In this way the child learns to understand the implications of her own choices and will develop the competence to take responsibility for her own actions.

There will be decisions where the need to override the child's wishes will be self-evident. No parent, for example, would comply with a two-year-old's refusal to have a seat belt done up, to run freely in a car park or to live on an exclusive diet of sweets, biscuits and crisps. All these issues require judgements on the part of parents on how best to protect their child and promote their best interests, but recognition of a fundamental respect for the child as a unique individual in their own right and not merely the property of the adults who have responsibility for them means that it is important to test each intervention to restrict those choices by the child, against a serious assessment of whether the exercise of the choice would seriously harm the child.

Similarly, a child faced with the need for medical treatment, however young, should be given an explanation, consistent with their level of understanding, of the implications of the treatment, the alternatives availiable, the implications of not having the treatment, the side effects and the prognosis, the likely recovery period. Parents and health practitioners have a clear duty under Article 12 to ensure that the child has been given both the time and the information she needs to help make an informed choice over the treatment. Only if she is genuinely unable to understand the implications of failure to agree to the treatment and the treatment is clearly necessary in the best interests of the child, would it be acceptable to override her refusal. Where a child is competent, the only exception to this principle would be where the consequences of failing to do so would result in very serious harm to the child. Where a child lacks the competence to understand the implications of the action, the decision which is made on her behalf must be made in line with the child's best interests. In other words the threshold for intervention is higher where the child is competent.

In summary:

- All children are entitled to express their views on matters of concern to them.

- If the child lacks the competence to understand the implications of the decision, a parent should only override the child if to do so is necessary to protect the child or to promote his or her best interests, e.g. insisting on teeth cleaning or restricting access to dangerous environments.

- If the child is competent, the parent should only override the child if failure to do so would result in serious harm to the child, e.g. refusal by the child to accept a life-saving treatment (although in Scotland, the Children (Scotland) Act 1995 provides that a child deemed to be competent has complete autonomy in health matters and therefore cannot be overridden).

- In all cases where the child's wishes are overridden, the child is entitled to an explanation of the reasons and acknowledgement of their concerns.

Issues imposing obligations on others

However, there are a number of other types of decision or choices which might be made which have implications not only for the child but for others within the family. In these cases, the competence of the child and a judgement of their best interests cannot be the only determinant of outcome. Many decisions in which a child might be involved or wish to be involved will have serious implications for others or will rely for their implementation on the actions of adults. A situation might arise, for example, where the parents are separating and decide that the children should continue to live with their mother. One of the children in the family might wish to live with the father. In this situation, the child, whatever age, cannot exercise this choice independently of his parents. In order for his wishes to be respected, the parents would have to consider the implications of splitting the siblings, and, particularly if the child was very young, the father would have to accept all the implications for his continued employment, the need for child care arrangements, and the financial implications. Clearly in this situation, it is not an assessment of the child's competence which would determine whether it was possible to respect their wishes. Rather, it would depend on a number of other factors such as the quality of the child's relationships with both parents, the strength of feeling expressed by the child, the capacity and willingness of the father to accept responsibility for the day-to day care of the child, the views of the mother and any other children in the family and so on. Even if it was not possible to allow the child to live with the father, it would be important to discuss the implications of the separation from the father with the child, to understand the depth of feeling and reasons for his views and to strive to understand and mitigate the consequences for the child once the decision was made. In other words the child's right to participate in the decision should be respected, and should inform the decision even where the child is unable ultimately to exercise a choice over the matter.

Similarly, a child might wish to take part in certain activities such as a dancing or drama class, or to buy particular clothes. Here the child's own capacity to make an informed and reasonable choice may not be in question, but the implications of the activity or purchase has financial and social implications for the parent. The extent to which the child's wishes can be respected therefore must necessarily be tempered by the parent's economic circumstances and available time. But the child is entitled to an explanation of the reasons for a decision which runs counter to his or her wishes and to be involved in exploring how and when it might be possible to find alternative solutions.

In summary:

- The child's wishes have to be considered alongside the obligations they impose on others.

- The child's competence to make a decision or exercise a choice is not the sole determinant of whether that choice can be fulfilled.

- As far as possible the parent should take account of the best interests of the child in responding to the views of the child.

- The child is entitled to an explanation of a refusal or inability to comply with their wishes and feelings.

Issues which interfere with the rights of others

Finally, there are issues where the exercise of a choice by one person, whether a child or adult, will have implications for the exercise of a right or freedom of others. In these situations, again, the extent to which the child is able to have their views and feelings respected will depend, not on their competence, but on a need to adjudicate justly between, for example, family members or children within a playgroup or class. In these situations it is the adults with responsibility for the child who will exercise those judgements both between children and indeed between the child and themselves. Such conflicts arise constantly within families, whether over access to particular toys, use of space within the house, choice of television programme, levels at which music is played or inviting friends to the home. If children are to grow up with a recognition of the importance of negotiation, of fair play, of respect for the rights of others, it is necessary to ensure that the way in which such conflicts are resolved involve the children in understanding how their rights are being acknowledged in this process. Listening to children, taking account of their feelings, finding ways of exploring compromise, ensuring that decisions are made which reflect what the child has said are essential components of respecting the right to participate embodied in Article 12.

In summary:

- Every member, adult and child, of a family, social group or community has the right to express their views and have them taken seriously.

- The wishes and feelings of different members of a family or group will not always coincide.

- Conflicting views have to be resolved by negotiation in which adults with parental responsibility will be the usual arbiters and, in seeking arbitration, must consider the best interests of all the children involved.

CONCLUSION

The recognition that children have the right to participate in decisions that affect them does cut across traditional notions of the power of parents to exercise complete control over their children's lives. It does necessarily involve a greater emphasis on negotiation, compromise and sharing of information. These processes imply a more democratic model of family life which is certainly not irreconcilable with cohesion and stability within families. On the contrary, mutual respect for all family members is likely to promote a greater capacity for long-term friendships and affection.

The UN Committee on the Rights of the Child, the international body established to monitor implementation of the Convention, which met in January 1995 to examine the progress made by the UK Government in complying with its principles and standards, expressed a concern that insufficient measures had been taken to ensure the implementation of Article 12 in this country. They recommended that 'greater priority be given to . . .

Article 12, concerning the child's right to make their views known and to have those views given due weight, in the legislative and administrative measures and in policies undertaken to implement the rights of the child', and went on to suggest that 'the State party consider the possibility of establishing further mechanisms to facilitate the participation of children in decisions affecting them, including within the family and the community.'

If we care about the welfare of our children, we must be prepared to listen to them. As adults who have consistently failed to listen to children, we have allowed untold harm to be perpetrated against them. In the name of their best interests, we have placed them in large long-term institutions, refused to hear accusations of physical or sexual abuse, allowed high levels of physical punishment, separated them from family members, denied them the knowledge of their identity or origins, tolerated bullying, locked them up for running away from children's homes, segregated children with disabilities, withdrawn entitlement to benefit – the list is endless. Obviously it will never be possible to guarantee adequate protection for all children. But many of those past and continuing abuses of children's rights could have been avoided or at the very least ameliorated by the simple expedient of listening to children and taking what they had to say seriously.

We do not have a culture of listening to children. Serious application of the principle of respecting children's rights to participate would require that we:

- Ensure that children have adequate information appropriate to their age with which to form opinions. Children cannot participate in decisions if they are not fully informed of the options available to them and the implications of those options. For example, children in a hospital setting need to be informed about who is responsible for telling them what is happening, what the implications of treatment are, side effects, options that are available, implications of not having the treatment, whether it will hurt, how long it will take.

- Encourage children to express views and demonstrate a willingness to take those views seriously. A serious commitment to respecting children's right to participate in matters of importance to them implies making the time necessary to ensure that the child has ample opportunity to explore the issues facing them. This applies whether they are at home, in school, in care, in hospital or any other environment. In assessing a young person's competence to take responsibility for decisions, it is important to consider the young person's own views about their competence. The ability of children to make decisions on their own behalf depends on the individual child but also on how much they are informed and respected by others concerned.

- Listen to their views with respect and seriousness and tell children how their views will be considered. They need to understand the process for decision-making, who will be making the decision, when, and what will inform the decision. There is obviously no point in listening to a child's views if you have no intention of taking them seriously. It is necessary to be clear about what aspects of the child's care or education or health or play he or she can be involved in.

- Let them know the outcome of any decision and, if that decision is contrary to the child's wishes, ensure that the reasons are fully explained.

- Respect and promote the child's right to take responsibility for those decisions which they are competent and willing to make.

A commitment to the basic human rights of the child, recognition of the responsibility to promote the child's welfare, and the need for a new generation of socially active and responsible young adults all require acceptance of the fundamental importance of the child's right to participation. It is a simple and self-evidently worthy principle which would, if taken seriously, have a profound impact on the nature of adult/child relationships in this country. Marta Santos Pais, a member of the UN Committee on the Rights of the Child, argues that

> Parents have a special role to play in promoting the capacity of their children to intervene responsibly in their family, school and social life. While it is essential to provide guidance and direction, parents are equally expected to assure to the child a positive and shared space for dialogue, which paves the way for the free expression of views and for serious consideration of those views.
>
> (Children's Rights Office, 1995)

Democratic decision-making processes are more time-consuming and can be frustrating and difficult to maintain at times but the long-term benefits will be the creation of an environment in which children have the optimum opportunity to gain in both the confidence and the capacity to participate in society as socially responsible individuals.

Further reading

Taking Part: the Case for Children's Participation (Lansdown, 1995).

Children First (Leach, 1994).

Children's Participation: from Tokenism to Citizenship (Hart, 1992).

Participation and Empowerment in Child Protection (Cloke and Davies, 1995).

Listening to and Communicating with Young Children (Pugh and Selleck, 1996).

PART 2
PRACTICE

5

CURRICULUM IN THE EARLY YEARS

Tricia David

The children were sitting on the 'story mat', their legs crossed. 'That way everyone can fit on,' the nursery teacher had explained. It was springtime, the theme for many of the children's activities, with the emphasis on exploring, representing, re-creating and creating (transforming) their understandings of the experiences offered. As they had been talking about baby animals, especially baby birds, a parent had produced a disused nest, which Diana, the teacher, was now holding out for all to see. She explained in hushed tones about the Mummy and Daddy birds she had observed going in and out of the hedge by her kitchen window, and how she had crept out, not wishing to frighten the birds, for a closer look.

'Imagine my surprise, children, there were four baby birds in that tiny nest, and sometimes the Mummy and Daddy too. I wonder, however could' holding up fingers now to help with the concepts involved 'one, two, three, four baby birds, and a Mummy, and a Daddy, all fit into a little nest like this?' Diana had intended her last 'question' to be simply rhetorical, indicating wonder at different aspects of life, but John, having reflected on his own experiences of the world, attempting to make sense of what he had just been told, offered the sage advice: 'I expect they all cross their legs.'

Sarah, aged four, was making delicate fingertip patterns to represent

---

flowers, describing as she did so what she was trying to create with the finger paints. She had gone through phases of using these experimentally, spreading, daubing, making squiggles, using lower arms and elbows as well as whole hands and fingertips. She had explored the characteristics of the paint, texture-wise, colour-wise, and the properties of different surfaces, such as a clear, vertical screen, as well as table-tops, paper, and so on. One could say that she had become an expert finger-painter, who had found lots of answers to the question, 'What does this do?' and had moved on to the question, 'What can I do with this?' The playgroup supervisor, Mary, a woman with many years of experience in work with young children, and sensitive to their emotional as well as their cognitive, social and physical needs, watched, ready to intervene, should a child need encouragement, or 'extension activities' to foster further learning. She held her breath as both Sarah's hands, palms outstretched, went forward to the two saucers of paint. Later, she told Sarah's Mum, 'I knew exactly what she was going to do, I almost stopped her, the flowers she'd painted were so lovely. But she did what was important for her, she had narrated the whole picture, how the flowers would grow, but because it's winter, they're all under the ground.' If Sarah had not verbalized during her totally engrossed finger-painting process, or Mary and Sarah's mother not taken interest in these concerns, maybe no one would have known that the swirls of paint covering the paper hid the delicately arranged flowers, nor understood the educational process this young child had experienced.

The above two examples of children in action in early years settings illustrate the ingredients Tina Bruce identified as the three elements required in the construction of an early childhood curriculum – the child and processes and structures within the child; knowledge the child already has; and knowledge the child will acquire competently but with imagination (Bruce, 1987, p. 65). Similarly, the examples illustrate how children try to 'make sense' of their experiences, how 'For the children themselves, the effective curriculum is what each child takes away. Schools and their teachers need ways of finding out what each child's experience is and how well they are learning what the school intends' (Schools Council, 1981, p. 1). If we, as a society, intend that all our young children have access to an appropriate early years curriculum for three- to five-year-olds, as a current entitlement and as a foundation for later learning, we need to explore what we mean by the term 'curriculum' for this age-group, why we so decide, and how such a curriculum may be available whatever type of setting a child may attend. However, we cannot take it for granted that opportunities for what we may consider 'worthwhile', appropriate, or positive learning will be available willy-nilly. Our children could be learning that one can be cruel to, or manipulate, those less powerful than oneself; that certain kinds of activity, people, abilities or attributes are accorded a higher value than others, despite the avowed intentions of the adults. For example, in one nursery, the staff realized that although their stated aims included 'developing independence, ... creativity', they actually stultified both these through their own behaviours, pre-structuring the activities and environment to such an extent that children were not allowed, or able, to override aspects determined by the adults.

Additionally, if we wish to assert that an early years curriculum is an entitlement for the present and one which should provide children with a foundation for later learning (now, partly 'delivered', through the National Curriculum), how are children to be afforded continuity – how will the early years (birth to five) and the post-five curricula link together?

WHAT DOES 'CURRICULUM' MEAN?

Although there are still disagreements among curriculum theorists, generally speaking, people discussing curriculum manage their thoughts about the interrelated aspects of school life, by suggesting that the whole curriculum is made up of the aims and objectives; teaching and learning styles, including assessment and evaluation; content; resources available (people, space, equipment); use of resources; relationships; and rules.

A decade ago, in the introduction to her book *A Curriculum for the Pre-school Child*, Audrey Curtis wrote:

> The main purpose of the book is to demonstrate that there is a recognizable curriculum for children under statutory school age based on skills and competencies to be developed in a flexible and child-centred environment, and that there is ample material with which to challenge and extend children without offering them a 'watered-down' reception class programme.
>
> (Curtis, 1986, pp. 2–3)

Audrey Curtis makes two significant points here, now of interest to us from an historical perspective: firstly, that a curriculum existed – something which, as David (1990, p. 72) was to assert, many preschool practitioners were loath to admit, because it 'smacked of subjects, set lessons, and a syllabus, rather than their own view of what was important in the lives of young children – holistic development through free and spontaneous play'; secondly, that a distinct curriculum, different from that in the infant school, and more appropriate to their developmental stage, is essential for children during this period of their, so far, brief lives. Put more bluntly, as Gwen Stubbs, formerly Staffordshire's Early Years Inspector, used to say, to bring home the uniqueness of this age-group, 'They aren't five-year-olds with their legs cut off.'

In support of this view of the settings for, and therefore the curriculum for, our youngest children being special, research indicates that

> The contexts of the nursery school, nursery class, day nursery and play-group may be said to share a common ideology. A nursery represents a recognizable social world which is clearly differentiated from the social worlds of the home and of the infant school. This social world of the nursery may be distinguished with reference to the ideas held by the nursery practitioners about the nature of young children and their learning processes . . . In the infant school the range of didactic methods is comparatively great, encompassing both formal instruction and discovery learning. In the nursery, although a certain element of structure may obtain, this tends to be covert; the emphasis is clearly upon play as the method of knowledge and skill acquisition.
>
> (Hutt *et al.*, 1989, pp. 227–8)

Burgess, Hughes and Moxon (1991) replicated these findings, although their observations were restricted to nurseries in the maintained sector of education, reception classes for four-year-olds, and combined nursery centres. The findings of this team suggested that there have indeed been commonly held principles for the implementation of a suitable curriculum for under-fives, but that the translation of these in practice varied according to the type of provision, and the social context in which the provision was operating. Their report raised concern that children in all settings may not have been experiencing coherence, continuity and equality of opportunity – for these were aspects in which discrepancies were found.

The members of the Rumbold Committee stressed, from a positive point of view, the importance of educators' awareness of context in relation to young children's learning, the 'people involved in it, and the values and beliefs which are embedded in it' (DES, 1990a, para. 67). They suggested that the principles upon which an under-fives curriculum should be based needed to complement those underpinning a curriculum for older children, and urged the use of a 'framework' rather than a 'National Curriculum' for three- and four-year-old children. Further, the committee argued that the aims of education for this age-group are basically the same as those for any other phase, as the House of Commons Select Committee had also stated, in their earlier report (House of Commons, 1989).

The Rumbold Committee (DES, 1990a) considered alternative ways of defining the curriculum and came to the conclusion that the best approach would be a framework based on areas of experience and learning; additionally, they stressed that the process of learning – how children are enabled to learn – was just as important as what they learn. This 'how' is usually expressed by early childhood educators as 'through play', and this view has been supported by official documents (e.g. DES, 1985b; DES,

1989a), by research (see Moyles, 1989), and by bodies such as the House of Commons Select Committee, as a result of their wide-ranging investigations (House of Commons, 1989).

Following the implementation of the National Curriculum for children aged between five and sixteen years, a number of factors impinged upon under-fives educators and caused them to realize that concerted action would be necessary in order to ensure appropriate curriculum entitlement for all under-fives. These factors include: access to provision, which continues to be variable; diversity in provision being endorsed by central government, thus reinforcing questions concerning co-ordination and collaboration across services; the fact that the majority of four-year-olds attend the reception classes of primary schools rather than nurseries; and research indicating that children who had attended nuseries with a play-based curriculum performed better than their counterparts in the assessments in maths and science at age seven (Shorrocks, 1992). Additionally, some sort of agreed curricular framework became imperative in the light of the impact of the new OFSTED inspections of schools. The anomalies arising from attendance at different settings and, in particular, the experiences of some four-year-olds in primary schools (OFSTED, 1993a) were the catalysts for the development of curriculum guidelines.

Thus it was that as part of the government's initiatives for 'expanding pre-school education' for four-year-olds (Shephard in SCAA, 1995), initiatives which include a parental voucher system (see Chapter 1), Sir Ron Dearing as Chairman of SCAA was asked by Gillian Shephard, Secretary of State for Education and Employment, to have the Schools Curriculum and Assessment Authority 'define a set of desirable outcomes for children's learning by the time they enter compulsory schooling and to consider the need for guidance to providers' (Shephard in SCAA, 1995, p. 3).

Meanwhile, a major project covering England and Wales, headed by Vicky Hurst at Goldsmith's College, had already been set up by the newly formed umbrella organization the Early Childhood Education Forum. Forum members represent 35 non-governmental organizations involved in work with children under eight and their families. With the help of funding from the Van Leer Foundation, the project, entitled *Quality in Diversity,* became the first to include parents and practitioners from a wide variety of backgrounds in discussions about the aims, structure and content of a curriculum for young children.

WHAT DOES OUR CHOICE OF CURRICULUM TELL US ABOUT OUR BELIEFS ABOUT CHILDREN AND CHILDHOOD?

Robin Alexander (1988) identified seven different types of primary school curriculum. Preference for one of these, or even a particular mixture, will be derived from one's knowledge and beliefs about children and society. Alexander's seven curricula are as follows: classical humanist (initiating the child into 'the best of cultural heritage'); behavioural/mechanistic (hierarchies of observable and testable learning outcomes); elementary (preparation for being a worker); social imperatives (1) – adaptive (enables children to adapt to meet society's economic, technological and labour needs); social imperatives (2) – reformist, or egalitarian (enables children to fulfil potential and contribute to the progress of society); progressive (an open and negotiable curriculum enabling children to achieve individual potential); developmental (underpinned by knowledge about children's psychological and physiological development and learning).

Drummond, Lally and Pugh (1989) offer ways of exploring one's own view of an appropriate curriculum framework for our youngest children by critically examining examples of curricula based on the following models: High/Scope; Rudolf Steiner; Maria Montessori; structured, pre-planned lessons, as in Peabody, Distar and 'Teach them to speak'; Portage; and HMI guidelines *Curriculum Matters 2* (DES, 1985a). The last is in fact the framework adopted by the Rumbold Committee (DES, 1990a) and it forms the basis for the SCAA (1996) 'desirable outcomes'.

Children under five are the most vulnerable and powerless group in our society. The way they are treated, their access to high-quality life experiences, whether at home or outside the home, is dependent upon those with more power than themselves, and in turn, their parents are often at the mercy of those more powerful than they are. For this reason it is important that those of us involved in working in, or promoting, early childhood care and education facilities should really examine questions about the curriculum that every individual child takes home. There is no such thing as a curriculum for young children 'set in tablets of stone' – it will be developed and modified according to what the people in a society believe it is appropriate for children to learn, and this will depend upon their view of early childhood, the position of children in that society, and the kind of people that society wants children to be and to become. In the early 1980s, Dowling and Dauncey (1984) suggested that an 'aims and objectives' model of curriculum may not be appropriate for children in this age-group, and that a set of principles, with ideas about their translation into practice, might be much more helpful. In fact, this is the type of approach to curriculum which those who have worked with and focused on the very young have often adopted.

In most of our European partner countries (David, 1993), the curriculum for children at this stage tends to be based on an areas of experience view of the curriculum and a constructivist model of the learner, that is, seeing the learner as an active participant attempting to 'make sense' of the world through relevant, meaningful activities.

YOUNG CHILDREN AS LEARNERS – CONTEXT AND PROCESS

It is often said that we should begin with the children and their needs. Do we believe this, and if so, how is this made manifest in our practices? Are the adults involved able to 'see through each child's eyes', because these adults have the ability to de-centre and have observed each child's learning patterns, or schemas (see Bruce, 1991; see also Chapters 6 and 10 in this book)? Do we believe in valuing what each of the children 'brings with them', as a result of earlier experiences, and if so, do we demonstrate this in ways that children and their families recognize? Is there a chosen body, or content, of 'worthwhile' learning activities, which we feel it is important for children in this age-group to have access to, and if so, what is it, and why do we consider it to be important? Are children given opportunities to control their own learning, through choice of activities and the availability of resources to enable the next steps in that self-chosen experimentation and discovery? What kinds of learning styles do we want the adults involved to encourage, who should these adults be, should they be specially trained, and if so, how? What level of adult–child ratios do we consider 'right'? What kinds of language, ways of talking to and with children, do we expect the adults to adopt, or to encourage among the children themselves? What kind of environment do we consider an appropriate setting for young children, what kind of hidden messages does each individual group setting convey?

All these items are part of the curriculum – factors from which children learn. Some are overt – they are factors from which it is intended children should learn – while others may be hidden. For example, many of us, over the years, have derived great benefit for ourselves and our children from playgroups which, because nowhere else was available, were sited in dusty church or community halls, with splintery floors, no outdoor play areas, and adult-sized, distant toilet facilities. I now ask myself whether this is a good enough way for a society to treat its youngest children and the dedicated women (for they are usually women) who work with enthusiasm, for 'peanuts'. What group of company directors would hold even one meeting in such a setting, let alone session after session? What messages are children picking up from such aspects of their provision?

Sally Lubeck's (1986) study of two early years groups in the USA showed how children from different socio-economic and racial backgrounds were learning different ways of interacting with each other and with adults, and learning different ways of 'being and becoming'. Children from an affluent, 'white' area were learning to be individualistic, competitive and independent. In the same city, children from a poor, 'black' area were learning to support each other, to co-operate, to be dependent, in the sense that they complied with adult demands. As Lubeck points out, there may be times in our lives when we should be capable of operating in each of these ways. We need to be aware of limiting children through the curricular context, or through failing to encourage the learning process.

The Early Years Curriculum Group suggested that the learning context for young children should provide 'a broad and stimulating environment which reflects the cultural backgrounds and interests of the children':

> Each child starts school with a unique set of experiences gained at home and in his or her community. A learning environment should respond to each child's need for something familiar, something new and challenging, and something which enables him or her to pursue a current interest. An environment and daily programme which offer maximum choice to individual children in terms of access to equipment and space, use of time, and opportunities for collaboration with others is most appropriate.
>
> (EYCG, 1989, p. 2)

Although some of the points mentioned above, such as space, or range of equipment, are aspects of the curriculum which may sometimes be out of our control, we need to be aware of their influence. We can, however, be particularly rigorous about those aspects for which we are responsible, so we need to be able to probe, individually and with other educators, parents, and the children themselves, what we really think our provision is helping children achieve and learn. This evaluative activity then helps us move on towards forms of provision which everyone involved considers high quality.

WHY SHOULD AN EARLY YEARS CURRICULUM BE BASED ON PLAY?

Even before the start of the twentieth century, pioneers, such as Robert Owen, Froebel, Montessori and Pestalozzi, had rejected, in both theory and practice, formal teaching for young children. Their espousal of play as appropriate activity for the young was reiterated by Margaret McMillan, and later, Susan Isaacs and the early members of the Nursery Schools Association (now BAECE).

They believed, and concluded from their observations, that small children needed time to play, with a variety of equipment, with opportunities to play alone, or with other children or adults, in order to learn. Furthermore, the kinds of activities children were afforded by their environment (Piaget, 1951), together with social interactions were an important part of the learning process. At around the same time, Vygotsky (1978), in Russia, was formulating his theory of the child 'as apprentice', suggesting that adults should take into account the affective aspects of learning (the emotions becoming overpowering when too much new learning is being presented), and act as facilitators helping children move on in manageable steps from what they already know and can achieve, to a new, self-chosen level of proficiency.

Although there continue to be those who challenge this view of early learning, expecting children during this phase of their development to be capable of long periods of adult-directed, formal or passive learning, for example from workbooks, the news from research carried out in the USA and the UK is that what is called 'the pressure-cooker approach' or 'the academic preschool' does not work (e.g. Osborn and Milbank, 1987; Katz, 1987; Zigler, 1987). During play, children are free to make choices and to follow interests, are self-motivated, engage in play about what is relevant to themselves and their lives, dare to take risks, learn from mistakes without any feeling of failure, and negotiate and set their own goals or challenges.

Perhaps as a reaction to those who have tried to restrict children to a narrow, inappropriate, formal curriculum, some early years practitioners, for example in Germany and Denmark, find it anathema to discuss the idea of 'play-based programmes' or 'a curriculum based on play'. They believe that this implies too much monitoring, interference and pressure on the part of the adults, and that young children should be 'allowed their childhood'. An example of this monitoring, interference and pressure, according to Danish colleagues, is the way in which many early years practitioners in the UK foster children's early literacy development. On a recent visit to Danish preschools, we were discussing children's early awareness of print, and I asked whether Danish preschool staff would help children set up a hairdresser's shop, together with appointment books, invoices, etc. I was told that children in the UK only ask for these items because our whole society pressurizes them into the acceptance that literacy is of over-arching importance. While we have convinced ourselves that we are empowering young children who demonstrate interest in learning about print, and that we are not committing the 'crime' of applying too much adult coercion, our Danish colleagues 'see' the implicit messages to which we may be blind – or is it that they are missing out, failing to spot an interest in, and thus failing to provide for, learning activities which children incorporate into their play, in relevant and meaningful ways?

ARE ALL PLAY ACTIVITIES EQUALLY VALUABLE?

Perhaps the previous paragraph will raise enough questions about why we think it important for children to engage in certain learning activities for us to recognize that we may value some experiences more than others. We have evidence from research (Bloom, 1964) that children's learning styles laid down at three years of age persist at age six. Children who display curiosity about their environment and who are able to explore, experiment, discover, then represent, interpret and evaluate their findings in the early years will be likely to continue to engage in these learning processes throughout life. Children who are afraid to go through such processes in early childhood may become the unquestioning adults of the future. Activities lumped together and labelled 'play' have been thought to offer opportunities for all those processes. However, in the last twenty years psychologists in particular have begun to observe children at home and in group settings, with a view to finding out what we mean by 'play' and if it does indeed afford children the valuable learning opportunities practitioners allege.

If we decide that we trust children themselves to be self-motivating, to decide when they need certain experiences, we make the assumption that they also know what is possible, or that they can imagine many things they have never seen.

Shane and Dawn, just three, and from highly disadvantaged families, began nursery school. While staff were busy with other children these two noticed some small sorting equipment and, never having seen anything like it before, but without spending time looking closely at the tiny replicas, began to have fun tossing the small, brightly coloured animals into the air above their heads, so that they fell like rain on to themselves and the surrounding floor. If play is a valuable learning activity, what did they learn from this episode? Some adults might think that the appropriate intervention would be authoritative, encouraging the two to pick up every piece and to examine them with a view to future sorting activities. What would such an intervention have helped them learn? At the other end of the scale might be the adult who decides to ignore the children's behaviour, it was self-chosen and fun, so let them get on with it. In between is an approach which recognizes the children's lack of experience, lack of close observation skills, but which acknowledges that this may not be the moment in Dawn and Shane's development to build on these. Intervention may entail the provision of a special space and a large sheet of paper on which to continue the activity without the risk of losing expensive small equipment, and with the excitement of a new way of clearing up the pieces from the floor, funnelling the piece of paper into the appropriate container.

Corinne Hutt (1979) built upon Jean Piaget's ideas about play and learning by suggesting that in the early years there are two equally important phases in children's play activities. She concluded from her observations that when something – a toy or material, clay for example – is new to a child, he or she will explore it, with serious and purposeful intent, as if asking the question 'what does this do?' Corinne Hutt labelled this the 'epistemic' phase – the child's search for new learning. In the next phase the child will engage in 'ludic', or true play, activity, when, according to Corinne Hutt, the child gains no more new knowledge about the toy or material, but becomes competent at using that gained during the epistemic phase. This means having fun, laughing with one's collaborators, sometimes using funny voices – as if asking the question 'what can I do with this?'

Work by Chris Athey (1990) and Tina Bruce (1991) has given even further insights into the ways children learn through play. Like Corinne Hutt, Bruce (1991) separates out children's need to explore, manipulate, discover, practise and represent, which she refers to as first-hand experience, as different from play. Bruce and Athey's approach demands not only careful observation of children during 'free-flow play' bouts, but close and positive collaboration between workers and families, since they suggest it has become clear that children have individualized patterns of learning interests to which they return in their play, and, given the opportunities, will engage in them in as many different forms as possible. These patterns are called 'schemas'. By knowing children's interests intimately, staff and parents are able to provide for, intervene in and extend children's learning according to individual needs and wishes, and not according to the adults' hierarchical, content-based idea of what should be learned next. Naturally, this demands expertise on the part of the adults fostering the children's learning. They need to be skilled at observing, assessing and diagnosing. When the curriculum is accessed through play, the ability of the adults to observe, assess, diagnose and record means they must also have a deep understanding of play, language and their learning potential. Research by Smith and Bennett (1995) is demonstrating the complexity of this task.

From the work of Piaget, Hutt, Athey and Bruce, then, it would appear that children need a balance between those activities offering challenge through first-hand experience following the introduction of an unthreatening yet unfamiliar 'starting point' (a new piece of equipment, material, outing, etc.), and those activities allowing for children's 'free-flow play'.

There have been numerous studies (e.g. Sylva, Roy and Painter, 1980; Smith, 1986; Meadows and Cashdan, 1988) demonstrating which types of play provided challenging learning activities, and the role of the adult seems to be crucial in determining whether this occurs, for as Parry and Archer (1974, p. 5) wrote concerning the distinction they made between two types of 'play': 'It is possible to detect the differences between occupational and developmental play experiences.' One merely keeps children occupied; the other contributes to their educational development.

Furthermore it is important to add, as Janet Moyles states (1989, p. 24), 'children can and do learn in other ways than through play, and often enjoy doing so.' Helping an adult bake, lay the table, wrap a present or feed the rabbit are simple examples of such non-play, enjoyable learning possibilities.

BREADTH, BALANCE AND DIFFERENTIATION

Discussions about appropriate curricula usually include questions concerning the steps which need to be taken to ensure 'breadth, balance, differentiation and progression'. While it seems clear that the authors of the SCAA (1996) 'desirable outcomes' have attempted to achieve what was demanded of them and at the same time adhere to their own knowledge and beliefs about early childhood, the resulting statements concerning Personal and Social Development, Language and Literacy, Mathematics, Knowledge and Understanding of the World, Physical Development, and Creativity, can be criticized as being too focused on product rather than processes of learning, too limited in their vision of children's powers, too lacking in recognition of the variations in patterns of development and learning. Breadth and balance seem to be lacking in what is called 'outcomes' but is implicitly a statement of curriculum. It is the letters in the SCAA (1995) consultation document, by Gillian Shephard, Secretary of State for Education and Employment, and Sir Ron Dearing, which betray the real purposes of the proposals – to *prepare* children for the National Curriculum, especially in the areas of literacy and numeracy. Such preparation is very different from *laying the foundations for later learning*, something we know from research evidence (Shorrocks, 1992) nursery education has been successfully achieving.

Breadth and balance

Breadth and balance means that providers should ensure that each child has access to a wide variety of experiences, in order to develop a range of skills and concepts, positive attitudes towards, and knowledge derived from different disciplines, and that no one area of experience predominates. The guidelines given in the Rumbold Report (DES, 1990a) provide useful information for planning ensuring breadth and balance in the early years curriculum, in all the areas of experience (aesthetic and creative; human and social; language and literacy; mathematics; physical; science; technology; spiritual; and moral).

For example, young children who attend a group where the adults are unable to provide any 'plastic' materials, such as clay, dough, sand, water, etc., may be missing out on science as an area of experience.

By observing the range of activities in which individual children engage, one can not only become aware of children's particular needs concerning breadth and balance, but also evaluate the strengths and weaknesses of the group's provision for particular areas of experience. Staff at one centre were worried because Yussuf spent most of his time with the Lego. They began to ask themselves why. Were they failing him because of their lack of his home language? Was he intimidated by an unrecognized undercurrent of institutional racism? What should they do, and how could he be encouraged to branch out, so gaining a broader and more balanced curriculum?

Differentiation

Differentiation means ensuring that the needs of individual children are met. When Emma began nursery at three-and-a-half, she was painfully shy and adult-dependent in the mêlée of large-group life, having spent the first years of her life as the focus of parental and grand-parental gentle adoration. It would have been easy in a formal classroom situation for a child like Emma to become one of 'the invisible children' (usually quiet and well-behaved little girls) who, although often unsure and nervous about what is expected of them, get on with what they have been ordered to do. In a nursery where children were expected to make choices and engage in first-hand experience and play, Emma seemed lost at first. As Woodhead (1976) and Hutt *et al.* (1989) pointed out, a nursery or playgroup in which everything is implicit, unplanned and not discussed makes overwhelming demands on the children to understand and take advantage of what is offered. In Emma's case, her teacher and nursery nurse discussed their observations and listened to the family's ideas. At home, Emma talked of her wish to play with other children, but could not find a 'way in', could not find 'a voice'. Her teacher decided to provide the children with a starting point which might mean some would make puppets, and she made sure materials for this were available. Emma was one of the children who made her own glove-puppet, and she then used the puppet as her intermediary, holding it in front of her face, speaking for it. The puppet gave Emma the confidence to begin communicating with other children. If a rejection occurred, it was the puppet, not Emma, who was being rejected – but fortunately, that did not happen.

Studies (e.g. Bennett *et al.*, 1984) in infant classrooms have shown that early years teachers are generally good at diagnosing, or assessing, individual children's needs, but find it difficult to address those needs. The problem is that in the situations observed in these studies, the children's activities were adult-directed. In contrast, other research (for example,

Sylva, Roy and Painter, 1980; Meadows and Cashdan, 1988) suggests that in guided play situations, where the children take the lead in making decisions about their own learning activities, there is a much closer 'match' of challenge and child. This is the result of the 'competent adult's' (Faulkner *et al.*, 1991) ability to 'scaffold' the child's learning through appropriately gauged discussion, questions and provision of materials. This point about scaffolding brings us on to 'progression' – each child should have opportunities to move on, developing greater competence and learning. In order for progression to occur, there is also a need for continuity, since children will not be able to 'make sense' of irrelevant activities which do not build on their earlier experiences.

CONTINUITY AND PROGRESSION

Children moving from one context to another

It is strange that our socity is not disturbed by the fact that during these first five years of life, when the most vital learning for life takes place and when children are at their most vulnerable, we think nothing of having them move from setting to setting as their parents seek provision with which they and the children feel content. Were we to subject our eleven-to sixteen-year-olds – an equivalent five-year age span – to the same number and type of changes of educators and curricula, we would no doubt be horrified. When children move from home to a group setting, or from one type of group to another, they can experience damaging discontinuities. Later changes can be equally traumatic, and for this reason the strategies which promote positive experiences for babies can be adapted for children in the three to five age-range, moving from group to group, or group to school, and even later – why are we not sensitive to the stress that change of school, home, work-place, team, etc. induces right through life?

In particular, however, I want to suggest that educators need to recognize children's entitlement to continuity in curriculum, irrespective of the setting. In order to achieve this, in the light of the Children Act 1989 and the Rumbold Report (DES, 1990a), there will need to be greater development of co-operation, co-ordination and collaboration between services; sharing and valuing of expertise and resources; greater investment in both initial and in-service training of early years educators. One of the most valuable contributions in all this, however, will come from the individual children's parents, who must be recognized as the first educators and the 'link people' between settings.

Children in primary school – the relationship to the National Curriculum for five- to sixteen-year-olds

The House of Commons Education, Science and Arts Select Committee reported that

> early education should be seen not as something separate and apart, but rather as the first step on the path into a relevant, coherent and integrated curriculum. . . 'The purpose of nursery education is the learning and development of skills, attitudes and understanding in order that children will have full and satisfying lives and become confident, useful, active members of a diverse, constantly changing society'.

> (House of Commons, 1989, paras. 2.5, 2.6)

I have referred to Audrey Curtis's (1986) delineation of the early years curriculum as distinct from curricula for older pupils, and Margaret McMillan certainly believed this early years curriculum should be available for children up to age seven. Thus we have a recognition not only that children in this age-group should be entitled to appropriate, high-quality educational experiences which complement home experiences, as entitlement and enrichment for now (that is, not pre- anything), but also that the curriculum offered in the statutory school years will build upon that early years curriculum: 'education is a seamless robe' (House of Commons, 1989, para. 2.5).

Vicky Hurst writes of the concern engendered by the requirements of the National Curriculum for five- to sixteen-year-olds and suggests that the subject-based learning in these documents

> adds to the impression that play is seen as separate from the high-quality learning that is aimed for. Yet it is possible that without the learning opportunities offered by play, the aims of the National Curriculum will not be achieved, since it is through play that learning becomes meaningful to children.

> (Hurst, 1991, p. 49)

By analysing the National Curriculum within the context of the early years principles and curricular framework (see Sylva and David, 1990), it is possible for educators to feel confident that they are providing children with a meaningful education, and at the same time helping them develop firm foundations on which later learning can be based. Research by Kathy Sylva and colleagues (Sylva, Siraj-Blatchford and Johnson, 1992) has demonstrated the importance of educators' own confidence and competence, developed through thorough training, to be essential in this approach.

ADULT ROLES AND RELATIONSHIPS

The roles and training of educators is discussed in the later chapters of this book and it is not my intention to debate this at any length here. However, it is important to reiterate the point made earlier about scaffolding, namely the ways in which educators facilitate learning. One vital aspect of this is, of course, language. The Rumbold Report (DES, 1990a) drew attention to the abundance of research evidence demonstrating the importance of talk. Children need access to adults who will behave in ways which stimulate and encourage dialogue, often about shared experiences (Wood, McMahon and Cranstoun, 1980). As Gordon Wells (1985, p. 73) put it, 'teaching thus seen is not a didactic transmission of pre-formulated knowledge, but an attempt to negotiate shared meanings and understandings.' In other words, the learning process is dynamic, and not additive, and children themselves shape the sequencing and pattern of that education process through these negotiations. The further implications of such a view of children's learning are that they need a setting and equipment which will promote opportunities to engage with other children. Further, for children whose home language is not English, equal opportunities for access to the curriculum on offer will be provided by the involvement of bilingual educators.

Providing a high-quality curriculum for young children is a complex and demanding task (Lally, 1991; McLean, 1991). Children begin learning from the moment they are born, perhaps even before, and we know that the first five years of life present an optimal learning period; further, that if the desire to learn is suffocated, or the variety of learning opportunities limited, children may come to later educational provision with neither the will, nor the ability, to benefit from that education. The level of education and training of the educators is therefore crucial, as research has shown (e.g. Clark, 1988; Whitebook, Howes and Phillips, 1990).

CONCLUSION

There is still much to debate about the idea of a curriculum for any age-group, let alone our youngest children, which is, even indirectly, dictated by government. That there are fresh, more democratic ways of looking at these issues is one of the stimulating challenges to be gained from exchanges with colleagues working on similar questions in other countries, as Dahlberg and Asen's (1994) work testifies.

The early years curriculum, while distinct, must be one which offers all our young children high-quality experiences which make sense to them because they are based on the curriculum already experienced at their earlier stage. And since children learn in individual ways, at individual rates, it is essential that the principles relating to early childhood provision are adopted and continued into the infant school, for older children but especially when there are four-year-olds in infant classes (Barrett, 1986; Brown and Cleave, 1991). These principles include: attention to the whole child; integrated (not compartmentalized) learning; starting from children's own concerns, abilities and interests; first-hand experience and play; the ensuring of time, i.e. self-regulated activity bouts; and access to adults and children with whom they can interact, and who show respect for all children as valued human beings with a right to equality of opportunity. The curriculum each child takes away should have been relevant, challenging – and fun.

Further reading and points for discussion

First, read

- *Preschool Education Consultation. Desirable Outcomes for Children's Learning and Guidance for Providers,* Draft Proposals (SCAA, 1995).

paying special attention to the letter from Gillian Shephard, the 'desirable outcomes for language and literacy' and the examples of practice in which language and literacy are central.

Follow this by reading:

- *Key Stages 1 and 2 of the National Curriculum* (DFEE, 1995, pp. 4–10).

- The forthcoming Early Childhood Education Forum curriculum framework *Quality in Diversity* (ECEF, forthcoming).

- The publications of the Early Years Curriculum Group (EYCG, 1989; 1992).

- Curriculum guidelines published by the local authority you work in.

To what extent do the different statements in the documents cited above 'fit together' and why?

What are the purposes of early literacy activities, according to the SCAA document?

In relation to literacy and language, how does the curriculum you offer to young children differ from that defined by the above documents? Why do these differences exist?

6

OBSERVING AND ASSESSING YOUNG CHILDREN

Mary Jane Drummond and Cathy Nutbrown

INTRODUCTION

In this chapter we will identify some of the questions that educators face as they engage in the process of assessment; we will discuss each question in turn, looking at its implications for practice; and conclude by offering a set of principles that educators might reflect on in developing practices for themselves that answer the questions we raise. We believe that this will be more worth while than attempting to give an account of observing and assessing young children that would tell educators everything they wanted to know. A step-by-step guide to observation and assessment in a few thousand words is not a realistic undertaking, and, perhaps, not a very useful one. Following other people's instructions is rarely the first step towards learning to think for oneself. We believe it will be more helpful for us to raise questions about assessment, rather than try to sketch in the full range of possible answers. Asking questions can stimulate thinking, while listing answers may forestall discussion and debate.

WHY ASSESS AND OBSERVE YOUNG CHILDEN?

When we ask ourselves 'why?' questions about aspects of our work with young children, we are looking for explanations and justifications of two different kinds. Sometimes we are trying to establish reasons for what we

---

do by drawing on our own past experience. We interrogate the understanding of young children's learning and development that we have, as a body of educators in different disciplines, built up over the past. Sometimes this accumulated experience does not offer substantial or sufficient reasons for our practices. Historical precedent is not always a convincing justification for some of the things we do, or do not do, although it may help us to understand how practice develops over time. For example, the lack of multi-disciplinary training opportunities in the past is no justification for their not being available now. We also try to establish, through 'why?' questions, the purposes and outcomes of our work: these questions are focused on the future, rather than on the past, on what will come of our work, rather than on what has shaped it into its present form.

Asking 'why assess?' and 'why observe?' will, in the same way, lead us to different kinds of answers, different kinds of reasons and justifications. One powerful reason for observing young children's development, and assessing what we see, is simple. Children's learning is so complex, rich, fascinating, varied and variable, surprising, enthusiastic and stimulating, that to see it taking place, every day of the week, before one's very eyes, is one of the great rewards of the early years educator. The very process of observing and assessing is, in a sense, its own justification. It can open our eyes to the astonishing capacity of young children to learn, and to the crucial importance of these first few years of our children's lives. But the process can do more than make us marvel at our children's powers – it can also help us understand what we see. Our own observations can help us learn from others who observed before us, and from whom we have learned in our own professional training. So, for example, the work of Piaget, Donaldson, Wells and Athey can be vividly illustrated for us by our own observations of children's activities: their drawings, their questions and their games with rules. Our own first-hand experiences of individual children's learning can help us to see more clearly the general principles that other researchers and educators have established as characteristic of that learning. Indeed some of the pioneers of early childhood provision worked in just such a way themselves, moving from the specific to the general, from single observations to generalized conclusions. Susan Isaacs, for example, ran an experimental school, The Malting House, in Cambridge from 1924 to 1927, and her gripping accounts of the day-to-day doings of the children in the school show clearly how her analysis of children's intellectual development is the product of a mass of detailed anecdotal insights. For example, she describes the development of the basic concepts of biology, change, growth, life and death, illustrating this process with a wealth of evidence:

18.6.25: The children let the rabbit out to run about the garden for the first time, to their great delight. They followed him about, stroked him and talked about his fur, his shape and his ways.

13.7.25: Some of the children called out that the rabbit was dying. They found it in the summerhouse, hardly able to move. They were very sorry and talked much about it. They shut it up in the hutch and gave it warm milk.

14.7.25: The rabbit had died in the night. Dan found it and said: 'It's dead – its tummy does not move up and down now.' Paul said, 'My daddy says that if we put it into water, it will get alive again.' Mrs I. said, 'Shall we do so and see?' They put it into a bath of water. Some of them said, 'It is alive.' Duncan said, 'If it floats, it's dead, and if it sinks, it's alive.' It floated on the surface. One of them said, 'It's alive, because it's moving.' This was a circular movement, due to the currents in the water. Mrs I. therefore put in a small stick which also moved round and round, and they agreed that the stick was not alive. They then suggested that they should bury the rabbit, and all helped to dig a hole and bury it.

15.7.25: Frank and Duncan talked of digging the rabbit up – but Frank said, 'It's not there – it's gone up to the sky.' They began to dig, but tired of it and ran off to something else. Later they came back and dug again. Duncan, however, said, 'Don't bother – it's gone – it's up in the sky,' and gave up digging. Mrs I. therefore said, 'Shall we see if it's there?' and also dug. They found the rabbit, and were very interested to see it still there.

(Isaacs, 1930, pp. 182–3)

The diary entries made by Isaacs and her colleagues were more than entertaining anecdotes: they formed the basis for her analysis of children's scientific thinking. Isaacs was able to learn about learning by intently studying her own detailed observations.

The importance of close observation is also illustrated by Goldschmied's work with babies under two (1987). Observations of babies playing with the Treasure Basket can give the watching adult valuable insights into the children's learning and into their interactions with one another. Other reasons for observing and assessing concern the adults' part in providing care and education. Young children's awesome capacity for learning imposes a massive responsibility on early years educators to support, enrich and extend that learning. Everything we know about children's learning imposes on us an obligation to do whatever we can to foster and develop it: the extent to which we achieve quality in day care and education services is a measure of the extent to which we succeed in providing appropriate environments for young children's learning and development.

The statements of criteria for quality in provision for young children, which have recently proliferated in response to the requirements of the Children Act, are attempts to identify and specify the necessary conditions for this learning and development. The processes of observation and assessment have a crucial part to play in achieving quality: they have important work to do in shaping the present, the daily experiences of young children in all forms of early years provision. The evaluative purpose of assessment is central for early years educators. We cannot know if the environments we provide and the support we give are doing what they should for our children, unless we carefully monitor the learning and development that take place within them.

Our observations can work for us by providing the starting point for reviewing the effectiveness of our provision: we can use our assessments of children's learning as a way of identifying the strengths, weaknesses, gaps and inconsistencies in the curriculum we provide for all children. Further, we can use the assessment process to plan and review the provision we make for individuals. We can identify significant moments in each child's learning, and we can build on what we see to shape a curriculum that matches each child's pressing cognitive and affective concerns.

Observation and assessment can also illuminate the future for us, as well as help us improve the quality of the present. This forward-looking dimension of assessment is the means by which we can explore the possible outcomes of our provision, curriculum, interactions and relationships. In this country, when pupils are sixteen, formal assessments are used to determine the type of education they will receive in the years sixteen to nineteen. We are not suggesting here that assessment at the age of two, three or four should be used to determine the type or quality of a child's statutory education, but it is important to be able to use the process of assessment to identify, for each individual, the learning that is just about to take place, in the immediate future.

This is the area of development that Vygotsky labelled 'the zone of proximal development', and he used this concept to argue passionately that assessment does not end with a description of a pupil's present state of mental development; in his own words, 'I do not terminate my study at this point, but only begin it' (Vygotsky, 1978, p. 85). Effective assessment is dynamic, not static, and can identify for the educator what the learner's next steps might be; assessment reveals learning potential as well as learning already completed. Vygotsky's arguments show how 'learning which is orientated toward developmental levels that have already been reached is ineffective from the viewpoint of a child's overall development. It does not aim for a new stage of the developmental process but rather lags behind this process' (Vygotsky, 1978, p. 89). Observation and assessment are the processes by which we can both establish the progress that has already been made, and explore the future, the learning that is yet to come.

WHO IS TO BE ASSESSED?

Other authors in this book (Moss and Pugh, for example) argue the case for a co-ordinated approach to services for young children, and demonstrate the need for equality of opportunity in terms of access and provision. The principles of co-ordination and equal opportunities also apply to the practices of assessment. If observation of children can increase educators' understanding, enrich curricular provision, and improve the match between individual children's development and the provision made for them, then observation and assessment must be part of the provision in every group setting for young children outside the home. If we take the Rumbold Report's conception of 'educator' seriously, it is no longer possible to categorize some forms of provision as more educational than others (DES, 1990a). Every child in every form of early years provision is a learner with a right to equality of learning opportunity. Every child's educators, therefore, have the responsibility of observing, assessing, understanding, and so extending that learning.

Through the process of assessment we have opportunities to enhance the individuality and the self-worth of each learner. The great educationalists, on whose work we draw in designing a curriculum for young children (see Chapter 5), have shown us some of the common characteristics of all young children's learning. However, the task of the educator includes the identification of differences, as well as similarities, between individuals. Through assessment we can distinguish what is unique and particular about a particular child: this distinction will make it possible for us to support each child's individual growth, as a learner and as a person. We can go further: by involving children in the process of assessment (see below, page 107), we can not only share our perceptions with them, but also help them to articulate their own perceptions; and so we can support them in the gradual process of synthesizing this self-knowledge, as they grow more truly independent, individual and autonomous in their learning.

Prosser (1991) studied her class of eight- to nine-year-old children in a primary school and found that just less than half the class (ten out of twenty-two) were prepared to state that they were aware of their teacher's assessment of them as learners. Seven children stated that they did not know, and five children did not know whether they knew or not! In follow-up interviews with individual children, Prosser investigated the complex thinking that surrounded the children's original statements, and revealed some surprising inconsistencies. For example, the interview with Chris (aged eight) contained this passage:

T.:   Chris, aren't you really sure what I think about your work?
Chris: I know you think I'm good at maths. I am good at maths but

I should be. My Dad's a maths teacher. But I don't really know about the rest of everything.

T.: Yes, you are very good at maths.

Chris: But I'm useless at reading.

T.: Chris, what a ridiculous thing to say. You're super at reading.

Chris: (Very animated and interrupting me) My Mum says I'm useless. I know you say I'm good at it but my Mum says I'm useless.

(Prosser, 1991, pp. 9–10)

Prosser's study, though small in scale, usefully alerts us to ways in which we may lose out on possibilities for fostering the growth of individual self-esteem. She shows how we need not only to make individual assessment an explicit, sensitively framed reality, but also to help children understand their own growing individuality as, in some ways, distinct from other people's perceptions of it. After further discussion, she encouraged her class to develop a self-assessment schedule, to which they gave the title 'What makes me, ME'. As they worked on completing the schedule, she was horrified by the children's anxiety as to whether they had fulfilled the task 'correctly', asking her several times if what they had written was 'right' or 'true'. Assessment practices that deny children individuality and autonomy as learners cannot be truly effective. Prosser's study suggests that some classroom practice in assessment may indeed have such an unintended outcome, and that teachers would do well to ensure that, from an early age, children start to contribute to the assessment process.

While all young children can benefit from the processes of observation and assessment, the focus of any specific act of assessment is always an individual child, whose uniqueness is revealed and reinforced in the process. Yet this account is not the whole story. Taken for granted at the heart of any statement about a child's individuality is a whole set of unquestioned assumptions about the concept 'child'. And taken for granted at the heart of many of our assessment practices are the very same assumptions. The ways in which we assess children's learning, and the purposes for which we do so, are based on an implicit value system, built up of beliefs about children, about what kinds of beings they are, what kinds of ways they behave, and what kinds of feelings they have, or are expected to have. A description of the normal child, or, indeed, the ideal child, is rarely made explicit in the process of assessment. Nevertheless, as we set about observing, assessing and evaluating young children's learning, we do have, deep in our mind's eye, some dearly held beliefs about what we are looking for. These beliefs are likely to be different for different groups of educators in different settings and different cultures; the exploration of such differences can be both challenging and rewarding (Tobin, Wu and Davidson, 1989).

WHAT DO WE OBSERVE AND ASSESS?

The short answer to this question is – children, and everything they do: exploring, discovering, puzzling, dreaming, struggling with the world, taking their place in it, and making their mark on it. The statutory requirements for the assessment of seven-year-olds, laid down in the Education Reform Act 1988, represent only a part of the whole process of assessment. There is much more to know about young children than their levels of attainment in Maths, English and Science at the end of Key Stage 1. The need for a broader view of assessment was explicitly recognized in the Rumbold Report (DES, 1990a), which warned that educators should 'guard against pressures which might led them to over-concentration on . . . the attainment of a specific set of targets' (para. 66). Assessment of six- and seven-year-olds for National Curriculum purposes is one small part of a more comprehensive process, in which educators assemble detailed and meaningful pictures of every child with whom they work.

What features of learning and development do these pictures contain? Bruce (1987) draws on the work of the pioneers of early childhood education to establish key principles for practice, one of which is directly relevant to the practice of assessment. 'What children can do, rather than what they cannot do, is the starting point in the child's education' (p. 25) – and so, by implication, it is the starting point of assessment too. Educators will observe and try to understand everything that children do, in their talk and in their play. Watching children at their work of interacting with their environment will tell their educators some of what they need to know about children's needs and development.

From their first days of life, babies are observed by their parents, not with a checklist and pen but with concern, interest, curiosity and love. They reflect on what they see and draw meaning from their observations: 'She's sucking her fist – is she hungry?' 'He turns his head when he hears me speak – can he recognize the sound of my voice?'

Such human, open and implicit observations are the cornerstones of meaningful assessment. As children grow older, the adults who observe them attend to everything they reveal about themselves. It is sometimes appropriate to observe a child with a very specific question in mind; for example, 'How do these three children co-operate when working in a group?' Or 'What objects does this six-month-old baby choose to explore in the Treasure Basket?' 'What does Rashid really do in the playground?' However, it is still important to keep a wider view as well, and ensure that our assessments of children are balanced, reflecting all that we can possibly know about their thinking, their knowledge and their understanding. This is a daunting task. Happily, early years educators can turn to the work of other educationalists who have shown us how the observer can learn to map the growing world of a child's understanding. The work of Athey

(1990) is of particular importance in this undertaking, not least because she also teaches us how our observations and assessments can enrich the curriculum we provide.

Athey builds on the work of Piaget, whose extensive and detailed observations of his own young children gave us a wealth of understanding of children's developing cognitive structures. Athey focuses on particular patterns of behaviour and thought – the 'schemas' of two- to five-year-old children. In Athey's use of the term, any particular 'schema' is at the core of the child's developing mind, and is thus a central element of intellectual growth. The vital corollary for the child's educators is that curriculum experiences can be provided to match this core, this growing point, this centre of the child's thinking and doing.

Nutbrown (1994) illlustrates how focusing on children's schemas can illuminate observations and understanding of their behaviour. The following observations show how a focus on children and their schemas can enrich both a short observation, and even more vividly, a series of short observations made over a period of hours or days.

> Adam (3:2) used stones and a thin strip of tree bark collected in the nursery garden to construct two pillars with the tree bark balanced between. He spent time testing which things could go under and which had to go over or across because they would not fit underneath. He said, 'this is a bridge, some can go over it and the little bits go under'.

What understanding of Adam's thinking can we achieve through reflecting on this observation of a child's play? If we consider the processes and not just the end-product, we see Adam describing, explaining, organizing, constructing, selecting materials, forming hypotheses, testing and categorizing. Adam used the natural materials he could find in the garden to develop his own forms of thought. It would seem that at the present, the schema that absorbs him is related to things that 'go over and under', simple spatial concepts, which will develop further in time. His surroundings enabled him to explore his schema, and the observant and listening adult could identify and support his actions and thinking. Much more is learned by reflecting in this way than by simply looking at the content of his work; so much would have been lost here, were the observation simply to record 'Adam made a bridge of stones and tree bark'.

Kate (4:1) was partially sighted. She was familiar with the environment of the nursery and used it to extend her own 'enveloping' schema. The following observations of her took place over two days on four separate occasions:

> (1) Kate was dressing up and wrapped first a sari and then a large shawl around her.

(2) She went into the home corner and pulled the ironing board across the gap, 'I'm here now – it's private.'

(3) She took a wicker basket and went around the nursery collecting objects such as shells, nails, screws, small boxes and paper bags. She felt each object, apparently exploring texture and shape. On reflection, the adult who made this observation realized that each object that Kate selected was either a form of container or, in the case of nails and screws, 'went into' something else.

(4) Kate was talking on the telephone, the line went dead. 'It's the inside that's broken I think,' she said.

These notes show a consistent thread of thinking over the two days, a thread running through four separate activities. Kate was exploring 'enveloping and containing' with all the experiences available to her. In the process she was collecting according to clear criteria and categorizing objects, using her senses. She was defining space, hypothesizing and using language to express her thinking.

Adam and Kate make it clear to us that children have their own agendas for learning, which can flourish in rich learning environments, where adults tune into children's forms of thought, meet their needs and extend and challenge their interests.

In order to build up a complete picture of every child's learning, assessments of cognitive developments, like those above, will be complemented with assessments of other aspects of development. The concern of the educator is with children in their wholeness.

Josie (4:5) was absorbed with 'connecting'. She chose activities which enabled her to explore this schema. She built 'a street with people going in and out of the shops' using large bricks. She put gates in her drawings. She liked making jewellery using beads and pieces of foil, threading them together to make them 'connect'. She made elaborate structures of tubes, funnels and valves in the water play which represented 'a factory making sweets'. Josie developed and extended her connecting schema with competence. There was an interesting development when Alan (3:2) wanted to use the construction bricks which fastened together. His manipulative skills were not such that he could fully master the materials he was using. Josie noticed his problem, and (possibly spotting the opportunity for more connection) offered to help:

> Josie: 'Give it here to me – I'll fasten them.' Alan seemed reluctant and held on to his bricks. Josie tried again: 'You tell me where and I'll click them on.' Alan pointed to one brick and held up another to be fastened to it. Josie: 'You want this on there – see it clicks on – give me another – where shall we put this one?'

Josie worked with Alan to make the structure. She talked with him skil-fully matching her words to the actions she was performing, probably mod-elling this on experiences she had had with adults reflecting her own actions back to her through talk. When both were satisfied with the process Josie took Alan to the teacher: 'Alan made this – he said what to do and I helped a bit – he tried hard.' She then turned to Alan and said, 'When your Dad comes you can show him.'

Josie shows us the way in which children can support each other, when the experiences they assimilate are appropriate to their thinking. The social interaction displayed here and the emotional support given by Josie to Alan is of a quality to be marvelled at. When adults attentively watch the children with whom they work, they can learn to provide a model for affec-tive as well as cognitive development, thus giving children, like Josie, the opportunities to co-operate and support their peers.

HOW DO WE SET ABOUT OBSERVING AND ASSESSING YOUNG CHILDREN?

For many practitioners, this is the sixty-four thousand dollar question. Questions of why, whom and what to assess have a certain abstract and intellectual appeal, but the question of how it is to be done is remorse-lessly practical. All early years educators are familiar with the cry: 'So how do you expect me to do all this and work with children?'

The most important task for educators considering how best to build observation and assessment into their practice is not to learn a handful of new techniques but to become more aware of their own, already existing powers: their power to think for themselves, to look for themselves, and to act for themselves. Early years educators can, we believe, develop a pattern of working which is not wholly dependent on instruction from outside. We can, through our own efforts, and through building on our existing skills, learn about our practice, and about our children's learning and development.

We will not discuss specific techniques of observation here as there are other sources for this purpose (for example, Walker, 1985; Hopkins, 1985; Sylva *et al.*, 1990). Although these are all concerned with observation in schools and classrooms, the insights of these authors can be applied in other settings where care and education are provided.

All early childhood educators already use observation as an integral part of their daily work. The implicit, covert skills of these acts of observing can be developed, and made more explicit; the fruits of observation can be stated more confidently as we learn to record, examine, reflect and act upon the knowledge we gain through observation and assessment. What do edu-cators need in order to develop in this way?

First, they need to know for certain that their assessments are worthwhile, important, valued and put to use by colleagues, parents, children and other professionals. Secondly, they need access to training whereby they can develop their already existing skills; this training should be available for all early years educators, with opportunities for cross-professional training whenever possible (Sheffield LEA, 1991a). Thirdly, although the activity of observation is inseparable from the other daily activities of working with children, and should not be confined to a particular time of day or week, educators need time to reflect on the meaning of their observations, time to select and record information. They need time to talk about their observations with colleagues and parents, and time to put their insights to work in building a richer and more fulfilling curriculum for young children.

WHAT NEXT? HOW IS ASSESSMENT TO BE USED?

All the preceding sections of this chapter have included some reference to the purposes of observation and assessment. We have noted a number of different ways in which observation and assessment are used: as a way of appreciating and understanding learning; as a way of recognizing achievement; as a way of distinguishing between individuals, identifying significant differences in their development; as a way of shaping and enriching our curriculum, our interactions, our provision as a whole; and as a way of identifying what children are going to learn next, so that we can support and extend that learning.

Under the Education Reform Act 1988, the assessment of children in primary schools and classes has become a statutory process, combining continuous teacher assessment with the results of a number of Standard Assessment Tasks (SATs) in Maths, English and Science. This process, specified in considerable detail by the Schools Curriculum and Assessment Council (SCAA), is intended to raise and monitor standards, nationally and locally, and to ensure the early identification of learning difficulties. In the years to come, as teachers of young children in primary schools learn to comply with the requirements of the Act, it will be important for early years educators to continue to carry out their own informal and non-statutory assessments for all the purposes we have described. In particular, the growing number of four-year-olds in school will not be well-served if assessments of their learning are confined to establishing numerical Levels of Attainment in Maths, English and Science. The educators of young children in schools can confidently assert the value of the whole range of their continuous and purposeful assessments; they will not be prepared to narrow their practice, or to restrict their attention to one small part of children's learning.

Two further important purposes of assessment remain to be discussed here: those of continuity and accountability.

Observation, assessment and continuity

The dictionary definition of continuity (*Chambers*, 1972 edition) includes the words: 'uninterrupted connection'. This succinct phrase contains two elements: the idea of interruption and the idea of connection. When we talk of continuity within any form of preschool provision, or continuity between one provision and another, we are bound to accept that some interruptions are inevitable. Children's preschool experiences are interrupted by illness, removals, weekends, snowstorms, holidays, changes of staff, family upheavals, and reaching the age of statutory schooling. We cannot do much to prevent these interruptions, but we can focus on connections, and thereby explore how it might be possible to establish 'uninterrupted connections', in other words, continuity. How can observation and assessment help us to do this? First, at the level of the individual child, we can see how regular observation and assessment can be used to establish and maintain connections within and between forms of preschool provision, in a variety of different ways. Daily observations in one setting have an important part to play in ensuring that each child's experience is stable and secure; daily efforts to watch, to reflect and to understand children's development can help us build on one day's events in planning the next, establishing fruitful connections between each day of a young child's experience.

Between settings, too, connections can be made. An understanding and appreciation of children's growing bilingualism, for example, will form part of a vital connection between different periods of their preschool experience. Parents who pass on knowledge of their children's current schema will enable the educator in a new setting to shape a curriculum that will continue to match their cognitive concerns. A set of detailed observations of children's fantasy play, showing how they are exploring a range of powerful emotions, will help other educators, reading a summary of those observations, to appreciate children's struggles and challenges, and to recognize and encourage the advances they have made and are making. Assessments of children's developing sociability, as they learn to interact in groups of different sizes, will ensure that young children moving to a large playgroup or classroom are not overwhelmed by a sudden change in what is expected of them. Records of children's developing physical skills will prevent children from being expected to start all over again, with equipment they have already outgrown, when they move from one setting to another. Babies who can feed themselves, or climb unaided on to a

changing mat, will not appreciate being interrupted in their development
by having these achievements ignored; connections between different
rooms, or different settings, informed by records and assessments, can sustain the babies' continuous development. As part of its developing co-ordination of services for under fives, Sheffield LEA has produced a variety
of record formats which can be used by educators in all domestic and group
settings (Sheffield LEA, 1991b). The use of such records can make a valuable contribution to the continuity of a child's early experiences.

Observation and assessment not only benefit individual children and
their educators: the process may also have a part to play in achieving the
continuity of some practices that affect the whole group of children who
are in transition, from year to year or from place to place. Observations
and assessments, made over a period of time, and summarized at the point
of transition, will also be a record of the values and belief systems of those
who made them and wrote them down. Assessments always say something
about what the assessors believe children should do, say, feel and understand, as well as recording what they actually do. These assessments, when
carefully read, could form an important connection between the values and
practices of one form of provision and the next. They could become the
first step towards a greater awareness of a set of beliefs that diverges from
one's own, or a further step towards a greater shared understanding of
what it means to care for and educate young children.

Some of the practices of assessment are themselves part of this value system, which may, and probably will, differ from setting to setting. The involvement of parents in the assessment process is an important example. Some
educators, who involve both parents and children in the assessment process,
would trace this practice to a core principle of partnership, underlying many
different aspects of their general practice. For these educators, making connections between their practice and other people's will entail making connections between principles too. The principle of parental involvement
cannot be seen, by them, as something that can be casually interrupted: they
will be prepared to work hard, through discussion and debate, establishing
practical connections, maybe small and apparently insignificant at first, until
a continuity of principle, across a variety of practices, is achieved.

Observation, assessment and accountability

All early years workers are accountable for their work, to one or more of
a variety of audiences: the management committee, the board of governors, the funding body, the community forum, the staff group, parents,
employers, children and so on. An effective working relationship between
educators and any one of these groups depends on the quality of the com-

munication between them. When educators set about explaining and justi-
fying their work, they will draw on their principled understanding of young
children's learning, but they will also speak convincingly of their daily experiences in their own setting. By rooting their beliefs in real-life events they
can explain how and why they care and educate as they do. By drawing
on their assessments and observations of learning they can demonstrate
clearly how principles are transformed into practice.

WHO IS TO BE INVOLVED?

A further step in ensuring the usefulness of their assessment will be for
educators to give some thought to the people who might be involved in
the process. Who can most helpfully contribute to monitoring the developmental needs and growth of young children? Which people are best
placed to do this? And who owns the process of assessment?

In schools and classrooms, it has traditionally been left to teachers to
carry out assessment. Teachers made the assessments, wrote the records,
held the records, and made decisions about how to communicate what was
in them and to whom. In recent years this monopoly has been broken. The
trail-blazing ILEA Primary Language Record was designed as a collaborative exercise in recording achievement. The development of the child's
language – or languages – in the home is seen as quite as important as
progress in school, and so the contribution of parents is an essential part
of the recording process (Barrs *et al.*, 1988).

In early years settings away from schools, there has been great interest
in the developmental record *All About Me* (Wolfendale, 1990), an anecdotal format for parents and other educators, who work together to build
up a vivid personal picture of many aspects of a child's development.

As parents, educators and teachers come closer together, discussing and
sharing their insights, the benefits for all concerned become clear. Nursery
teachers in Sheffield have worked on a joint approach to assessment, sharing records with parents and giving them the opportunity to comment
(Sheffield LEA, 1986). They report an opening-up of the whole process of
recognizing and reporting development. Parents made comments such as
the following:

I never thought she was as clever as that – it's good – to say that she's
only three!

It just shows how much they learn, even when you think they're playing, and to see it written down.

Some of this he does at home, drawing and things, it was nice to have
the chance to write a bit myself on his record sheet.

Over the past few years, the development of records of achievement, which started in the secondary sector, has stimulated the development of similar approaches in primary schools. These records are based on the continuous involvement of pupils in their own assessment. This initiative, now endorsed by SEAC (1990) for all primary schools, has the effect of giving assessment a much wider ownership: parents, pupils and teachers are all active partners in the process. Even very young children can talk about their learning and development, and so make positive contributions towards their own assessment profile: 'I can write' or 'My book is about a dog, I like reading it', are comments which four-year-olds might make about their developing literacy. Young children can be encouraged to comment on themselves in this way, playing an active part in recording their development, and laying the foundation for further, more evaluative contributions later (Nutbrown, 1991).

Another initiative, the Sheffield Early Literacy Development Project (Hannon, Weinberger and Nutbrown, 1991), suggests that when educators work with parents to share the children's experiences at home, their understanding of young children's literacy development is enriched and extended. Parents were invited to watch and to comment (often in some detail) on their children's early literacy activities. The comments from parents make clear their perspective on the value of such involvement:

> I noticed his writing more by going to the meetings than I think I would have ... one time when he was drawing it was all lines. Then after a few weeks he changed and started doing circles.
>
> (*ibid.* p. 15)

> I didn't make a point of reading with him before – then I did. He looks at books a lot more now.
>
> (*ibid.* p. 18)

The project team considered ways in which parents might reflect on and record their children's development. They devised a way of providing pointers to different aspects of writing development which could be combined with a method of recording a child's progress. Parents were offered a record format resembling a jigsaw, with each piece representing one small element of literacy development. They found this a valuable exercise, and one parent commented:

> I got a surprise when filling in the jigsaw bit. It surprised me how much he could do. There was only one blank.
>
> (*ibid.* p. 16)

These initiatives show how observation, assessment and recording can be more widely shared, more openly discussed and so become more reflective and evaluative. We can learn from these examples how the purposefulness of the educator's assessments can be enhanced by the contributions of others.

CONCLUSION

In this chapter, we have tried to indicate some of the questions that face early years educators engaged in assessing young children's learning, without suggesting that there is only one possible set of answers to these questions. However, the answers that educators arrive at, in the process of reviewing and developing their practice, will not add up to effective assessment unless they are based on a coherent set of principles, which can provide justification and explanation for particular practices. By way of conclusion, we will take a more personal note, and outline four fundamental principles that we believe should underlie the practice of assessment in the early years.

The most important of our principles is that of respect. We believe that assessment must be carried out with a proper respect for the children themselves, for their parents and other carers, and for their educators. This respect will be expressed in actions, in words and deeds, in our daily interactions and in our attitudes. So that, for example, in respecting ourselves as educators, we will acknowledge both our expertise and our fallibility; we will respect our judgements enough to build on them in practice, but without elevating them into infallible dogma. We will respect our determination to work hard for our children but also the physical limits of our energy and endurance. We will respect each other's judgements, even when differences arise, and we will respect our own professional ability to have our judgements challenged and questioned. Our skills in observing and assessing children will be used by others with respect for their accuracy and validity; we will be able to build confidently on our own work.

Our second principle that we see as central to the practice of assessment is that the care and education of young children are not two separate, discrete activities. In our work as educators, we both care and educate. Quality care is educational, and quality education is caring. Children's enhanced learning and development are the outcomes of our work in whatever setting. Our assessment practices will recognize the close relationships between these concepts; and we will struggle to develop a pedagogy that recognizes learning and development in all their human manifestations, as processes in which all the child's faculties and powers are employed. In our assessment practice, we will recognize children learning to love one another, as well as children learning to count.

Our third principle concerns the awesome power of the early years educator. We believe that it is important, first, to acknowledge that power, and second, to use it lovingly. The psychotherapist David Smail (1984) writes of 'the loving use of power', in his discussion of relationships within families. We believe that the 'loving use of power' in the assessment of young children is an absolutely central principle.

Our fourth principle is that the interests of children are paramount. Assessment is a process that must enhance their lives, their learning and development. The educators' needs are secondary to those of the children they work with. Assessment must work for children. Their minds and their futures are entrusted to our hands for the brief years of childhood. We must do all in our power to serve them well.

Further reading and points for discussion

For further discussion on observation and assessment, readers are referred to *Making Assessment Work: Values and Principles in Assessing Young Children's Learning* (Drummond, Rouse and Pugh, 1992). This pack will provide starting points for numerous discussions about observing and assessing young children and can be used as a staff development programme.

Getting to know you – a guide to record keeping in early childhood education and care (Bartholomew and Bruce, 1993).

Assessing Children's Learning (Drummond, 1993).

Threads of Thinking – young children learning and the role of early education (Nutbrown, 1994).

Baseline Assessment – a review of current practice, issues and strategies for effective implementation (Wolfendale, 1993).

7

WHY UNDERSTANDING CULTURAL DIFFERENCES IS NOT ENOUGH

Iram Siraj-Blatchford

The States Parties to the present Convention shall respect and ensure
the rights set forth in this Convention to each child within their juris-
diction without discrimination of any kind, irrespective of the child's
or his or her parent's or legal guardian's race, colour, sex, language,
religion, political or other opinion, national, ethnic or social origin,
property, disability, birth or other status.

(Article 2, Part 1, The Draft Convention
on the Rights of the Child, Unicef, 1989)

The United Nations recognized that it is the right of every child and his/her
guardian to be free from oppression and discrimination, and that every
state has a duty to ensure this. While the state may articulate policies and
shape provision, it is of course the service providers and those in daily contact with children on whom the ultimate reality of providing a discrimina-
tion-free environment depends. It is beyond the scope of this chapter to
attempt an analysis and to provide practical strategies for early years educators to overcome all discriminations. (Note: the term 'educators' is used
to refer to all those who care for and educate young children; c.f. Rumbold
Report, DES, 1990a.) What I will attempt, however, is to deal with one area,

racial prejudice and discrimination, as a case study. Readers may well find parallels with other forms of discrimination under the sub-headings that follow, and indeed would be encouraged to transfer concepts.

RACIAL DISCRIMINATION: WHY WE VALUE SOME RACIAL GROUPS MORE THAN OTHERS

It will not surprise most early years educators to learn that Britain's relationships over the last four hundred years with Africa, the Caribbean, South East Asia and other countries nearer home such as Cyprus were grounded on the subjugation of the people of these areas and that vast human and material resources were exploited. The wealth created by black slavery and colonialism was, and still is, to a large extent, enjoyed by British society. Britain is no longer the imperialist power it once was but the beliefs and institutional and cultural practices which were normalized in past centuries still exist and manifest themselves in discriminatory beliefs and practices today.

As a country we have recognized the existence of the more crude and apparent effects of racism in the Race Relations Act 1976 and more recently the Children Act 1989. This legislation acknowledges and offers practical measures for removing racially discriminatory practice and procedures in early child care/education provision (Lane, 1990). What may surprise early years educators is how well we continue to absorb both subliminal and overt racism in our lives today. We shall look more closely at the effects of this on young children's lives later. It is true that we no longer celebrate Empire Day in our schools (a common practice until the 1950s), and that it is unlawful to discriminate against people on the grounds of 'race' in care, housing, employment and education. So how is racial discrimination still normalized? Why do many British people still continue to hold negative beliefs and attitudes about South Asian and African-Caribbean people? It is worth considering some of those ideas we take for granted, accept without questioning and do not notice in our omissions or transmissions about black, ethnic minority and white people. (Note: the term 'black' is used to refer to all those groups which share the common experience of racism, in particular African-Caribbean and South Asian people.)

Our environment is a hothouse for propagating notions that present black and ethnic minority people as a problem and inferior. It will be useful to consider a few examples of this:

(1) *The press.* The press largely sensationalizes and focuses on black and ethnic minority people only when writing about items of violence, famine, political unrest and sport.

(2) *Television.* Viewers are continuously presented with negative images on the news. Old Hollywood movies are shown where black people act as servants or martyrs to white people. Repeats of many popular comedy programmes from the 1960s and 1970s also contribute.

(3) *Books.* Our literature is read uncritically, e.g. in Robinson Crusoe the labour relationship between 'Man Friday' (a name given to him) and Crusoe is absorbed by generations of children as normal. School biology, history and geography texts in particular have been shown to convey racist messages.

(4) *Grafitti.* There are rarely positive images of black and ethnic minority people in large advertising displays in our environment, but almost everyone has seen racist grafitti. It is significant that very few individuals take active steps to get it removed, because it is accepted as an everyday occurrence.

(5) *Jokes.* Racist jokes about black people, Irish people and Travellers are commonly heard and usually accepted as innocent fun. The fact that they degrade, hurt and humiliate certain groups is often ignored. Racist jokes are only funny if you share the underlying stereotypes and assumptions.

(6) *Language.* Our culture accepts that 'black' is generally negative (blackleg, blackmail, black mood, etc.) and that words such as 'nigger' should be part of our stock of dictionary words. In the English language there are dozens of disparaging words to describe people who are not white and English (e.g. Taffy, Paki, Kraut, Yid and Wog). Name-calling is a 'normal' part of our children's experience.

(7) *Traditional British tolerance.* Employers and landlords/ladies are often tolerant of intolerance, accepting without question the assumed or expressed xenophobia desires of their employees and tenants. Such cynical and fatalistic attitudes by those with the power to effect change yet seeking a 'quiet life' may be the greatest barrier to equality.

Through these dynamic and continued happenings racism is perpetuated and absorbed by all around. The continued overt and subliminal messages to children and adults alike is that there are groups of people in our society who are inferior from birth because of their racial background. Simultaneously the message of assumed white superiority is constantly promoted. This kind of stereotyping leads to gross inequality at an institutional level. Where white people wield power over other people (e.g. educators over children and parents, teachers over children, employers over employees, policy-makers over practitioners and housing and social workers over the public) the consequences can be devastating for the lives of black and ethnic minority individuals and families.

We carry with us our baggage of experience and part of that experience is growing up in a racist society. Racism affects our attitudes and beliefs. However, the real damage occurs when more covert institutional practices result in the conversion of people's personal beliefs into action. Early years educators are not exempt from these influences. We need to understand what our own past experiences have been and how and why we feel the way we do about tackling racial equality issues. Unfortunately our experiences feed into each other and this may not be such an easy task. The model in Figure 7.1 may be useful and can be added to further.

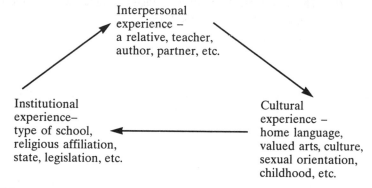

Figure 7.1

We must understand that if our home language is English then that gives us more than a national identity, there is also a global significance. I shall try to unpack some of the assumptions upon which the foregoing is based before going on to the next section.

YOUNG CHILDREN'S IDENTITY AND ATTITUDES

'Research shows that racism damages the emotional, intellectual and social development of black and white children' (Brown, 1990, p. 9). Many early years educators believe that racial equality is exclusively about black and other ethnic minority children, but racial equality is as much an issue for the ethnic majority. The dehumanizing effects of racism on white British ethnic majority children is an issue which must be raised and addressed. If educators remain unconvinced about this and fail to analyse the facts, racial equality cannot, and will not, be achieved in the early years. This is a serious responsibility which all of us have. Further explorations of the link between culture, language and the complexity of identity reformulation has been discussed elsewhere (Siraj-Blatchford, 1994, 1995, 1996).

Very few educators would dispute that young children learn from their environment. If we are to believe that the early years are the most formative in a person's life, a time for learning through associations in the environment and through observation (Sylva and Lunt, 1982), then we should accept that children inevitably absorb racist values too. The work of some social psychologists shows that children demonstrate a clear awareness of 'race'. Three- to five-year-olds learn to attach value to skin colour (Milner, 1983). They are aware of a pecking order which places white at the top of the hierarchy and black at the bottom. The inevitable impact on some children's self-image can be very damaging.

Apart from white being the norm, children also witness and learn to accept the position of black people in our society. Ian Menter cites an example from a nursery school where

> A four-year-old child was showing a painting, which she had just completed, to her teacher and some other children. She had painted a wide brown border all around the large piece of kitchen paper. Inside this frame was a large yellow sun, a human figure and some yellow 'ground'. She explained that this was a picture of Africa. The frame, she said, was because she had seen Africa on the television, in a programme about hungry people.
>
> (Menter, 1989, p. 95)

Menter goes on to analyse how this image may consolidate into a stereotype of Africa and black people.

In the absence of any positive black role models, either in the early years care/education setting or in the immediate community, a young white child may have no choice other than to absorb negative views about black and ethnic minority people. These will be further reified by the media at home and in school as the child grows older. The cognitive development of black and ethnic minority children may be seriously damaged if they encounter adults with stereotypical and racist views about their culture, language, skin colour or learning abilities.

In one infant school a four-year-old continued to struggle with a knife and fork at lunch times over a period of several weeks. At home his parents ate Pakistani food, chapattis and rice were eaten by hand, as is normal practice. The child was learning for the first time that food could be eaten using implements other than hands. The teachers encouraged his development. One lunch time, after struggling to balance baked beans on his fork for some time he resorted to using his hands. The school secretary (who collected payment for meals in the lunch hall) shouted across the hall to this little boy, 'Stop eating with your hands, only animals eat with their hands!' The look on the four-year-old's face was one of bewilderment, hurt and embarrassment. He and all his black and white peers were interpreting the secretary's words to make meaning of them. She had indicated not only that his behaviour was deviant and animal-like but by implication so was his parents' and that of his community. Anti-racist work must include all those working with young children, for they are all in a sense 'educators'.

The cumulative effects of discrimination and stereotyping can leave some children feeling isolated, angry or rejected. It can leave some white children with false notions of superiority and encourage the perpetuation of racism through bullying and name-calling. Fundamental concepts of justice, fairness, equality, co-operation and sharing are distorted. Children are denied the opportunity to learn, appreciate and value the aspirations and achievements of others. All those involved are in effect being dehumanized and disadvantaged. If we accept that all our children have an equal right to achieve their full human potential then we need to move on to look at what specific changes are needed in early years education.

POLICY AND RACE EQUALITY ACROSS EARLY YEARS PROVISION

There is little doubt that most power in our society is held by white, middle-class males (Epstein and Sealey, 1990). Our policy-makers at national and local authority level are not therefore generally drawn from any of the oppressed groups in our society and have little experience of discrimination. In fact, their experience has been, and continues to be, one of positive discrimination towards their own group. If we do not believe that women, ethnic minorities, working class and disabled people are inherently inferior, and I suggest that very few people would actually argue this, then policies aimed at sharing power and a wider experience of life must be a prime democratic objective.

Of course, power is a relative concept. At a micro level we need to focus attention on the power of educators. Educators are not generally powerful in economic or policy terms; indeed, given that most are women, they may often feel relatively powerless. However, educators are powerful in terms of the power they have over the children in their care. If educators are to exert any influence over economic and policy decisions they need to apply their understandings of government policy and legislative effects at both a national and local level within whatever voluntary and private sector groups they have access to (e.g. National Childminding Association, Preschool Learning Alliance, Council for Awards in Childcare and Education, etc.). Policy statements are gradually beginning to incorporate 'race' equality issues as part of the agenda. The policies do, however, vary in terms of commitment and extent, and the practicalities of implementation need to be explored.

Government legislation

There are three major Acts of Parliament which can effect change for racial equality in early years care/education.

Race Relations Act 1976   This legislation outlaws racial discrimination which is defined in four ways: 'direct' and 'indirect discrimination', 'segregation' and 'victimization'. This has clear implications for exclusions from and admissions to the care and education of young children and for the training and recruitment of staff. It is widely acknowledged that black people are under-represented in the field of early years care and education and that provision and service practices can be racist (Lane, 1990). The Commission for Racial Equality (CRE) booklet, *From Cradle to School* (1996), which is a practical guide to 'race' equality and child care, provides a clear framework for analysing the role of local authorities and highlights the research evidence, indicating widespread discrimination in local policies.

Children Act 1989   This Act appears to be an exciting move towards equality as it is the first piece of legislation on the care of children which refers specifically to catering for children's racial, religious, cultural and linguistic backgrounds. The Guidance, Volume 2, *Family Support, Day Care and Educational Provision for Young Children* (DH, 1991), is a particularly valuable document for local authorities (LAs). Ethnic monitoring is now required by law and services will be evaluated according to the extent that they are non-discriminatory. LAs will need to set up monitoring and evaluation procedures and guidelines.

LAs will also need to develop a framework with clear guidelines and criteria for the registration and cancellation of day care provision if it does not meet the 'race' equality criteria of the Children Act. A 'fit person' to look after children should, for example, have 'knowledge of and attitude to multi-cultural issues and people of different racial origins' (para. 7.32, p. 54). LAs have been given the power to cancel registration if 'the care being offered to an individual child is considered by the local authority to be seriously inadequate having regard to his needs including his religious persuasion, racial origin and cultural and linguistic background' (section 7,4(1)(b) and (2)(b), p. 60, para. 7.51). Many examples are cited to illustrate the need not only to rethink provision and services but also to reconsider training and the kind of knowledge needed to be able to offer services free from racial discrimination.

LAs will need to review their training schemes and the expertise required of day care advisers, childminders and others. Those in positions of power as directors of social, health and education services will need to re-evaluate their own commitment to 'race' equality. 'Race' equality should now be the responsibility of someone with 'status and commitment'. The experience and perspectives of black staff are crucial and recruitment practices that lead to increased participation are considered essential to progressive change.

Education Reform Act 1988 (ERA)   Under the ERA schools are required to cover multi-cultural issues across the curriculum and section 1(2)(a) of the ERA requires that a broad and balanced curriculum should be provided which 'promotes the spiritual, moral, cultural, mental and physical development of pupils at the school and of society'. This legislation applies to all five- to sixteen-year-old children in our schools but the ERA is vague regarding the practicalities of such provision and there is some evidence to suggest that schools are too worried about the assessed elements of the National Curriculum to bother very much about multi-cultural/anti-racist education which is often perceived as a 'bolt-on' inconvenience.

Policy initiatives

For children under five the Department of Education and Science (DES) has published the following statement:

> Good social relationships are often fostered by planning a curriculum that provides opportunities for the children to learn more about the lives and work of the people in school and the wider community. The children's awareness of diversity in custom and culture and their respect for and understanding of cultural differences are effectively developed through planned activities and the use of carefully selected stories and picture books, artifacts and materials.
>
> (HMI, 1989, p. 12)

We will focus our attention more closely on such specific planning and practice later in the chapter. Education and care practices and policies that may contravene the Race Relations Act are monitored and continuously acted upon by the Commission for Racial Equality (CRE). Government Acts lay down edicts and these can be used to increase accountability and promote change.

Many of the changes that have taken place are the product of grassroots action, where educators with a firm belief in, and commitment to, achieving racial equality have recognized inequalities and have been determined to effect change in their organizations and institutions. In the past five years a number of early years organizations have asserted their commitment to achieving racial equality. The National Childminding Association (NCMA), for example, has produced a bold statement of commitment and local regions such as Warwickshire have provided training for their childminders on race equality. So far such activities have been voluntary, but the Children Act may change this. The NCMA subcommittee on equal opportunities is working towards an implementation policy:

> NCMA is committed to a childminding service which views children as different but equal and which strives to meet the needs of the whole child, physical, emotional, intellectual and cultural.
>
> To this end, it is the responsibility of all childminders to acknowledge that racism exists, and that it harms all children in their care.
>
> Good quality child care involves valuing each child equally and affirming the positive value of different skin colours, cultural and family backgrounds. It involves giving children a realistic picture of the world they live in and correcting the distortions and prejudices about that world.
>
> Good child care is anti-racist child care.
>
> (The Anti-Racism Subcommittee of NCMA)

The Council for Awards in Child Care and Education (CACHE) formerly National Nursery Examination Board (NNEB), faced this issue well and reviewed their recruitment and selection processes with the help of the CRE. The NNEB had an equal opportunity statement and worked on integrating this statement throughout its practice. An active equal opportunities working party monitored and advised on racial equality as well as on other equal opportunities issues.

The NNEB's policy was:

(a) that it is committed to promoting equal opportunity throughout its activities;

(b) that no applicant for a course of study leading to one of its awards should be disadvantaged compared with another by virtue of class, ethnic origin, gender, marital status, race or religion;

(c) that no student undertaking a course of study leading to one of its awards should receive less favourable treatment than another by virtue of class, ethnic origin, gender, marital status, race or religion;

(d) that in the examination of students, both internally and externally, teaching institutions and the Board should ensure that no student receives less favourable consideration or treatment than another by virtue of class, ethnic origin, gender, marital status, race or religion; and

(e) that the curriculum for all its schemes should reflect a commitment to promoting equality in all the aforementioned aspects and so help to establish a concept of equal opportunity amongst all sections of the multiracial society to be found within the United Kingdom.

(NNEB, 1990, p. 16)

The NNEB is now part of the Council for Awards in Childcare and Education (CACHE), and the above policy remains part its commitment to a high quality service.

Similarly, the Preschool Playgroups Association (PPA) had for some time had progressive regional activity (e.g. in Camden) and a national working party has been looking at racial equality in their practice. The PPA has sought advice from the CRE and has now integrated some of its deliberations into its guidelines for practice (PPA, 1990a, b). Although there are several sound attempts to promote racial equality through statements appearing in pink and green at the end of most sections of the guidelines, e.g. on management, staffing, play activities, etc., these provisions do suffer from such presentation which suggests that they may have been added as an afterthought. It is hoped that future editions will provide an integrated and proactive approach to equal opportunities central to the text. That said, the PPA guidelines do cover a broad range of issues related to equal opportunities and are still well worth reading. Now as the Preschool Learning Alliance (PLA) they continue to carry this commitment.

The National Children's Bureau Early Childhood Unit has developed a clear policy and commitment through its working group on anti-racism, and this is now monitored by its advisory group and by the Bureau's Equal Opportunities Committee. It is interesting to note that the NCB as an organization now has a Bureau-wide policy. The Bureau's policy statement highlights its positive approach: the Bureau recognized that passive policies will not in themselves provide equality of opportunity and that specific positive programmes of action are needed. More recent publications with a sound, integrated equal opportunities perspective include the training pack, *Ensuring Standards in the Care of Young Children* (National Children's Bureau, 1991) on the registering and development of quality day care, *Young Children in Group Day Care* (Cowley, 1991) which offers guidelines for good practice, and most specifically *With Equal Concern* ... (Elfer, 1995), training materials designed to ensure day care and educational provision for young children takes positive account of the 'religious persuasion, racial origin and cultural and linguistic background of each child' (Children Act 1989).

The European Childcare Network has one funded project looking at racial equality and child care in Europe, and this project is being led by Britain. There is a need, while continuing to work towards racial equality in Britain, to raise the standards of early years racial equality throughout the European Community.

It is clear then that an increasing number of early years educators and policy-makers have felt this issue to be of utmost importance and approximately 80 per cent of local education authorities now have a policy on multi-cultural or anti-racist education. Unfortunately, many schools have still failed to respond and there is a growing concern that with the ERA, as the power of LEAs has been eroded and combined with the effects of local management of schools (LMS), which is leading to increasing competition between schools, the gains in recent years may be lost and it is difficult now for LEAs to implement any policies. Many of those working towards greater equality of opportunity are working in isolation. Wider support and training is thus needed at a regional and national level, and such support should be provided by all organizations which work with educators.

PRACTICAL IDEAS FOR RACIAL EQUALITY

Policy initiatives are useful exercises and do convey commitment, but policies can be seen as mere paper exercises without any impact on the daily practices of practitioners (Cole, 1989). If parents and children are to benefit, a well-intentioned belief in racial equality is not enough, action is necessary. It is the responsibility of every organization that deals with early years education and care to provide training for this area and for every educator to seek training.

A curriculum and environment free from racial discrimination has to pay attention to the ethos and ambience within which children grow up and learn. It is not enough to offer a narrow multi-cultural curriculum which focuses on the diversity and difference of 'exotic' cultures. Such a tokenist form of curriculum promotes what has been referred to as the 'zoo' effect or the 'tourist' curriculum. Derman-Sparks is critical of educators who depend upon information gleaned from celebrating festivals, school visits and exchanges and holidays:

> Children 'visit' non-white cultures and then 'go home' to the daily classroom, which reflects only the dominant culture. The focus on holidays, although it provides drama and delight for both children and adults, gives the impression that that is all 'other' people – usually people of colour – do. What it fails to communicate is real understanding.
>
> (Derman-Sparks, 1989, p. 7)

The multi-cultural curriculum is problematic when it focuses on information about Indians or Chinese rather than on British-Indians or British-Chinese, for such an approach focuses on differences more than upon similarities. One of the most worrying aspects of a multi-cultural curriculum is that educators often assume that it is only relevant to multiracial settings. When it is applied to white children, multi-culturalism assumes that there is a set content of knowledge to be transmitted to children about 'other' groups. The fact that 'other' groups may be as diverse as 'we' are is ignored. While few educators would attempt to explain Christianity in all its forms in a twenty-minute discussion, drama or story, this is precisely what is attempted with major world religions in many schools.

There are many areas to review when developing a racial equality approach, whatever the situation (childminder's home, playgroup, class-room or hospital). This chapter can provide little more than an overview of some of the issues and references for further study. I have argued that every adult working with young children holds power and acts as a role model. If the adult stereotypes, omits or provides inaccurate information about our multiracial society, children will learn what is important to their educator and emulate those behaviours and attitudes. If we are to avoid this we need to consider how an early childhood setting can promote racial equality in practice.

The visual environment

While young children are still struggling with language, the impact of images is all pervasive. Images provide the means by which they absorb symbolic understanding of who 'belongs' in our society. There should be images, in our posters, books, jigsaws and other resources, that demonstrate and celebrate our racially diverse society. The images should be positive ones of children and families involved in normal, daily activity, e.g. meal times, in the park, visiting the dentist. Images which are negative, e.g. poor hungry children from areas of Africa or South America, should be coun-terbalanced – children receive enough of these images from the media. Children will, of course, at times want to talk about famine, water short-ages or war and adults must respond to these issues in a well-informed and honest manner appropriate to the child's age. The visual environment should not be tokenist with only one or two black faces – there should be a numerical balance of different racial groups. In fact, Derman-Sparks (1989) recommends that more than half, although not all, of the images and other materials should reflect black people to counter the predomi-nance in society generally of images of white people.

Language

Children should have the opportunity to hear and see various languages, and alternative scripts including Braille and sign. Children will only develop an awareness of the literary achievements of other cultures if we present the product to them. Language is the single most important factor in shaping a child's self-identity, esteem, culture, social, emotional and cognitive development. It is essential that educators value the whole linguistic resource that a bi/multilingual child brings with her/him. It is not enough to value only the English part of it; any such neglect of the home language will impart negative messages to the child about a part of them that is also a part of their whole identity and community. The educator does not require fluency to show they value their pupil's language. Monolingual educators can support bilingual/multilingual children in a variety of ways (Siraj-Blatchford, 1990). They can use bilingual story tapes, learn a few everyday words in the predominant minority language in their setting and encourage activities which allow children to use their home language. Monolingual children's awareness of other languages should be encouraged through bilingual labelling. Alphabet and number posters, dual language books, songs, rhymes and finger games are all things that all our children can join in, enjoy and ask questions about.

Educators require knowledge of the languages in use in our communities. They need to understand what it means to be bilingual/multilingual. That means understanding that words carry culturally specific concepts; for example, the word 'saucepan' may mean 'something to cook food in' to most English children and while it may have the same meaning (although involving different food) for a South Asian child it will also be the receptacle that tea (Chai, a special spiced, sweet tea) can be boiled up in. An incident in a nursery setting illustrates the need to understand this sort of thing well. A nursery nurse observed a Pakistani child 'making tea' in a saucepan in the home corner and demanded that the child use the kettle! One cannot suggest that all culturally specific meanings should be equally understood by everyone – that is neither possible nor perhaps desirable – but we can avoid making value-laden assumptions. The nursery nurse could have asked the child why she was using the saucepan or how she was going to make the tea. Through this process she would have learned the child's culturally specific understanding of 'saucepan'.

It has been noted by a number of nursery workers that where extra visual, auditory (puppets, sound effects) and bilingual resources are used, it helps all the children in their language development and not just the bilingual children. This is an interesting issue for us to reflect on. We need to recognize that bilingual and race equality education is simply good practice.

Books are a mixture of language and images and they reflect social values and attitudes. Since books and reading activities make up such a significant part of young children's lives in school and care, texts should be selected and used very carefully. The Council on Interracial Books for

Children (1980) provides a clear set of criteria for selecting and evaluating books on the basis of racism and sexism.

Toys and activity materials

The issue of toys is not as simple as buying black dolls or getting rid of the golliwog. As Bob Dixon (1989) suggests, the toy industry is strong and thrives on exploiting sexist and racist 'norms' in our society. Toys are a very strong socializing force in children's lives.

Dolls should be reasonably authentic in their shades of colour when representing black and brown skin tones. Unfortunately, some manufacturers believe that there is little demand for black dolls and therefore little profit is to be made. In the present circumstances, if we want black dolls we need to urge our local department stores to stock them. We also need to explain the kind of authentic looking dolls we wish to have in our education and care settings. It is clearly unacceptable to buy dolls with black faces which have the same European features as white dolls or dolls which have black/brown hands and faces but a pink body. Such dolls exist and suggest to children that black people are pink under their clothes! Dolls and puppets should represent a balance of the major groups in Britain, e.g. Caribbean, South Asian, Chinese, as well as white.

Dressing-up clothes should represent everyday clothes from a range of cultures rather than 'national' costumes. We would be shocked if the only English clothes in an Indian nursery were those of Morris dancers. Similarly, black people are often surprised to find what they consider rare dressing-up clothes from their own cultures being promoted as 'normal'. It is also worth considering why children dress up and what it means to them. Being a 'Red Indian' involves playing out a stereotype, offensive to Native Americans. What sort of knowledge could a young child possibly have of 'Red Indians' other than from the many aggressive and racist wild west films? Similarly, any early years topic based on 'Red Indians' is misconceived at best and discriminatory at worst. The children could only be misinformed. Dressing-up clothes should be chosen carefully and, if at all possible, with the consultation of local minority groups.

Arts materials should always reflect the home background of children and a wider community. For collage work such materials as mustard seeds, a range of legumes, rice, paints (brown, tan and black) and crayons can be provided. Mirrors should be on offer so that children can learn about, and articulate, their physical features and how best to describe them. The educator has much to offer here in helping to develop a child's self-identity.

All toys should be checked against clear guidelines to promote anti-sexist and anti-racist practice. The Working Group Against Racism in Children's Resources has produced an excellent set of Guidelines (1990) for the evaluation and selection of toys and other resources for children.

Food and festivals

As a society our attitudes about food have changed considerably in the last twenty years. A diversity of restaurants is commonplace in most towns and cities and most supermarkets stock an international range of foods. Nevertheless, there is still a lot of prejudice against certain foods and against the people who eat them regularly. Children at a very early age should be introduced to a range of foods within and across cultures. Children can learn that all groups have staples in their diet such as potatoes, rice and breads. A good time to introduce a commonality of experience is at harvest time. Many early years settings display a range of breads – these could include chapatties, wholemeal bread, French stick, pitta, etc.

British society is particularly concerned about smells and children should be encouraged to cook with a range of herbs and spices. Young children enjoy cooking as a real activity in which they participate in a process from start to finish. Engaging in baking and smelling pizzas, sweet rice with saffron or fresh chapatties is not only a delightful learning experience but one in which language can be developed and the senses (both smell and taste!) enhanced.

Children are often asked about their favourite food and many children from non-English cultures may feel they can only give the answers which the educator (if white) will understand. Therefore the way we phrase questions is important. We could ask children what they have to eat or drink every day, or what foods they can eat with their hands, e.g. fruit, samosa, sandwich, pizza, chapatti (roti) and curry (salan), etc.

Festivals are strongly associated with food and celebration as well as religious ritual. Many early years settings only celebrate a few festivals, e.g. Chinese New Year, Eid ul Fitr, Diwali and Christmas. Educators need to question what children learn from these experiences. Is it merely promoting a 'tourist' curriculum? Children need to understand why they are celebrating. Stories and the educational part of a festival need to be seen as much more important than simply an excuse for celebration in itself. Many infant schools start Christmas celebrations several weeks before Christmas Day, with the children making cards and decorations, writing letters to Santa, talking about presents, rehearsing their plays, holding discos and so forth – by the time the nativity play/story comes round they are all too 'high' and excited to learn anything! Similarly for Eid and Diwali, a one-day celebration with dancing and spicy food is hardly an educational experience for any child.

Early years settings need to set clear guidelines on the purpose of festival celebrations, on the use of foods and on cooking policy. We need to question who cooks with the children. Must it always be the Bangladeshi mother who cooks Bengali food with the children? The children would have a more balanced world view if the English teacher cooked a curry with them and the Bangladeshi mother made fairy cakes. Role models are important.

Interactions which promote race equality and deal with racist behaviour

If our early years learning environments reflect the black presence in our society, we are working towards 'race' equality. It is not enough to leave things at that. Children are naturally curious and have absorbed values from outside. Educators will want to read stories and have discussions with children which raise the issues of racism and sexism and allow children to express their feelings, views and experiences in this area. These issues will inevitably arise in the children's minds. When they are expressed they learn about their educator's views on the matter. They learn whether she/he thinks racism acceptable or very unacceptable. It is vital for all children to know that they are safe, secure and loved by their educator.

Children's indoor and outdoor play should be monitored carefully and their interactions listened to. Adults often assume stereotypes about boisterous Afro-Caribbean boys who do not concentrate or quiet Asian girls who never speak. The adults' interaction with children should also be monitored. All children should be offered a great deal of encouragement to engage in the full range of activities.

Many educators fear dealing with incidents of racial abuse, name-calling or ridicule. This is often because they do not have enough knowledge to deal with the issue with clear explanations or are ignorant of the damage this form of behaviour causes. Racist behaviour and name-calling is a form of mental violence on the victim. If a child is called 'Paki' or told 'you can't come to my party because my mummy doesn't like blackies', how can the victim react? The hurt, humiliation and damage is done. The message is that the child's colour/racial background is by its very nature unacceptable and inferior, and by implication that white/English is superior. Educators must learn to handle these situations. Victims must be supported with love and care and shown that we recognize the gravity of the crime committed. The perpetrator should witness this support and be talked with. Punishment is not enough, the reason why what the perpetrator said was wrong and unacceptable should be clearly and gently explained by the educator.

All these issues are equally applicable to parents. Parents should be involved in developing and understanding the educators' policy, and the reasons why racist behaviour is damaging, wrong, unacceptable and against the law!

A PROCESS FOR CHANGE: FIVE STEPS FORWARD

(1) *Staff personal commitment*: develop children's learning through racial (and gender, class and disability) equality and develop a learning programme with all your colleagues. This approach ensures the ownership and commitment of all those involved – it will be your own ideas you are all working towards. A typical group might convene ten meetings over one year by which time a policy could be written and put into practice.

(2) *Looking at resources*: look at existing materials using anti-racist evaluation sheets. It would be helpful to identify the gaps and the existing good practice in the curriculum, and check thoroughly what messages the hidden part of the curriculum conveys (e.g. childminders may become alerted to the value of keeping some dual-language books), including resources used to assess children.

Educators will want to try out anti-racist materials and resources and discuss and research the potential of new resources. Human resources should also be considered. Local authority multi-cultural/anti-racist education support services may well be able to contribute.

(3) *Learning from others*: it is always worth inviting speakers to give their experiences and knowledge of working in an anti-racist context or speakers who will clarify one area of concern, e.g. how to support bilingual pupils, or working in an all-white area.

Try to develop a library collection with useful books, journals, any union literature on racial equality, newspaper cuttings and specific guidelines and addresses. The local authority may also offer specialist help. If it cannot, you are in a position to recommend it should.

(4) *Role models*: who is employed in your organization? What does this convey to young children? Schools often find that the only black person in their school is a cleaner or a helper; all other people who have real authority are white. Similarly, you should look at your local playgroup organization, childminders' association, private nursery staff, etc., and ask yourself how this affects our children's lives.

Once we recognize that role models are important and that inequality has resulted in the exclusion of black people from our workplaces, then we have to do something about it. Policies which discourage black applicants should be discarded in favour of those which encourage, and we can campaign both locally and nationally for fairer recruitment procedures.

(5) *Monitor and evaluate*: policies and practices need constant evaluation so that practice is improved. We need to identify what to monitor, e.g. schools may want to look at teaching styles or language use while day care advisers may prioritize looking at value-laden child-rearing practices. From this process a new set of steps should emerge for staff development. There are no simple solutions to eliminating racial inequality but accepting the need to take the first step is the most important.

Further reading

Issues relating to the theory and practice raised in this chapter are argued more extensively in the following references:

The Early Years: Laying the Foundations for Racial Equality (Siraj-Blatchford, 1994).

Challenging Inequality and Promoting Respect (Siraj-Blatchford, 1996).

Educating the Whole Child: Cross-Curricular Skills, Themes and Dimension (Siraj-Blatchford, 1995).

For further support, see the training materials published by the Early Childhood Unit:

With Equal Concern . . . (Elfer, 1995).

Managing to Change (Cowley, 1995), training materials for day care centres, including a module on *Equal Opportunities*.

8

MEETING SPECIAL NEEDS IN THE EARLY YEARS

Sheila Wolfendale and Janine Wooster

INTRODUCTION

This chapter provides a review of recent developments in special needs in the early years. We examine a number of concepts, principles and values and put these in the context of special needs legislation. We plan to appraise progress in identification of special needs and intervening with or on behalf of young children with special needs. These areas are illustrated first hand, using one LEA as an example together with three child case studies. Concepts of quality assurance conclude the chapter.

VALUES AND PRINCIPLES

It is a mixed blessing that, in a book devoted to a diverse range of perspectives on the early years, there should be a chapter on special needs. The dilemma for early years/special needs workers is encapsulated by the presence of such a chapter, integral to the book but with a title that potentially marginalizes 'special needs' into being an adjunct to mainstream day care and early education.

Aware of the paradox, we feel that readers might wish to know our stance at the outset. We plan to acknowledge and celebrate achievements in special needs/early years, commensurate with early years issues becoming higher on the education agenda. So we shall chronicle a number of notable developments. At the same time we want to demonstrate a broad responsibility on the part of all early years practitioners towards the distinctive learning and developmental needs of all children, in creating opportunities for them to flourish.

Rights and opportunities

It is a recent phenomenon that special needs and disability areas have been perceived to come within the orbit of equal opportunities, belatedly joining 'race, sex and class' as the major educational and social issues over which positive action was seen to be needed (Roaf and Bines, 1989). The language of the Warnock Report (1978), the Education Act 1981 and its accompanying Circular 1/83 was not couched in equal opportunities terms but these in part paved the way for the perspective propagated within the Education Reform Act 1988 that pupils with special educational needs have a fundamental, inalienable entitlement to the National Curriculum. These rights to access to all available curriculum and educational opportunities have become a bedrock principle permeating educational thinking (Rieser and Mason, 1990) including those working in preschool and multidisciplinary settings (Cameron and Sturge-Moore, 1990).

The broadest universal context for these developments has been the moral imperative provided in the International Convention on the Rights of the Child (Newell, 1991). This convention adopted by the United Nations General Assembly in 1989 has now been signed by the majority of countries. It is a set of international standards and measures that recognizes the particular vulnerability of children, brings together in one comprehensive code the benefits and protection for children scattered in scores of other agreements and adds new rights never before recognized. Once the Convention has been signed and ratified by twenty countries (and this has been attained), it has the force of international law.

This will and should have implications at every level of policy, decision-making, provision and practice for children from birth, if the fundamental premise is to protect and guarantee children's rights. A number of Articles within the Convention are explicitly geared towards special needs and disability (Children's Rights Development Unit, 1994).

Definitions and terminology

The debate on the meaning, purpose and adequacy of the terms 'special needs', 'special education needs', and disability has often recurred (Wolfendale 1993a, 1994). A term that started out, pre-Warnock in actual fact, as intended to be benign and advantaging towards children perceived to be vulnerable and educationally at risk, has become contentious. At its worst, 'special needs' has been perceived as being a separate area, with its own panoply of procedure and personnel, and in education, 'SEN' is too often used as a shorthand label that does indeed encapsulate this view (see Norwich, 1990).

The Children Act 1989 had its own definition of 'need', relating particularly to the early years. Woodhead (1991) challenged a number of 'givens' that he says have informed policy-making in the early years and beyond. His thesis is that it behoves early years workers to 'recognize the plurality of pathways to maturity within that perspective' (Woodhead, 1991, p. 50).

Such social and cultural imperatives need to inform our practice as an influential backcloth to the need to provide for a range of 'conditions' listed by Cameron and Sturge-Moore (1990) in their definition of 'special needs' and their justification for using the term within early years contexts.

For the purposes of the chapter, our 'early years' go up to school entry at five years and the first couple of years in school.

THE PLACING OF SPECIAL NEEDS IN THE EARLY YEARS ON THE AGENDA

The public and legislative agenda: focus on education

The Warnock Report in 1978 gave under fives and special needs a higher profile than that area had hitherto had by recommending it as a priority area in terms of teacher training and increased provision. Emphasis was given to the proven effectiveness of intervention programmes, including Portage, partly to justify this call for increased investment in the early years as both a preventive and 'remedial' measure. Equally, the Court Report published a littler earlier (Committee on Child Health Services, 1976) had focused attention on health and development in the early years and had recommended implementation of local early screening and surveillance systems to detect developmental delay and early-appearing disability.

Other government reports on early years included the Select Committee on Educational Provision for the Under Gives (House of Commons, 1989) and the Rumbold Report (DES, 1990a), which includes brief mention of special needs.

The Warnock Report paved the way for the legislation that amended existing law on special education, namely the Education Act 1981 (implemented from 1 April 1983) which conferred new duties on local education and health authorities in respect of identifying and assessing young children with possible special needs. The accompanying circular to the Education Act 1981, updated in 1989 (Circular 22/89) to take account of the Education Reform Act 1988 as well as recent developments, had a whole section on under fives with special needs, doubtless influenced by the (1987) Select Committee criticisms into this phase of education and provision.

The Education Reform Act 1988, whilst not statutorily covering preschool of course, nevertheless had implications for the education of four-year-olds in infant schools (Dowling, 1995) and for the applicability of the National Curriculum for young children with special educational needs.

The latest and most significant legislative landmark is the Education Act 1993, Part 3 of which refers exclusively to special educational needs. This Part of the Act repeals the Education Act 1981, retaining core principles and formal assessment procedures, but strengthening a number of parental rights and clarifying the processes. Schools are now required by law to have written accountable SEN policies. The 1994 Code of Practice constitutes a set of guidelines to which LEAs and schools must have 'due regard' in the planning and delivery of SEN services. It adopts a five-stage model of identifying and assessing children with special educational needs (summarized in Figure 8.2).

The Code of Practice acknowledges the importance of partnership between LEAs, child health and social services in working together to meet the needs of children under five with SEN. Parents of children under five with SEN will also be able to express a preference for a particular maintained school to be named in their child's statement, so will have priority access to available nursery provision.

There is now plenty of evidence to show that at every level of practice, management and policy-making, special needs in the early years is in receipt of more attention, resources and provision that at any other time.

Personnel working within these areas are bound to implement and have due regard to the legislation, such as the Children Act 1989 and it emphasis upon needs definition, service provision for young children 'in need' and with disabilities, registration and review (Allen, 1992; Bull *et al.*, 1994). The preceding section briefly outlined the impact of SEN legislation.

Strong encouragement is given to these various Acts of Parliament for practitioners to work together more effectively. For example, multi- and interdisciplinary liaison is urged at each Stage of the Code of Practice. Some local authorities are beginning to consider and implement joint commissioning of early years, mental health and children's services (Audit

Commission, 1994; Health Advisory Service, 1995; and see Jones and Bilton, 1994).

Service provision ideology in the 1990s is certainly driven by concepts of corporate and collective responsibility wherein each professional has a number of identified if not prescribed duties and functions, and liaises with parents and carers, who likewise have areas of involvement and responsibility (see next section below). The chart in Figure 8.1 has been assembled by one of the authors, working with practitioner groups over a number of years. It represents and illustrates inter-connections as well as individual and collective responsibility in the area of SEN.

Despite this agenda, however, and the fact that there is some kind of consensus over the importance of the early years, the known variation in provision reflects the lack of co-ordination and commitment to explicit policies at government levels, and the anomalous status of non-statutory preschool provision (except for under fives with a statement of special educational needs which must be met and provided for by the LEA).

The parents' agenda

Each of the reports mentioned above emphasizes the importance of parent–professional dialogue, and the various Acts have enshrined and latterly strengthened a number of parental rights. Many parents themselves have translated rhetoric and principles into a number of realities and practical action which include:

- Finding a collective voice: a number of local, regional parents' groups have emerged, within, now, a national umbrella and parents of children with SEN have begun to share their views and concerns more widely (Gascoigne, 1995).

- Empowerment, via the emergence of parent advocacy, representation, self-help, and parent–professional coalitions (Armstrong, 1995; Garner and Sandow, 1995; Hornby, 1995).

- Participating in assessment processes (Wolfendale, 1993b).

- Parents as educators, as in Portage and other home-based early learning schemes (Leadbetter and Leadbetter, 1993; Daly, 1994).

The Code of Practice lays out a number of key principles for establishing and facilitating parent–professional partnership, and illustrates how this can be effected throughout the Stages of the Code. The 'message' is further reinforced via the existence of Department for Education and Employment grant (GEST) to LEAs and schools to set up and maintain Parent Partnership Schemes (the grant runs from 1995 through to 1997).

Appendix

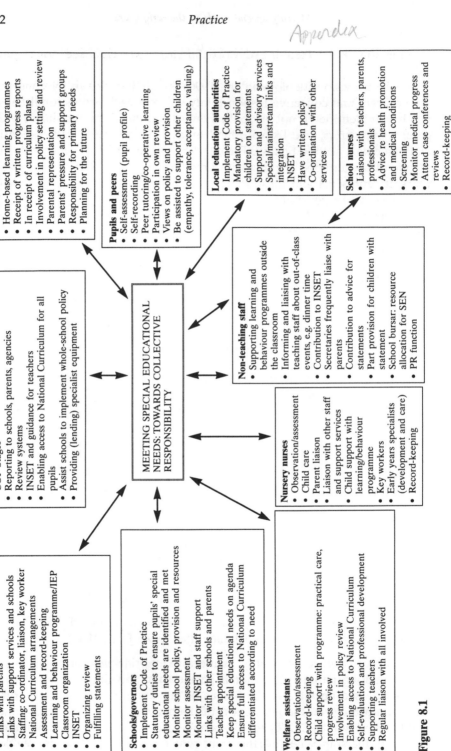

Teachers/schools (via SENCO)
- Implement Code of Practice
- Set policy and implement (special needs, discipline, pastoral, equal opportunities)
- Links with parents
- Links with support services and schools
- Staffing: co-ordinator, liaison, key worker
- National Curriculum arrangements
- Assessment and record-keeping
- Learning and behaviour programme/IEP
- Classroom organization
- INSET
- Organizing review
- Fulfilling statements

Support services
- System of links with and between schools and teaching collaboration
- Procedures for assessment and school support at COP Stages
- Reporting to schools, parents, agencies
- Review systems
- INSET and guidance for teachers
- Enabling access to National Curriculum for all pupils
- Assist schools to implement whole-school policy
- Providing (lending) specialist equipment

Parents
- Contribution at COP Stages
- Contribution to assessment and record-keeping
- Contribution to child's review
- Home-based learning programmes
- Receipt of written progress reports
- In receipt of curriculum plans
- Involvement in policy setting and review
- Parental representation
- Parents' pressure and support groups
- Responsibility for primary needs
- Planning for the future

Pupils and peers
- Self-assessment (pupil profile)
- Self-recording
- Peer tutoring/co-operative learning
- Participation in own review
- Views on policy and provision
- Be assisted to support other children (empathy, tolerance, acceptance, valuing)

Local education authorities
- Implement Code of Practice
- Mandatory provision for children on statements
- Support and advisory services
- Special/mainstream links and integration
- INSET
- Have written policy
- Co-ordination with other services

School nurses
- Liaison with teachers, parents, professionals
- Advice re health promotion and medical conditions
- Screening
- Monitor medical progress
- Attend case conferences and reviews
- Record-keeping
- Home visits

MEETING SPECIAL EDUCATIONAL NEEDS: TOWARDS COLLECTIVE RESPONSIBILITY

Non-teaching staff
- Supporting learning and behaviour programmes outside the classroom
- Informing and liaising with teaching staff about out-of-class events, e.g. dinner time
- Contribution to INSET
- Secretaries frequently liaise with parents
- Contribution to advice for statements
- Part provision for children with statement
- School bursar: resource allocation for SEN
- PR function

Nursery nurses
- Observation/assessment
- Child care
- Parent liaison
- Liaison with other staff and support services
- Child support with learning/behaviour programme
- Key workers
- Early years specialists (development and care)
- Record-keeping

Schools/governors
- Implement Code of Practice
- Statutory duties to ensure pupils' special educational needs are identified and met
- Monitor school policy, provision and resources
- Monitor assessment
- Monitor INSET and staff support
- Links with other schools and parents
- Teacher appointment
- Keep special educational needs on agenda
- Ensure full access to National Curriculum differentiated according to need

Welfare assistants
- Observation/assessment
- Record-keeping
- Child support: with programme: practical care, progress review
- Involvement in policy review
- Enabling access to National Curriculum
- Self-evaluation and professional development
- Supporting teachers
- Regular liaison with all involved

Figure 8.1

POLICY INTO PRACTICE: DECISION-MAKING IN KENT

Assessment of young children with special needs has fundamentally changed in the light of the Education Act 1993 and specifically the Code of Practice which already has had many effects on processes for assessment within schools and local education authorities. The most dramatic change has probably been in the time-scales for action; the timing of events during the process of statutory assessment has become much tighter, the intention being to try to obtain a more streamlined process that is clearer for all concerned. The Code has within it a specific section devoted to the under fives which is a new element within legislation. It develops the principles featured in Circular 22/89 and gives clear guidance for providing under-fives services.

The advent of the Code of Practice has served to validate existing good practice and it provides a starting point for the occurrence of further good practice. The Code gives clear guidance as to the roles of all professionals in implementation and its effectiveness depends to a greater extent on partnership. Fragmentation is minimized at all stages by bringing together all the professionals involved in that stage of the decision-making process so that everyone feels ownership and roles are clearly defined enabling each player to see the way forward for him/herself. The challenge to local authorities has been to maximize the effectiveness and positive aspects of the new procedures whilst minimizing the disruption caused by realigning procedures and practices yet again. In order to provide some practical examples of the issues raised in the earlier parts of this chapter we have decided to look at the way in which Kent has organized its local decision-making process and how this has affected specifically the young child with special needs.

The decision-making process for young children begins after they have been identified (usually by medical staff, but sometimes by parents or other professionals) as having some kind of special need which is likely to evolve into them having some kind of special *educational* need. The child will be seen in Kent by the preschool adviser, who is a professional with experience of working with children in the early years and who is skilled at giving advice to parents and other professionals as to what the child's needs are and how they can best be met at that particular moment in time. When the preschool adviser has got to know the child and family by visiting them the child will be referred to a preschool review, which will also be attended by the preschool adviser, and an educational psychologist. A member of the special needs support team, a representative of the health authority, representatives from social services, teachers from the physical/sensory service will be invited as seems to be appropriate. The review team meets at least once termly. The preschool adviser has the responsibility for co-ordinating the meeting and a person is nominated from the review to discuss the outcome of the meeting with the parents/carers of the child. Decisions will be made according to the child's individual needs; for some the outcome will be to recommend a placement in a nursery or playgroup, for others it will be to recommend further specific assessment, and for a further group it will be a referral on for consideration of the need for a full statutory assessment under the Education Act 1993. The preschool review will try to develop multi-agency interventions to support the child and family before he/she begins school.

The preschool adviser works to obtain a clear picture of the child's needs and what the family want for the child. Given relevant information, the school and teacher will be able to formulate plans for the child well before the day they start school.

The Code of Practice comments that all schools will wish to assess pupils' current levels of attainment on entry to school in order to ensure that they build upon the pattern of learning and experience already established during the child's preschool years.

The older children not eligible for discussion at the preschool review will be discussed at an 'in-school review'. The basic membership of the in-school review will be the headteacher, the school's special needs co-ordinator (SENCO), a member of the county special educational needs support team, and an educational psychologist.

The school may elect to invite other members of its own staff and/or representatives of health and social services as appropriate in individual school cases. For most children who have not been discussed at a preschool level the in-school review will be the start of the process of regular discussion, planning for the curriculum and referral to other agencies as necessary.

The in-school review will place children on the audit (see Figure 8.2) and can refer them on to the local advisory team (LAT), which forms the next stage in the decision-making process. The basic membership of this body will be a senior caseworker, a member of the special educational needs support team, an educational psychologist, and a representative headteacher. Other professionals can be invited to the LAT if it is considered necessary and/or appropriate.

The role of the LAT is to apply consistent criteria in deciding whether or not a statutory assessment should be carried out. A standard format is used and all decisions are recorded clearly and fed back to the referring agency and all of those who have given evidence. Written evidence is requested to support all requests for statutory assessment. The LAT may move forward to a statutory assessment or turn down the request, stating at which audit level they feel the child can be supported, or defer the request asking for more evidence.

If at this stage it is decided that a statutory assessment should be begun,

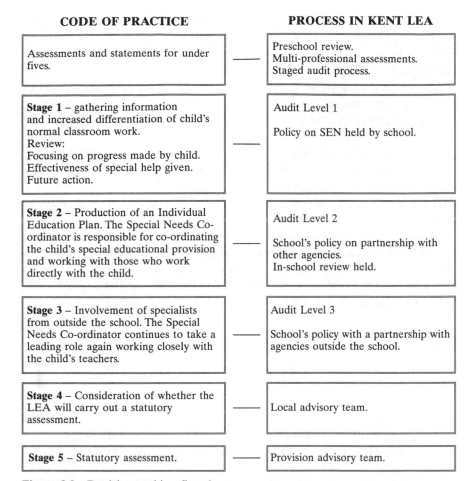

CODE OF PRACTICE | PROCESS IN KENT LEA

CODE OF PRACTICE	PROCESS IN KENT LEA
Assessments and statements for under fives.	Preschool review. Multi-professional assessments. Staged audit process.
Stage 1 – gathering information and increased differentiation of child's normal classroom work. Review: Focusing on progress made by child. Effectiveness of special help given. Future action.	Audit Level 1 Policy on SEN held by school.
Stage 2 – Production of an Individual Education Plan. The Special Needs Co-ordinator is responsible for co-ordinating the child's special educational provision and working with those who work directly with the child.	Audit Level 2 School's policy on partnership with other agencies. In-school review held.
Stage 3 – Involvement of specialists from outside the school. The Special Needs Co-ordinator continues to take a leading role again working closely with the child's teachers.	Audit Level 3 School's policy with a partnership with agencies outside the school.
Stage 4 – Consideration of whether the LEA will carry out a statutory assessment.	Local advisory team.
Stage 5 – Statutory assessment.	Provision advisory team.

Figure 8.2 Decision-making flowchart

then the parents will be informed of the decision and they will be invited to come along to an informal workshop to discuss how the process takes place, what their part is, what they can expect to receive from the local authority, what the formal procedures are and what they should do at each stage if they disagree with what is happening.

A database is used to keep all this information efficiently and in an easily accessible format. Each child being assessed is allocated a caseworker who has responsibility for ensuring that the system operates as efficiently as possible and that the assessment is carried out within the given time. Reports are requested for all of the statutory agencies and they are collected and logged onto the database as they arrive. Once all the required reports have been collected a Statement of Need is drafted which is sent, together with the received reports, to the provision advisory team (PAT).

The membership of the PAT is the special educational services manager, the assistant county educational psychologist, a county development manager, a representative headteacher (who changes termly) and other representatives on request.

As well as discussing draft statements, the PAT considers the results of annual reviews and requests for changes in provision.

PAT decides upon the placement or additional resources both human and otherwise. The function of PAT overall is to match the provision to the need at the level of each individual child. It determines what the statement of need for the child will say. In some cases a more multi-agency input will be required; this is provided through a regular JPAT or joint provision advisory team – comprising the usual PAT team and representatives from social services and the health authority.

If the PAT or JPAT recommends a residential or 'out of the county' placement for a child the papers are forwarded to the residential advisory placement panel (RAPP) which meets on a county basis. The RAPP can give advice on the relevance of residential placements and/or suggest alternative placements to the PAT team.

The whole decision-making process is regularly reviewed by all of those involved on the Panels – thus the whole process is evaluated and updated.

Three illustrative child case studies follow – each demonstrates a different facet of the decision-making process and each highlights issues of assessment and provision.

Case study 1: Child put forward to local advisory team for statutory assessment but assessment not approved

Tim's mother wrote to pupil and student services, who referred the letter on to the preschool adviser, saying the family (herself, Tim and two older children) was moving into Kent from Essex and that the local school and nursery class she had approached was full. Mum has chronic asthma and is unable to escort her children very far. Tim had been attending a family centre in Essex for language development.

On further discussion with his local authority, it was discovered that Tim was due to be seen by the preschool adviser with a view to possible formal assessment after a visit by an educational psychologist because of Tim's language, learning and associated behaviour difficulties.

Tim's case was presented to the preschool review and he was found a place in a nursery. Within a few days of his move to Kent in February 1995, he started at the nursery, aged four years and three months.

He was seen by the preschool adviser in March and was recommended by the preschool review in April as a child who would need to be assessed formally. He was due to start school the following September and Level 3 support (see Figure 8.2) was recommended whilst the assessment procedure was under way. His case was considered by the local advisory team in June, who did not consider statutory assessment to be relevant in his case and recommended he enter school for one term and be discussed through the in-school review process.

The receiving primary school was informed of the LAT's decision and relevant notes and papers were sent to them. The school's special educational needs co-ordinator (who is also the reception class teacher) and the headteacher contacted the preschool adviser to ask for her attendance at the first in-school review as they were finding Tim very difficult to manage. He refused to follow instructions and had hit and bitten the teacher and other children on several occasions. His latest developmental assessment by the clinical medical officer outlined his continuing difficulty with language and short-term auditory memory, affecting his ability to follow instructions.

The decision of the in-school review was for the school to collect more information concerning his cognitive ability and language skills and how these related to the behaviour displayed in school. The educational psychologist is to become involved in working with Tim in school and at home. A referral has been made to child and adult mental health services and Tim's case will be re-presented to the next in-school review in November.

Case study 2: Child has undergone statutory assessment and is in a mainstream reception class with support

Jane was referred to the preschool adviser in 1992 at age one year ten months as presenting with mild to marked hearing loss, some speech and comprehension delay and mild microcephaly.

At two years five months she was discharged by ENT (following surgery) but was reported as having made no progress in her receptive language and expressive speech. Jane was mainly making herself understood by sign language and gesturing. She was also displaying signs of limited attention and listening skills.

Jane was visited in her playgroup and presented to the preschool review. A nursery placement was found for her where she could be assessed. Her case was presented to the local advisory team and her parents also wrote to the local authority to request statutory assessment.

In July 1995 her assessment was completed with the recommendation that she should enter her local school's reception class along with her peers in September, with fifteen hours per week classroom assistance and six hours per term tutor time.

Case study 3: Child referred to preschool adviser
and placement found via preschool review

Paul was referred to the preschool adviser at age two years four months
by a senior clinical medical officer following a developmental assessment
which highlighted concerns about his short concentration span, behaviour,
sleeping and eating problems. Paul was also being seen by a speech ther-
apist who indicated that he had mild/moderate speech and language delay.
He had just had six teeth extracted and suffered from eczema. He also had
inner raises for both shoes. He was still in nappies.

The preschool adviser contacted Paul's mother, who was finding him
increasingly difficult. She has cancer and was very tired – she has two children from a previous marriage and three step-children. Paul was referred
for Portage but this referral was not taken up by mum. PSA referred Paul
and mum to the clinical psychology service. Mum welcomed this intervention, which is ongoing.

A playgroup place was found for Paul immediately and a support assistant paid for to work with him on his listening, attention, speech and language skills.

Paul's case was presented to the preschool review and a five-session-a-
week educational nursery place was allocated to him. He has been attending the nursery for three-and-a-half terms and is due to start mainstream
school in January 1996. It is anticipated that he will need Level 2 support
(see Figure 8.2) for his speech and language but that all other areas of
development have improved to an age-appropriate level. He is still, however, presenting problems for mum at home.

Paul will continue to be monitored once he enters the reception class.

DELIVERING QUALITY SERVICES FOR
YOUNG CHILDREN WITH SPECIAL NEEDS

At the time of writing, early years provisions is set to expand, but in directions that are not totally predictable – it remains to be seen how the
voucher system proposed by the government during 1995 works out in
practice. It seems to be the wish of the government that the SEN Code of
Practice should apply to all early years establishments within the voucher
scheme.

Talk of expansion parallels recent focus upon the criteria that define and
constitute good quality early years provision, be it in nursery school, day
nursery, day centre, playgroups or other forms of voluntary and private
provision.

Calls for expansion come accompanied by discussion on establishing and measuring quality (Ball, 1994). A recent House of Commons report on educational provision for the under fives took due note of some of the literature on quality, citing key factors, such as appropriately qualified staff, an adequate adult–child ratio, the right kind of facilities and resources and a curriculum which will meet the needs of the children (House of Commons Education Committee, 1994, p. viii). These quality characteristics are echoed and indeed elaborated in other literature – see, for example, discussion on *equality* in Moss and Pence (1994), and the involvement of parents and children in assessment (Abbott and Rodger, 1994). Williams (1995) provides an overview of ten contemporary approaches to the definition and measurement of quality in early years provision – these include observational rating scales, coding schemes, use of the the British Standards Institution scheme, development of performance criteria, and of course the criteria contained in the OFSTED Framework for Inspection (OFSTED, 1993b).

Indeed the latter, which was reissued, amended and updated, in late Autumn 1995, provides guidelines and criteria for inspectors to collect and assess evidence of the quality of provision within schools, including nurseries. The SEN area is integral to the OFSTED Framework.

Within day care services, the triennial review, required under the Children Act 1989, provides opportunities for assembling an evidence-base to be matched with performance criteria. However, recent research (Bull *et al.*, 1994) suggests that the majority of such reviews were primarily descriptive rather than analytical. Opportunities for using the data collected critically to assess quality of provision in day care settings were not yet being fully taken up, in part doubtless reflecting the reality that it takes time to build up the necessary expertise and methodology to carry out such rigorous exercises.

This is the broader context within which quality in the delivery of early years SEN services is also to be judged. However, there have also been attempts to focus specifically upon the SEN area. For example, the National Portage Association produced a code of practice (reproduced in full in Wolfendale, 1994) which enumerates twelve criteria underlying a service like Portage. In Carpenter (1994) Mittler is of the view that the Children Act 1989, the Education Act 1993 and the associated Code of Practice provide an opportunity to rethink the aims and objectives of early intervention and he poses a list of five questions to facilitate this exercise. Russell (also in Carpenter, 1994) lists factors in developing early identification and intervention programmes which constitute not only an agenda but a blueprint for applying quality criteria.

The notion, then, of 'quality audit' is becoming accepted and is gradually becoming widespread in practice.

In conclusion, we return to themes outlined at the beginning of this chapter, namely values and principles, and collective responsibility. Any auditing arrangements must not only provide the basis/criteria for the collection and analysis of evidence of effectiveness, but also be grounded within a set of articulated principles and values around the provision of early years/SEN services. The Code of Practice provides a beacon, but it behoves all early years practitioners working within a diverse range of settings to identify key *aspects* of values/principles and determine which key *elements* of these can best express and realize in practice true collaboration, partnership and shared responsibility.

Area	**Key elements** (examples, which can be expanded)
Principles and values	Commitment to working with parents as partners. Equality of rights for parents. Family culture seen as central. Shared assessment and diagnosis. Family involvement in intervention. Use intervention of proven effectiveness.
Entitlement	Children with special needs are entitled to preschool learning opportunities. Children and their families are entitled to quality services of proven effectiveness. Children have the right to learn in mainstream settings.
Responsibilities – professionals	To be available to parents, to provide information, explain decisions. To provide services, the quality of which can be assessed by practitioners and parents. To keep appointments, be punctual, be honest.
Responsibilities – parents	To keep staff informed. To act on behalf and in the interests of their child. To play an active part in decision-making and service delivery. To keep appointments.
Evaluation of effectiveness	All providers and users to be involved in review. Regular monitoring and review. Collection of evidence of effectiveness. Continue to research/use research findings to inform practice.

Figure 8.3 Identifying values and principles as the basis for a 'Partnership Charter'

The grid in Figure 8.3 was formulated during 1995 by one of the authors and is offered to readers as a basis for a 'Partnership Charter' between parents and professionals in services for young children with special needs.

The statements in the right-hand column are examples, which can be amended, expanded, added to if using the grid. It has been formulated, with due regard to contemporary literature, some of which has been referred to in this chapter.

Acknowledgement

The authors wish to acknowledge, with thanks, the involvement and co-operation of Ann Warn, Kent LEA, in preparing this chapter.

Further reading and discussion points

Implementing the Children Act for Children Under Eight (Bull *et al.*, 1994): focuses on how local authorities have implemented the Act and looks at areas such as co-ordination, regulation, provision of services and equal opportunities.

Working with Parents of Children with Special Needs (Hornby, 1995): provides an overview of recent and current parent–professional initiatives, covering communication, group work, intervention programmes.

Valuing Quality in Early Childhood Services (Moss and Pence, 1994): quality issues covered in this book include involving staff, parents and children in defining quality, equal opportunities, and other quality criteria.

Assessing Special Educational Needs (Wolfendale, 1993b): a range of assessment perspectives from preschool to school-leaving are provided in this book. Of particular relevance to readers of this chapter are chapters on preschool and entry-to-school SEN assessment, working with parents on assessment, and multidisciplinary approaches to assessment.

These areas are suggested as being amenable for discussion and lively debate between practitioners, policy-makers, researchers and students:

* inclusive education;
* ensuring quality early years/SEN services;
* equality and equal opportunities;
* effective means of recognizing, identifying and assessing SEN;
* skills needed to work with under-fives and SEN;
* collecting evidence and providing accountable services.

9

QUALITY FOR THE UNDER THREES

Dorothy Selleck and Sue Griffin

INTRODUCTION

This chapter explores two issues relating to the care and education of children under the age of three, and their families. These issues apply to a range of play and learning environments, in a variety of communities:

- children's needs for relationships with significant responsive adults;

- children's needs for developmentally appropriate learning experiences.

There are many criteria for defining quality, and because values and beliefs vary in a pluralistic society, so do ideas for giving a priority to any issue. We have settled on these two issues as they are of contemporary concern to a broad range of providers as well as to parents.

This chapter considers issues relating to children under three because of the distinctive development and learning needs of this age group, and because of a number of current developments. These include:

- A need to consider the continuity of learning from birth onwards. There has been much discussion in joint forums for education and care about learning from birth onwards. After many years of working separately and often in competition with each other, representatives of all the different providers of services for young children have come together to form the Early Childhood Education Forum (ECEF). The project *Quality in Diversity* is establishing an agreed framework for early learning in England and Wales. Part of this project concerns details of the birth-to-three curriculum based on a common set of principles and foundations for early learning (ECEF, forthcoming). The increase in numbers of combined nursery centres and childminders, and growth in the private sector to meet the needs and wishes of working parents, makes the interrelatedness of education and care a priority for discussion. A vision for combined services for young children and their families requires the development of quality provision for the under threes (Duffy and Griffin, 1995).

- The duty (Section 19, Children Act 1989) requiring local social services and education authorities to work collaboratively to ensure quality standards when reviewing all childminding and day care for young children (see Elfer and Wedge, Chapter 3 in this book).

- The links which are becoming more effective with colleagues in Europe and internationally (for example, Melhuish and Moss, 1990; Moss, Chapter 2 in this book). We have much to learn from international exchange and networks which will challenge, enrich or inform traditional practice in Britain.

- The demands of integrating children with special learning needs into all early childhood settings. This reinforces the need for all educators to have detailed knowledge of the characteristics of learning and development of all children, and to be skilled observers using understanding of the continuum of development to inform curriculum planning for children whatever age they may be.

Definition and clarification is required of two key terms used in this chapter: 'educators' is used to apply to people who care for and educate children in a variety of settings. These people may be parents, grandparents, childminders, workers in day nurseries or family centres, teachers, preschool and playgroup leaders, nannies, home visitors and so on. All these adults affect children's development and learning, and so we use the term 'educator' to refer to them all (Rumbold Report, DES, 1990a). Education and care are inextricably linked. Quality care is educational, and quality education is caring.

Children learn and develop as a result of a set of experiences which are provided consciously or unconsciously. We shall use the term 'curriculum' to include:

- all the activities and experiences provided for babies and toddlers by educators;

- all the activities children devise for themselves;

- the gestures, vocalizations and the languages that educators use to communicate with children, and all the representations that children use to communicate with other people;

- all that children see and touch and hear and taste and smell in the environment around them.

It is from this curriculum, however planned or unplanned, consistent or inconsistent, explicitly based on particular theories of how children learn or derived from observations or respected responsive colleagues, that children learn and are educated (Drummond, Lally and Pugh, 1989).

We begin from the premise that children have a right to good quality care and education in whatever setting their parents choose. Children in group day care, children with childminders or in the family home all have the right to experience responsive education and care which has been sensitively arranged to meet their distinctive developmental needs from birth onwards.

The fundamental principle of the Children Act 1989 is that the welfare of the child is paramount. We examine children's development and learning in the context of their rights to 'individuality, respect, dignity' (DH, 1991) and to equal opportunities in their play and learning experiences.

The purpose of this chapter is to identify imaginative practices for improved quality care and education. It is not enough to provide 'adequate care' or for a 'fit person' to work with children (Children Act 1989). Children deserve the best we can offer them.

QUALITY RELATIONSHIPS BETWEEN CHILDREN AND ADULTS

It is recommended that staff use a key persons system. Each staff member will have responsibility for an identified group of children and their families, and will be able to form a close attachment with them. Babies should spend most of their nursery day in the care of their key adult.

(Cowley, 1991, p. 42)

These National Children's Bureau day care guidelines clearly describe policy and practice for working with young children and emphasize the accepted ideology in the UK that the provision of responsive and sensitive educators allows children the opportunity of familiarity with, and attachment to, their significant adults.

More than a generation ago, Bowlby (1953) cautioned mothers about the negative aspects of institutional group care and the dire consequences of maternal separation. More recently, Belsky (1988) offered further evidence that full-time day care of more than twenty hours a week before twelve months of age may have detrimental effects. On the other hand, Andersson (1990) points to the benefits of early educare, particularly where educarers have more and better quality education and training themselves. These conflicting views can be confusing, on the one hand deeply worrying and on the other constructively hopeful (Melhuish, 1991).

Earlier research (Ainsworth *et al.*, 1990; Bowlby, 1953; Schaffer and Emerson, 1964) supports the view that a close emotional tie between young children and their day-to-day carers is the solid base, a secure safety net, a protection against strange and overwhelming experiences, and a comfort in coping with new sensations and relationships. This concept of attachment underpins all good practice. Secure attachments to educators are thought to increase the chances of developing successful relationships in later life. The films of James and Joyce Robertson in the 1950s will haunt all who witnessed the distress of children like 'John' who was seventeen months old when he was separated from his mother for nine days, in a situation where no individual or continuous care could be provided. John was not able to feel attached and safe with a particular trusted adult. The conclusion of these studies of early separation is that separation in infancy can have long-term effects which may disable children in forming successful, warm, responsive relationships later in life. This frightening warning still lingers and means that we place heavy emphasis on the importance of secure attachments. Later studies, however, show clearly how flexible children can be. Experience has shown us that little children are able to form attachments with a constant small group of care-givers including childminders, and fathers as well as mothers (Schaffer and Emerson, 1964).

Recent literature stresses the need for constancy in key people to support children's emotional learning, and their developing ability to manage their feelings. There is also evidence to show that children's cognitive develpment is supported by a child assignment system where key adults who know children intimately can respond to their curiosities and concerns and support and extend their ideas, thoughts and feelings (Rouse Selleck, 1995). Further formative research is needed to investigate the effects of key persons systems in different forms of provision (see Elfer and Rouse Selleck, forthcoming).

We believe that children need trusting, dependent relationships in order to be able to learn to love, and to venture out and learn from the curriculum available to them. However, we recognize that not all cultures develop the quality of their provision for babies and toddlers from this premise. Alternative philosophies offer us the opportunity to examine these long-held views.

Le Vine (1989) shows that societies in which 'insecure' and 'avoidant' attachments are more typical than 'secure' attachments are not marked by greater incidence of psychopathology than are countries where 'secure' attachments are typical. Indeed, Japanese child development experts, in a discussion on spoiling children, describe the attachment-like behaviour of mothers as narcissistic, over-involved maternal investment in children. This occurs when mothers are isolated and emotionally needy and so look after their children to provide gratification otherwise lacking in their lives. In China, group day care is regarded as a benefit because children can get away from the dangers of spoiling (over-attachment?) in a single-child family, and so be liberated from smothering maternal attention and love (Tobin, Wu and Davidson, 1989). In Italy, key relationships with a significant adult are not seen as necessary to children's successful development in group day care. Group settings may be seen as attempts to counterbalance the clinging, suffocating closeness of mother and child. An alternative ethos to the key person system is the system of reference rather than the person of reference (Rouse, 1991b). Children are encouraged to respond to the environment and to a small group of adults and children rather than to a key adult.

When parents share their parenting role they need the complementary support of educators. It is not enough for educators to tide things over until the parent returns, unless the arrangement is only as an occasional 'babysitter'. A day educator must also develop a strong and complementary attachment with the infants and toddlers in her care. She will not be a replacement or substitute for mothers or fathers or grannies, but she must be able to form a special relationship which can nourish and protect, and is available on a regular and predictable basis during the day. The quality of these complementary attachments depends on a number of features including:

• responsive and loving attention by a key person (Goldschmied and Jackson, 1994);

• opportunities for children to develop a positive self-concept, personal identity and interdependent relationships (Roberts, 1995).

The educators in the baby and toddler unit in a nursery for children aged 0–3 in Italy demonstrate their responsibilites in their loving, physical attention to a baby who was causing some concern. The baby, from a family of Chinese immigrants, cried pitifully and clung to her mother during the initial transition process from home to school. The arrangements to meet the needs of the baby and her family included:

- the educators learning to carry the child in the same way as established by the family, the baby's legs astride and seated on the adult's hip with her arms clasped around the adult's body. Every effort was made to let the child lead while the adults responded to and supported the child's body. This was an opportunity to value the significance of parents' preferences and to learn about their child-rearing style;

- the educator noting that the Italian intonational pattern of her voice was distressing for the Chinese baby. So she babbled and made up songs and rhymes for this baby by imitating the intonational rhythms of the Chinese language. The baby found this comforting and was reassured by the educator's voice;

- tapes being made of the father singing lullabies in Chinese. These were played to help the baby feel tranquil at siesta time but were enjoyed by all the other children too.

As children develop language it is important that adults should be verbally stimulating and responsive. There was a time when we were told that we should bathe the child in language and surround them with books and stories. If this were sufficient, it would be enough to settle a two-year-old in front of the video or with his own sackful of tapes. However, quality experiences which support children's language development need to be reciprocal exchanges; responses should follow the pattern, tone and rhythms of the child's own communications.

Language and communication are closely interrelated with all other aspects of development, especially emotional well-being, social competence and the child's sense of distinct, capable self. Therefore it is important that educators give time for individual turn-taking games, songs and activities with even the youngest babies. Children need adults who can attribute meaning to their utterances and gestures, who are sensitive and responsive in their physical movements, and in the intonations, rhythms and pace of their interactions. Educators must develop the ability to follow the initiatives of needy, vigorous infants, to meet their needs for security and conversational exchanges of gestures and movements.

Holding on and letting go

Physical care and loving attention is required in different ways as a toddler becomes mobile. The child still comes close to the educator – approaching, following, reaching out, cuddling in – but exploratory behaviour also takes the child away as she crawls, walks and inspects the world about her. The educator is required not only to protect the child through closeness, but also to let go to encourage growing autonomy.

The toddler can explore from a safe base, returning for solace if stressed, in danger or feeling apprehensive, and have the experience of an adult containing their powerful emotions, before moving off again (Lieberman, 1991; Elfer, in press). If her foray into separation brings her up against too unfamiliar or unexpected circumstances, she may cling and be cuddled; as she grows in self-reliance, she may need only to check that her special adult is still close by if needed. Where babies and toddlers experience the opportunities and challenges of groups in the company of their educators (parent and toddler groups, childminder drop-ins), thoughtful arrangement of adult furniture, carpeted areas and play equipment and materials can enable the child to have control over holding on and letting go. The educator should remain alert, watchful and ready for action, but the child must not feel constrained or under constant observation (Ruddick, 1989).

Educators should never lose sight of the prime role of the parents in the child's life. They should think about managing the separations and reunions at the beginning and end of each session. The childminder who accompanies the child and the parents along the garden path each day to the car, making almost a ritual of parting and farewell, is marking the boundaries of her complementary but not usurping role. The child, the parent and the educator are all clear about the extent of that role and of the sustained central role of the parent.

Educators are required to make a commitment of attachment to children they nurture, to be open to intimacy, not only with the children, but also with other members of families. They are also required to relinquish the care of the children to their parents each day, and eventually to subsequent educators. People selected to be educators should therefore be adults capable of attachment to children without clinging, suffocating closeness. They must not be seeking to compensate for their own unresolved early experiences of separation and instability (Bain and Barnett, 1980; Hopkins, 1988; Elfer, 1995).

Opportunities for children to develop a positive self-concept, personal identity and interdependence

The significant key adult has a many faceted role in supporting children's identity, interdependence and positive self-concept. Through the interactions and physical closeness described above, the young child learns the boundaries of her own identity, her separateness, and her competence to influence and affect the people attached to her through touch and interactions. As children learn to do things for themselves and to become autonomous, they define their own sense of self. By trying out the boundaries of their skills, children are defining themselves. Adults need to support children to manage this on their own while also recognizing, describing and valuing each child's individual contribution and interdependence.

The arrangement of space, furniture and play materials also plays an important part in this relationship between children and adults and their evolving capacities to belong in groups. These settings have a profound influence on the opportunities and constraints for enabling children's exploration of their own capabilities. A number of nurseries in Emilia Romagna in northern Italy are imaginatively designed, built and arranged together with architects, teachers and parents. They include a number of features which suggest ideas for developing quality practice in this country even if they are not all ones we would emulate directly.

The sleeping rooms in one nursery for the under threes are arranged to give even the youngest children a sense of control. The cots are not cages on stilts which small children have to be hoisted in and out of by adults, but baskets with children's own entrances. Babies can help themselves to sleep or comfort. In each sleep 'nest' are the child's personal bedding and comfort objects. These arrangements are evidence of the respect and support children receive to help them to take initiative and responsibility for their own needs. In the nappy-changing and toileting areas, children able to climb are provided with little steps to the changing mats. The towels and nappies are stored in low cupboards. Children can help themselves, and adults are able to avoid unnecessary lifting and back strain.

The outside play area has scope for solitary exploration. One child (about fourteen months) on a piece of equipment (a series of toddler-sized steps and ramps) repeatedly practised the techniques needed for scaling the stairs, and then tackling the more challenging task of coming down again. She worked for twenty minutes at this task with perseverance and absorption, playing alone. No adult stood within twenty metres. The adult's role was to plan and create the environment containing safe, stage-appropriate equipment, in an inviting setting. The adults were not waiting with outstretched hands to catch her fall, nor was it necessary to praise her for being a 'clever girl'. The adults remained behind the scene, observing unobtrusively, not directing. This child was given the space, the privacy, and the opportunity to learn a new skill. She enjoyed the feeling of efficacy of testing her own capabilities and achieving her own goals. An adult's praise or protection would have been superfluous (Sylva, 1994).

A primary educational feature in their nurseries is the development of identity. Children's need to identify themselves as individuals, and their need to know and use their own bodies, is central to the curriculum. This philosophy is evident in large wall mirrors from floor to waist height for babies and toddlers, and often two or three metres long, fixed behind an arrangement of mattresses and cushions; a rail for grasping, for babies to pull themselves up to an upright position, a common fixture in front of the

big mirrors; at skirting board level and on the baby's 'nests' large head-
and-shoulder photographs of the babies, covered with wipeable film with
a mirror above of the same size. Mirrors and photographs are also a regular feature in the sleeping and changing areas so that children can see
themselves and others.

Supporting the development of positive
self-image for themselves and others

Educators play a crucial personal role in helping children develop a concept of self, a positive image incorporating realistic self-knowledge, and
self-esteem rising out of the valuing of each child's own abilities, gender
and own particular combination of skin colour, facial features or hair type.
Children learn to have equal concern for the other people in their communities (Elfer, 1995).

The damage done to children's perceptions about themselves and others by absorption of discriminatory and mistaken concepts and values
about gender, racial origin and disability are well rehearsed in other places
(CRE, 1996; Siraj-Blatchford in Chapter 7 of this book). In the context of
this chapter, the significant consideration is how early the development of
such concepts begins.

It would be more comfortable and less threatening to believe that the
youngest children somehow have an innocence which means that 'they
don't notice' differences amongst themselves and the adults around them.
However, we know that this is not true. There is clear evidence that by the
age of three, children not only distinguish between skin colours, but also
give different values to them, with 20 per cent of two-year-olds and 50 per
cent of three-year-olds making such distinctions (Milner, 1983). Whilst
there is less striking evidence available about gender differentiation by
such young children, there are indications of gender-stereotypes in choices
of toys as young as eighteen months (National Early Years Network/Save
the Children Fund, 1995).

Issues of combating discrimination and prejudice and ensuring equal
opportunities for all are significant in the nurture of a child's self-image.
The differences and shared characteristics of children and families should
be recognized, described and valued. Careful selection of materials and
activities for play and learning should reflect and celebrate the racial, cultural and linguistic diversity in Britain. Images and models of all people of
various racial origins and cultural backgrounds, gender and/or disabilities
should demonstrate active, responsible, influential and caring roles. In particular, educators working with babies and toddlers must be knowledgeable about a range of child-rearing practices, and demonstrate that they

respect and value each family's preference, so that their own practice can follow the lead of the family and be in harmony with it.

Educators should look inside themselves at their basic assumptions, values and beliefs about children and childhood, and think about where these ideas come from. Perhaps professional training provides us with a theoretical framework for working with children, but personal experiences of childhood, and early experiences of playing, learning and loving, will also have had an effect on the way educators understand and interact with children. Attitudes, beliefs and values have been forming from our own childhood onwards. If we look after and work with other people's children, we have to be able to recognize and explore these values.

The development of a child's positive self-image is affected by our perceptions, prejudices and attitudes to children. Educators should explore and reflect on their personal assumptions or 'labels' so that we can ensure that every child is positively valued.

When you see a child with a dummy, do you see a tranquil child being comforted, a child enjoying the erotic sucking on the teat, or do you see a child with an unhygienic object stuck in her mouth which will inhibit her language development . . . or something else? Do you see the physical features of Down's Syndrome on the baby who holds out her arms to be picked up, or do you respond firstly to a child who is asking for a cuddle and then secondly do you notice the signs of a child with a disability? Do you see a black toddler, boisterous and undisciplined, or a toddler who is black, and enthusiastic to join in the game? When a child is pouring sand down the drains do you see one of the 'terrible twos' being naughty and unbiddable or a bright, curious infant investigating the properties of sand and water? (Drummond, Rouse and Pugh, 1992.)

DEVELOPMENTALLY APPROPRIATE
LEARNING EXPERIENCES

What does education for the under threes mean? Some people who work with the youngest children have traditionally been seen, and have seen themselves, only in a 'caring' role. Their overlapping role as educators must be acknowledged – it is central to their job in offering and extending play and learning experiences. We are learning more about the distinctive learning needs of children from birth to thirty-six months old – as a group of educators look at the foundations for children's learning in all age phases (Early Childhood Education Forum, forthcoming).

Education, training and care are interrelated. Caring for very young children involves a number of activities like the rituals of nappy changing, bathing, dressing and soothing children to sleep. Other activities might seem to be more directly 'educational', like sharing a picture book with a child or explaining the habitat and habits of the bumble bee that the two-year-old tries to pull out of a foxglove. 'Training' is about teaching children 'no' so that they don't put the poisonous digitalis leaves of the foxglove in their mouths, or so that they don't offend social conventions by their child-like inclinations to explore, to pick the flowers in hedgerows, public parks or other people's gardens. Training is establishing the rhythms and patterns of daily routines for health, hygiene, safety and for establishing codes of behaviour so that families and communities can live together where each member's needs and rights are considered. The rituals of bedtimes, naps and night-time sleep may be matters for training so that the whole family or day-care group can rest during a siesta, or during the evening, or so that adults can alternate their other work with child education and care as a child sleeps in a nest basket, a crib, a back bundle supported by a wrapper, or a coach-built perambulator. Training is particular to the customs and conventions of each family.

So, if we take the definition of curriculum as identified in the introduction to this chapter, then in practice it becomes impossible to separate education, training and care. As an educator dresses a child they may discuss the woolly texture of her jersey (learning about the properties of different materials), or count the buttons on her shirt (numerical experiences contributing to basic mathematical concepts). While explaining about the bee's search for nectar to make honey (new knowledge for the child related to her previous experiences of eating honey for breakfast), the adult would also protect and care for the child by restraining her from clasping the bee for a closer inspection as well as training her not to pick or eat foxgloves.

Education, training and care are interrelated in:

- *All aspects of the child's development*, including emotional, cognitive, sexual, social, physical, moral, aesthetic, and the development of self-concept. All these aspects of the child's development demand nurturing, are complex and require 'maternal thinking' (Ruddick, 1989), or educators who are knowledgeable and reflective about the distinctive learning needs of the under threes.

- *All areas of learning and experience*. Children's knowledge and skills evolve from mathematical, moral, physical, scientific, spiritual, techno-logical, aesthetic, creative, linguistic, literary, human and social early learning experiences (HMI, 1989).

  (Watching the bumble bee in the foxglove is certainly an aesthetically rich experience. Watching the furry, round body bustle and delve into the cerise trumpet and listening to the intermittent buzzing of the tiny creature in the sunshine may well have been a formative sensory and aesthetic experience for the toddler. The child could also have had mathematical experiences and formed mathematical concepts as the bee's vertical movements are described by the adults. 'The bee is going up and down the stem to look in all the flowers.' These words could feed a child's emerging thinking about spatial awareness. The explanation of the bee's work could be noted as learning about the 'process of life'.)

- *All aspects of the child's play.* As children track the movements and reflective lights on a mobile, when they splash water, examine the tickle in their belly button, gaze at their own image in a mirror, manipulate play materials by sucking, banging, fitting, filling, emptying, piling, demolishing, poking, and pulling out all the contents of the kitchen drawer, their childminder's handbag or the 'Treasure Basket' in the day nursery which is overflowing with a range of household and natural objects (Goldschmied, 1987), so they learn. Each of these bits of play represents specific stages in the child's learning, and in their education.

A number of individuals and groups have identified distinctive curricula for the under fives, some with their own formats for assessing children's learning; for example, High/Scope Key Experiences (High/Scope, 1986); identifying patterns of play or 'schema' (Athey, 1990); others have identified 'subjects areas', 'topics', or 'processes'. For a summary, see Section 9 in *Making Assessment Work* (Drummond, Rouse and Pugh, 1992).

However, in this chapter we are concerned with the learning needs of children up to thirty-six months. Too many books and training materials bunch the needs of under fives together, but we must take care to perceive the needs of each child as unique, and to acknowledge that they have special learning needs at different stages in their development. Just as schools must ensure that the curriculum meets the needs of four-year-olds in reception classes, we must also take care to see that two-year-olds have particular materials and activities which support their stage of learning. Children's interests and abilities change rapidly during their first three years, and it is only through careful observation and with imaginative use of resources that it is possible to create the stimulating, inviting, purposeful activities that will offer children opportunities to concentrate, to discover and to achieve, and for us to celebrate their achievements.

Much has been written about the stages of 'normal development' or 'developmental milestones' and there are copious checklists to note down 'desirable outcomes' (SCAA, 1996), or in some cases to worry about the empty boxes with no ticks. However, all these lists are arbitrary, especially when applied to children's behaviour, play and development. Only the child's basic physical perceptions, functions and growth should be noted and checked out as universal conditions. All development must be observed in context. All milestones, normal development or 'desirable' behaviour are recognized in the context of the educator's values, beliefs, cultural and

social expectations of particular families and social groups. There is nothing that children ought to do unless we decide it must be so. Why is it
important that children learn to say 'thank you', or kiss their grandmother,
or dress themselves, or eat with a spoon, or avert their gaze when an adult
is talking? All these things are 'normal' or expected, or discouraged in some
families. It is our duty to socialize children into our kinds of families and
communities so that they may 'fit in'. But does it really matter if children
learn to manage without nappies before they are three? Why must they
learn to stack bricks or play pat-a-cake? What do we want our children to
learn, to know, to be and to feel? The kind of education we envisage is
rooted in our own childhoods and in our values and beliefs. Accepting this
plurality will enrich our early childhood programmes as well as accord
respect for the rights of individual children in particular families.

It is also important to distinguish, theoretically at least, between the
training of infants and the education of infants more clearly so that the
latter can be examined in more detail.

Training is about belonging to a family or group's customs, morals, man-
ners and routines. It is learning to adopt the patterns of behaviour which
promote 'peace in the home or group' and which is acceptable in supermarkets, restaurants, the mosque, grandma's garden and society in general.
Until or unless society changes to become more tolerant of children and
is able to revere and extol the state of childhood, then even very young
children will have to learn some of these patterns of belonging in groups.
Of course, children should learn to be courteous and considerate, and this
learning is interrelated to education. The training and socialization of
infants will continue to be the kernel of educators' discussions and a focus
for their energies and imagination for our future citizens. There are many
contradictions for an educator to ponder. When groups of practitioners talk
about the children they 'train' there will be feelings of guilt, amusement,
controversy, indignation, self-righteous superiority, crushing inadequacy,
joy, despair, frustration and accomplishment. The debate is philosophical
and personal. We must draw up a curriculum based on children's distinctive learning needs but we must constantly make decisions which involve
moral dilemmas, which require knowledge about children's perceptions and
cognitive learning structures, and which have no clear-cut answers.

We are at the beginning of a new era of exploration and understanding
of how babies and toddlers learn, and more importantly how we can meet
their learning needs. Most of the literature on early education has concentrated on three- to five-year-olds, but some new research and discussion is opening up new concepts of education for infants and is illuminating
our understanding. At last, the focus of research is building on from earlier formal laboratory experiments (Bower, 1977; Papousek, 1969; Moore,
1975) and practice-based new 'research' in natural settings is beginning to

identify the distinctive patterns of children's play and behaviour which will inform education practice. The work of Bower and others has long indicated that babies are brilliant thinkers. He concludes his fascinating and detailed scientific study of infant development by suggesting that this new knowledge can be used to 'judge what kind of inputs are appropriate or necessary' (Bower, 1977, p. 166).

It is the 'inputs' that we are interested in, not to raise a brighter baby, not because we think plenty of stimulation must be better, not because we make the erroneous assumption that by identifying the distinctive learning needs of babies we shall be able to accelerate development. A faster rate of development does not necessarily guarantee a higher level of cognitive functioning in the long run as far as we know. Instead we want to indicate how imaginative provision of materials and developmentally and culturally focused and choreographed experiences can broaden and enrich development and facilitate newly emerging patterns of activity and thought in young children (Korner, 1989).

Chris Athey's *Extending Thought in Young Children* (1990) is a milestone in describing the continuum of education from birth to the primary school. This work describes the development of patterns or commonalities of action and thought in young children which she calls 'schemas'. Examples of continuity in education include: how the infant behaviours of looking and gazing can be the first steps to map-making in the nursery class; and how the spontaneous vertical and horizontal linear patterns made with bricks, beads or toy cars in a toddler's play are the 'connecting schema' (or thinking and playing by joining things together) which can lead in turn to tessellation, measuring and numerical concepts. The Athey ideology has indeed inspired many educators to develop their practice by identifying patterns of play, behaviour and thinking in young children's activities. The adults then use their observations to make curricular plans, 'to feed the child's schema' with appropriate talk and play materials so that they may support and extend the child's play activity and thinking (see Chapters 6 and 10 in this book). This approach of observation and support for children's play has many possibilities for the curriculum of children under three.

Stroh and Robinson (1991), in their therapeutic work with children who show many signs of developmental delay, describe their educational approach of enabling children to 'learn-to-learn'. They do this in the context of a psychotherapeutic and child/family therapy process which does not lose sight of the child's emotional needs whilst attending to their learning needs. Their work is based on an optimistic belief in the creativity of individual children and on detailed observations of children's intrinsically motivated play which can be concentrated, intense, persistent and enjoyable.

The work of Elinor Goldschmied has built on this philosophy. In her work in creating early play and learning experiences for babies who are sitting up, but are not yet crawling or mobile, she has invented a 'Treasure Basket'. This is a sturdy basket overflowing with a range of household and natural objects. Goldschmied (1987, 1996) demonstrates with video material how babies explore, concentrate and use the materials for interaction with other children of the same age. The video has a riveting sequence of two babies having a turn-taking game, a 'conversational' type exchange, by handing objects from the basket to and fro to each other. This material clearly demonstrates the potential abilities of babies to be able to interact with their peers. Many parents, child care 'experts' and educators have underestimated the capabilities and possibilities for sophisticated social behaviour of infants when they have company, and when they are given stimulating, developmentally appropriate play materials (Goldschmied and Selleck, 1995). Goldschmied's work with sitting babies shows how children explore play objects of differing weights, textures, sizes, colours, tastes, temperatures and smells. They do this with their mouths, their eyes, and with the energy of their whole bodies from their groping, sucking lips to their toes curling with pleasure and concentration. Babies are shown to be using all their senses to learn about the properties of objects in the presence of their trusted adult.

When a child becomes mobile, but before language alters her pattern of thinking, a new challenge is presented to the educator. Goldschmied's concept of 'Heuristic Play with Objects' explains how children move on to think about what they can do with the play objects. They discover or reach an understanding of what they can do with things in their spontaneous play (Goldschmied and Hughes, 1994).

These ideas for curriculum development and those of other innovative educators must be the basis of further observation and research so that we can extend our knowledge of how the youngest children learn.

As the child develops language, her play alters. Instead of wanting to find out what she can do with an object, she will explore the object's function in the real world. She will want to join in with adults' activities, to assist and copy the real world. Next the children will imagine what their play objects will become, will begin to pretend and later to fantasize.

If we were to observe a child's play with an object, for example, a chain, over the first thirty-six months, it is possible that a continuum of learning would emerge. At a few months old John will play with the chain by sucking it, shaking it, dropping it and banging it and so discover what it is. As a toddler John may fill up a cup with it, rattle it round in a tin, drop it down a cardboard tube, flap it on a tin tray, coil it into a match box or dangle it over the banisters to see what he can do with it. At a later stage, he will explore what they really are for. He will imitate the adults around him. He will pull the chain to unplug the bath and empty the water, he will fasten the gold chain round his neck like his mother and he will hang the dog's chain on the hook at the back of the kitchen door as Grandpa does. By the time John is two years old he will use his imagination. The chain may become a wriggly worm, a garden path for his Duplo people, or a pretend rope to moor his boats in the bath.

Such phases are not distinct or an invariant sequence of play behaviour. They overlap and are part of a continuum of learning. Some objects are used as real ones at the same time as other objects are used imaginatively to represent something else. Two-year-old Rosie sits on the bottom stair, a doll sitting on the stair behind, an old handbag beside her, a toy radio in front of her and a teething ring/rattle which happens to be round and have spokes clutched in her hands. She is driving to the shops with her little girl in the back seat. The bag is a real object being used in an imitative way, the radio and the doll are toys representing real things, but the rattle is a play object from earlier sensory/discovery learning phases which has now been transformed in the child's imagination to a steering wheel. Rosie's play is imitative and imaginative and reflects her own needs to understand events as well as to explore objects.

There is also further evidence to illustrate how crucial friendships with other children are to children's development and learning. Children from a few weeks old are able to use vocalizations, gazing, touching, and later exchange of objects to develop loyalties and attachments to key children in their group. These relationships also need to be valued and respected by carers and educators (Rouse Selleck, 1995; Goldschmied and Selleck, forthcoming).

Each of these phases in play demands knowledgeable and understanding adults to sustain the children's explorations, their learning work, and their imagination. There is a whole new language evolving to help us to think about our observations and assessments of children's behaviour and play so that we can find new ways to develop a curriculum which meets the needs of children at each phase as they move rapidly through changing patterns of thinking and understanding. As educators plan for children's learning, whether they talk about 'learning tools', or heuristic play, or 'sensory motor key experiences' (High/Scope, 1986), or 'schemas', the important thing is to distinguish the learning phases and needs of babies and toddlers, and to grapple, to find words to enable discussion (not to create barriers) and to talk and think together about the distinctive role of the early childhood educator. This work is in progress with the research and development project *Quality in Diversity* (ECEF, forthcoming) and in practice in the best quality early childhood centres.

CARING FOR THE EDUCATOR

Educators have the responsibility, the awesome power, and the challenging task of organizing learning opportunities for children. Each child is unique, and has individual needs as well as common developmental patterns of learning and development shared by all babies and toddlers.

The interactions between young children and educators are mutually enriching but are also demanding. Educators can support, extend and nourish children's development, or conversely thwart, stunt and damage children's beginnings, the beginning of their sense of self-worth, and the onset of their capabilities as confident learners. To minister to needy, vigorous, demanding infants is significant and worthwhile work. This work can be a pleasure, and may leave the adult satisfied and emotionally replete. Young children are sensuous creatures who drape and cuddle, who smile enchantingly and fit the contours of our ambitions to love and be of service to humanity! Conversely, young children are eternally demanding and can drain care-givers' physical strength, and can evaporate the best intentions of conscientious adults. The insistent and continuous greedy gobbling of infants into adult time, love and patience can empty an educator of energy and imagination.

Educators must also be responsible for their own psychological welfare. They are emotionally vulnerable, their work involves them in repeated cycles of relationships with and commitments to young children. The demands of children and of parents can drain the emotional and physical resources of the adults. If educators are to maintain the levels of communication and intimacy needed for effective practice, with both children and their families, then this commitment and involvement must be respected and cherished. The distinctive demands on educators of the under threes cannot be taken for granted if personnel are to sustain their health and well-being. The educators themselves have great needs for support in 'letting go'. They need time to reflect on their practice and to share concerns with colleagues. Such needs may be met through sensitive supervision and in-service training, or through mutual support meetings and networks. Working with young children is often isolated as well as demanding, and careful planning may be necessary to create times and spaces for refreshing and strengthening philosophy and practice (see Whalley, Chapter 10 of this book).

CONCLUSION

We must have the courage to insist on the best, not just an adequate quality of education and care with 'fit persons' for babies and toddlers. We need the vision to plan for whole human beings who have a clear and realistic personal identity whatever combination of cultural or religious background, racial origins, gender, ability or disability that may be. Children who know who they are will have the confidence to love and learn and communicate in a world of mathematical, scientific, aesthetic and technological experiences. Children who can collaborate and learn together in harmony with other people are likely to respect and value differences. Children who are able to have intimate responsive relationships with their significant adult will have better access to relevant early learning experiences. Children who play in inspirational, safe and challenging environments will take these values into adulthood and pass them on to future generations. An ethos of respect for and dignity in childhood may be set from the cradle.

Points for discussion

From the perspective of babies and toddlers, think about the significance of:

* the quality of the relationships with adults who care for and educate them;
* their opportunities for developing friendships with other children;
* the physical environment for their learning; and
* the objects and materials they have access to for learning.

What features and characteristics of each of these have significance for under threes:

* emotional well-being;
* development of self-knowledge and self-esteem;
* exploration and developing understanding of the physical world around them;
* development of skills of contributing, participating and communicating?

Which features and characteristics would you expect to be beneficial to very young children's welfare, learning and development, and which would you expect to be detrimental?

Why? What has led you to conclude that these are the significant matters, and to see each in a positive or negative light? What part has been played in the formation of your views by your own experience of childhood, of being a parent? How much has been derived from professional training and experience? How much have you drawn on knowledge of practice in cultures and settings other than your own?

10

WORKING AS A TEAM

Margy Whalley

The feeling of power and confidence achieved by powerless groups
who challenge their ascribed position in society by acting collectively.
(Dominelli, 1990, p. 126)

INTRODUCTION

In this chapter I want to outline the belief system that underpins the way
we have worked at Pen Green since it opened in 1983. I want to look at
the structural and pedagogic implications of adopting a community development model. I want to show how we evaluate our work and ensure that
what we are offering is a quality service that can respond to constantly
changing community needs. I want to describe how we work with parents,
volunteers and workers from other agencies and to look in some detail at
our staff development programme and our in-service training. Above all I
want to celebrate the many mistakes we made, mostly with good intentions, and to be clear that making mistakes has become a very important
part of our learning process. Making mistakes implies that we have taken

risks; taking risks assumes that staff have the self-confidence and the ability to make decisions and to take on personal responsibility. I want to encourage children, parents and under-fives workers to believe in themselves and to congratulate them on taking risks and taking charge of their own lives.

I am aware that being a strong, assertive, challenging child or parent, or under-fives worker, may not make for an easy life. The children who leave our community nursery have been described by one local teacher as having 'the Pen Green Syndrome'. This is an interesting psycho-social disorder which presents in four-year-olds going up to big school – children who are not interested in what their infant teacher has decided to put out for them, assertively or subversively (depending on your viewpoint) put it away and take out activities that they really want to do, maybe even something they had planned to do on the way to school. The Pen Green Syndrome manifests itself in parents who boycott or protest at governors meetings called at inconvenient times, or at parents' meetings that have no crèche facilities, or where they are asked to sit on little chairs. It manifests itself in staff who challenge the assumption that they can plan and develop quality work for children and families without the non-contact time that professional colleagues with older children assume.

THE BACKGROUND: A SEARCH FOR A CONCEPTUAL FRAMEWORK

The Pen Green Centre for Under Fives and Families was set up in 1983 in an empty comprehensive school on a 1930s estate. The Pen Green estate is made up of thirteen streets backing on to the now defunct steelworks. The houses were only separated from the blast furnaces by a railway and a sixty-foot strip of land.

The 'bad news' for those of us who set the Centre up in those early days, was that the closure of the local comprehensive school had been much resented by the local community. The proposed new 'preschool centre' was viewed with a great deal of hostility by both local people and other professionals. The most active voluntary group locally was a Community Action Group which had strongly protested at the lack of consultation between local community and county council.

The two lead departments were social services and education and neither had a clear understanding of how the Centre would work in practice. The education department described it as an extended-day, year-round, nursery school with some parental involvement; social services saw it as a day nursery for referred children. Corby then and now has no local authority day nursery provision. The two departments had no shared conceptual framework or language and geographically Corby was very isolated from the administration in Northampton. The district health authority, which had contributed to the capital costs of the new centre, became immersed in a reorganization and was unable to contribute to running costs, but retained its policy and management role.

The 'good news' outweighed the bad and still does for those of us working in Corby. There was strong local political support for the new project and the steering group that had been set up had strong councillor support. The steering group was truly multi-disciplinary having representation from the LEA, social services, the health authority and voluntary groups in the community. This steering group visited a well-established combined centre in London, read the limited amount of research available on joint provision, and resolved to put all staff on the same conditions of service, since differentials in holidays and hours of work appeared to be a real block to a creative partnership.

Social services locally was organized on a patch basis and local social workers were working as community development workers in the local community association. They influenced the decision to make it a local community resource rather than a town-wide service. Since the closure of the steelworks, male unemployment in this patch was as high as 43 per cent and there was a good working relationship between agency workers and the local community group – a 'partnership in adversity'. Many of those parents involved in the action group against the centre had already been involved in local housing campaigns and were very ready to express their concerns about the nature of the proposed centre for under fives. They were clear that they did not want it to be a 'dumping ground for problem families'. This action group was critical to the development of the Pen Green Centre for Under Fives and Families. Several of its members became vociferous spokespeople *for* the new centre and used it on a daily basis. Parents, staff, children and community groups were all brought on board; 'parental involvement' was *not* an optional extra – it was integral to the way we worked.

Most significantly, some of these parents were involved in the initial recruitment of staff and these staff, as a consequence, felt directly accountable to them. All newly appointed staff then had between two and six months to work together while the alterations to the building were completed. Much of this time was spent walking the streets, getting to know local people and local resources and visiting other centres. Parents and staff remember that blissful period when everything was open to negotiation; when we had an empty nursery waiting to be filled. People were invited in and started using the centre whilst the concrete was still wet, and rooms undesignated. Staff who remember that period are thankful that time was spent in finding out what was needed rather than imposing a predetermined 'neat and tidy' plan. In the life of an establishment it is rare to get that kind of quality time.

RECRUITMENT AND STAFF DEVELOPMENT

What we started with in 1983 was a commitment to set up a community-based, multi-disciplinary centre. The brief included offering year-round nursery and day-care facilities with provision for an extended day, a service for supporting families and a health 'resource'. Contextually we were working in a socio-economically depressed community with an active and critical community group, and some very creative professional colleagues well accustomed to working co-operatively in adversity. Some of the structural obstacles to a creative team approach had been removed, such as differentials in conditions of service, but some still remained. Chief among these were the grossly differentiated pay-scales between care workers and teachers or field social workers; and the inappropriate pay-scales for key workers like secretaries, cooks and other support staff (mostly women).

Most of the research on combined provision emphasizes the difficulties experienced when integrating staff who have always focused on the needs of children in a care capacity and those who see themselves as educators. Our experience was very different. In the first place we were recruiting staff from many different sectors, not only from education and day care but also from social work, health and the voluntary sector. They had a vast range of different qualifications including CQSW, B.Tech, NVQ (Level 3) and PLA courses, PGCE, B.Ed, NNEB, SRN, and they were accustomed to different styles of working and different models of supervision and support. The varied backgrounds of many of the staff (some qualified in more than one discipline, some with no formal qualifications but enormous amounts of experience in the private or voluntary sectors) meant that there was no simplistic polarization between education and care. All their different experiences informed our practice, and made it possible for us to set up an appropriately flexible management structure and support system for staff working in a challenging and innovative way. We tried to take the best from all the different models of supervision and support.

The critical difference between our centre and those that had been modified from already existing schools, day nurseries or children's centres, was that we could be clear at interview about what the job involved. Even our adverts were 'different' and usually required major debates and sanctions from whichever personnel department was handling them. One department found them so idiosyncratic that they refused to handle any of the process and left it entirely up to us.

Parents who have been involved in interviewing, over the years, have found it to be a fulfilling and challenging process. Some parents have even been motivated to make career decisions on the basis of interviewing others! Parents were not 'pre-selected' for interviewing so that applicants met many different members of the community: some shy, some assertive and some negative. A tradition was soon established that meant that when there was a vacancy, parents would interview for the member of staff who would subsequently be working directly with their child. It became clear that parents who had appointed staff continued to root for their chosen candidate throughout their time at the centre and quickly introduced the new member of staff to other parents in their 'family group'. Interviews were always informal and candidates were told that this would be the case. On some occasions interview panels were very unwieldy. My own interview was conducted by the two chairmen of the social services and education committee and twelve other officers, employees and members of the community.

All posts are advertised as 'family worker' posts, a generic title which embraces those primarily working with children and those who are chiefly concerned with adults. Some posts are more senior than others but we do attempt to distribute the unpleasant and mundane jobs fairly evenly.

All family workers in the nursery have a responsibility for up to ten families and they are the key workers for those families. They home visit 'their families' and keep developmental records on 'their' children. With some families, family workers liaise with the statutory social worker, attend case conferences and attend court. No new member of staff undertakes this sort of work without support and/or training. They need to feel both confident and competent. The important point is that staff are encouraged to take on that level of responsibility where they are involved as the key worker. Family workers in the nursery are also given the opportunity to work directly with parents by each offering one session a week as part of a group work programme; again with appropriate training and always with a co-worker. Other family workers recruited to work primarily with parents are asked to spend time in the nursery, to home visit families and to spend time with the children at lunch time.

There was no assumption that a teaching or NNEB qualification implied any differentiation in the core family worker role. Teachers appointed to family worker posts needed to be prepared to take on additional responsibilities commensurate with their substantially higher salary and different training. The responsibility that an individual teacher was able to take on had to be negotiated on the basis of what skills and experience they brought with them. Clearly a probationary teacher, leaving a one-year PGCE course, would only have a very limited experience of curriculum planning and development; they might, however, have a strong specialism such as dance and music or other life experience that they wanted to offer.

All staff when appointed are given some time to get to know the different aspects of the centre's work. In the early years staff had an enormous amount of freedom to visit other centres all over England. Such visits are still encouraged and most staff, including ancillary and support staff and many parents, will have been to a variety of different types of centre within their first few years in the job. Over the last few years staff have visited early years provision in Italy, Denmark and Madrid. Most staff have been involved in what has now become a rich exchange programme. All the nursery staff and several parents have had these opportunities, and so have support staff such as our cook and administrative assistant.

It soon became apparent that since the majority of new staff came from a teaching or nursery nurse background, most had a vast range of experience with young children but felt less confident in working with adults. Having said this, all three senior staff in 1983 had either PGCE and CQSW or PGCE and extensive community work experience. Overall, staff tended not to come from either mainstream education or social services but rather from residential/special schools, child and family guidance, or community nurseries.

We quickly realized that no single qualification could provide all the skills and knowledge needed for working in this new way. We had an enormous skills bank to call on for our own in-service training but we also needed a comprehensive in-service rolling programme that staff could opt into on the basis of their level of confidence and competence. Some key areas of work had not been addressed in any initial training course and these were management and team-building skills and budgetary control. Some training needed to be on-going, some addressed current issues (such as the AIDS awareness programme in the mid-1980s). Table 10.1 gives a rough outline of our staff development programme.

We do not view staff development as an optional extra. It enables us to provide a quality service. As Professor Tomlinson said in an open lecture (1986), what we need are 'confident and secure professionals well trained in their own service who can co-operate and see the part to be played by other services'. Centres for early childhood education with care should be 'learning organizations'. Because we are committed to staff development, we currently have staff studying and writing assignments for the Advanced Diploma in Nursery Nursing; BTEC course in social care; the Adult Education Teachers Certificate; Advanced Counselling courses; Contemporary dance; NVQs in Working with Children and Families; GCSE Maths and English; an MA in Early Childhood Studies; an MA in Action Research; a Phd in Management Studies and so much more! Of course there is some reduction in the quality of services when staff are attending courses or taking time back for courses they have attended in their own time but we inconvenience parents and children as little as possible. In the

Staff development programme

	Content	Geared to
Stage 1 (during the first eighteen months)	Listening skills Counselling Family dynamics Home visiting Working with parents	Most relevant for NNEB, teaching staff and support staff volunteers
Stage 2	Assertiveness Group work Marital counselling Boundaries with co-workers	For all staff colleagues from other agencies working with adult groups
Annual programmes	Gender issues Race issues Violence First aid	All staff
Child focused (on-going)	Child psychology and child development Early years curriculum Working with troubled children Assessment Record-keeping – an educational model Record-keeping – a social work model Child abuse/child protection	As part of planned individual programmes/all nursery staff
Responding to new legislation (when it comes out)	NHS White Papers *Promoting Better Health*, *Working for Patients* National Curriculum Children Act	As appropriate
Training relating to co-operative working (on-going)	Working with other agencies Working with volunteers Management, team-building Supervision/appraisal	All staff

long term, staff are enabled, through training, to feel confident in and to challenge their own practice. They have no need to put up a front of so-called 'professionalism'. Senior staff spend a great deal of time in supervision and support, encouraging staff and setting up in-house training courses. Training is the carrot that keeps us all motivated. When we feel out of our depth we can reassure and revitalize ourselves by attending a course or a study day and understand a little more. Training is also one concrete way of showing low-paid workers and volunteers that they are valued and that they too have choices and career prospects. We rejected the traditional model of training whereby emotionally fraught teachers or burnt-out social workers were sent off on expensive secondments. We believe staff have the right to a properly structured staff development programme which involves training, supervision and support, the majority of which should take place in work time.

MANAGING SERVICES

What I have tried to do is give an impression of an environment where:

(1) Decisions are made as a response to the expressed needs of the local community and not their *assumed* needs. When we have set up groups or activities because, as a staff group, we thought they were 'a good idea', they rarely took off. Our rather self-conscious health food pantry was a disaster!

(2) Staff were given time to get to know the local neighbourhood and parents were invited in from the word go. Parents helped to make the decisions about room allocation, use of space and what equipment we needed to buy.

(3) Parents were on the interview panels for all staff appointments – not only the parents who might have had the confidence to fight for a seat on the school governing body, but also parents who were too afraid even to attend parents evenings in mainstream school.

(4) Staff needs are seen as central and staff working in a different way need a whole range of training courses and a lot of personal support. All staff are involved in team-building, and 'all staff' includes ancillary support staff whenever possible. They also need to be given time in lieu when they have given up weekends or evenings on training courses.

(5) Everyone is learning – children, staff and parents.

The staff we appointed were committed to on-going training and development. They didn't believe that their initial qualifications meant they had 'arrived'.

To enable all this to happen whilst maintaining an extended-day, year-round provision for up to 70 families in the community nursery and 300 plus families in the 'drop in', parents' groups and health facilities, involves a lot of organization and a healthy and committed staff who enjoy shared responsibility. When I was first appointed I misread the advert and thought when it stated all staff would be on the 'same conditions of service' it meant we would all have the same pay! My naïvety must be attributed to having worked overseas on multi-disciplinary pre-fives projects for over six years and having earned 'local wages'.

Clearly the pay structure at Pen Green implies some sort of hierarchy with teachers' salaries being the most advantageous. Whilst it is obvious that differentials in salary do affect how people perceive their role, it is even more important that people feel valued for what they are doing. Staff also believed that what they were doing was important and that their personal contribution made a difference. It is fair to say that most of the staff had already experienced hierarchical work settings. They were attracted to posts at Pen Green because they wanted to take on more responsibility and wanted to see rigid inter-agency role definitions relaxed.

The management structure that we established involved a co-operative approach. In our first naïve attempts to work together we sometimes skirted uncomfortably around issues involving those who earned more and those who were willing to take on more; sometimes we confused democracy and accountability. 'Team work' and 'collegiality' seemed to imply no management at all. We also at times avoided dealing with the 80:20 factor that our management consultant highlighted for us, i.e. 20 per cent of the people in most organizations end up doing 80 per cent of the work! Once or twice we did recruit staff who, like many in the caring professions, hoped to 'find themselves' through helping others, who were ungrounded and demanded too much personal support; usually they did not stay long. Very occasionally we recruited staff who despite the extensive interview process really did not understand how hard (emotionally and physically) the work was and who found the job just did not give enough back. The majority of staff we recruited have managed to balance their personal and professional lives. Perhaps in the early days when we were struggling to empower traditionally passive low-paid under-fives workers and families who felt deskilled, we underestimated the need for senior staff to have time together to reflect on how they were working, set targets, and review progress on a regular basis.

Instead of a hierarchy we established a 'side-archy' (Whittacker) which allows staff to focus on their strengths. Even in the early days we saw conflict as healthy, and felt that anger and resentment were better expressed than stored. Staff who work with young children and families almost always see themselves (and are defined by others) as 'nurturers', but that does not mean they have to be 'nice' all the time; consensus was not always the most desirable outcome. We have also learned to recognize the fact that there is a manipulative and controlling part in all of us.

Staff meetings

In practice, then, we spent time in pairs or small groups visiting other centres and seeing how they worked, bringing back ideas and arguing over
'good practice'. Staff quickly realized that with the wide range of views and
experience we had amassed, we needed to continue to carve out time for
ourselves as a staff group even when the centre was fully operational. We
had seen many different models in practice from hurried after-school staff
meetings and lunch-time meetings in educational settings, to interminable
and unfocused team meetings in social services establishments.

We decided that a mid-week break was the answer and this has been
the pattern for eight years. Nursery education, day care and family work
take place on Monday, Tuesday, Thursday and Friday, and Wednesday
became a community morning. This meant we could offer a session to any
family on the waiting list and to foster parents and childminders.
Wednesday afternoon was set aside for staff development, team-building
and sometimes training events. It was the one time in the week when staff
could work together without interruption, with clear heads and lots of
energy. Professional colleagues from the LEA and other local authority
day nurseries looked on it with some suspicion. Some felt we were 'neglect-
ing' the children's needs. In fact, nursery children were getting far more
time and continuity in the nursery sessions we did offer which gave them
the opportunity for extended uninterrupted play. Children and parents
accept the weekend break and just as easily learned to accept the
Wednesday afternoon break and welcomed the choices and flexibility we
could offer them at other times.

Having fought for it, how did we use the time? Our initial staff group
of six permanent staff (plus four support staff) met in one group for the
whole afternoon. When numbers increased to around sixteen permanent
staff, it became important to split the time available so that staff could
work in small groups, meeting as a whole group for a relatively short period
for an information exchange, diary dates, and general business session. Staff
spend most of the time in two groups; those primarily concerned with the
nursery children and those mainly working with adults. Senior staff try to
move between groups but the head of nursery spends all her time with the
'nursery group' since they are planning and exploring the nursery curriculum. This is a fairly crude division of staff since all have concerns for and
are involved in working with both adults and children. Both groups use
part of the session to focus on 'people' issues like problematic staff relationships, people's feelings about their work and sometimes personal issues.
The rest of the session is task oriented, sometimes with an agenda that has
come from personal support sessions or management meetings, sometimes
coming from individuals within the group.

Meetings are informal with a rotating 'chair' and a minute taker. Minutes are essential both to remind us of what we committed ourselves to, and for sharing information between groups and for staff who are on leave or attending courses. Over the years chairing the meeting has been a real issue and the structure of the meeting has changed many times. Most recently staff decided to vote for five or six staff who could run the meetings most effectively and this worked well for a time. We also recognized the fact that seniority in terms of length of experience or formal qualifications did not necessarily imply greater competence in running an effective staff meeting with a large staff group. There is always a real tension between getting tasks completed and giving time to individual members of staff who need to share difficult work situations. Sometimes the balance is wrong and we go round in circles or become self-indulgent; when it is working well a great deal gets achieved. Whatever happens it is almost always the most demanding and stressful session of the week! Because we were often working with large numbers of staff (up to twenty-eight at one time, including our community service volunteers and social work students) and because it seemed important to increase our awareness of each other's different work-loads, we set up a tradition of 'Not the staff meeting staff meetings'. The main agenda of these meetings, which were planned by small groups of staff who did not usually get the chance to work together, was team-building and fun and the learning was kept light.

Feedback from colleagues and trainers who have taken part in staff meetings has been amazement at the energy and diversity of views, and the assertiveness of even fairly new staff when working in small groups. We realize that this is quality non-contact time and we do not see it as a privilege but as an essential part of our staff development plan. One vital lesson we learned within the first few months was that parents did resent the closure, for one afternoon a week, of their new play facility. They also welcomed the opportunity, when the space was handed over to them, and some staff support was offered, to set up their own playgroup one afternoon a week. Parents who used the service the rest of the week became service providers on Wednesdays; they went on courses and from 1985 set up two playgroups offering sessions in the next-door building, five days a week for about sixty children.

Staff meetings have been discussed in some detail because that is where most ideas are generated or debated, where policies are revised and where staff share knowledge and give each other support. Nursery staff also meet from 4.30 to 6.00 p.m. every Monday night. This time was spent in the early years of the life of the centre in making the environment attractive and welcoming to parents and children. We were in an old, poorly maintained building which seemed to be falling down around us! We set up wonderful displays which disguised the unfortunate state of the plasterwork. Over the last four or five years the building has been renovated and made more attractive; formal displays were largely overtaken by attractively mounted photographs of the children's learning process. Monday nights are now spent sharing our observations of children, writing formative and summarative assessments of the progress and planning a rich early years curriculum and allocating responsibility for putting it into effect. Other aspects of our organizational structure are shown in Figure 10.1.

Parents' meetings

Parents in the first two years were encouraged to attend the part of the main staff meeting where general issues were discussed. Some did attend and brought a friend along. It seemed important, however, that staff should have their own time.

It also seemed important for parents to have a meeting, preferably chaired by a parent, where they could give critical feedback, exchange views about what was going on in the centre and share information with staff. Access to the group which runs in the evening was made easier by the centre covering the cost of babysitting fees and by staff offering transport on winter nights. The meetings were always informal with coffee and wine. One regular attender would always arrive half an hour late and the meeting would have to stop for a five minute summary of *EastEnders* before business could be resumed. Most recently an evening crèche is on offer, for in the current climate of anxiety over child abuse many parents are reluctant to leave young children with babysitters even when babysitters are available.

Both because of the change in employment patterns and because some parents said they would find it easier to bring criticisms and share information in smaller family group meetings, these have now been set up during the day with a crèche. This gives parents an opportunity to discuss issues about their own child's education and care with other parents who share the same family worker. The family worker running the meeting is supported by a senior member of staff so that they can listen and get support during and afterwards, if the discussion has been difficult or painful. These meetings give parents a real opportunity both to understand how the centre works internally and how it is managed by the two lead departments and the policy group. Parents nominate representatives to go from the family group meeting to the monthly parents' meeting. Two parents who attend this parents' meeting are then elected to represent all users on the policy group and in this way have a voice in the overall policy-making and management of the centre. The parents' meeting is primarily concerned with day-to-day events, staff appointments, training, social events, budgets, fundraising and suggestions for the group work programme.

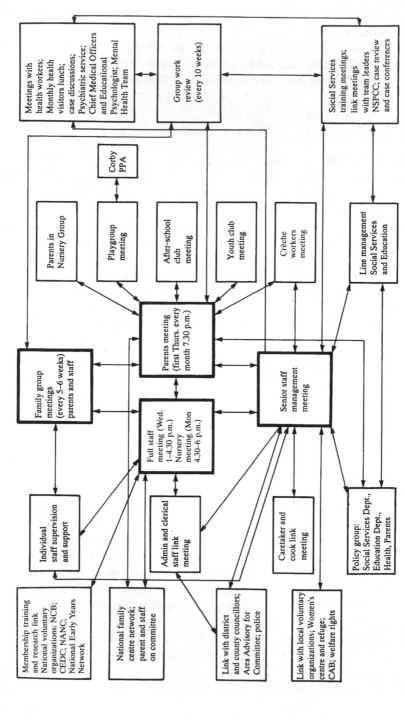

Figure 10.1 Towards communication, co-operation and collaboration: a management 'side-archy' and communication network (Pen Green, 1991).

Sometimes it deals with more contentious issues. On two occasions the parents' meeting has formed itself into a community action group to protest at cuts in services and the possible closure of the adjacent building. On these occasions parents have become vociferous campaigners and have made many representations to the county council. Interestingly, parents who have been actively involved in the centre have moved on to become governors in the three local schools.

Staff support and supervision

At the same time as setting up staff groups and parents' groups to discuss central issues, we also looked around for the best possible model of supervision and support for individual members of staff. It would not have been possible for staff to remain open to criticism and to appraise their own work critically if they had not received consistent professional support. We set up a system where most staff receive supervision/support every three weeks from a senior member of staff. Senior staff then receive support from the Head of Centre who in turn has a monthly consultancy session with an external consultant (a lecturer in the University Social Work Department). This level of supervision is essential for staff working in centres for under fives and families which combine a social work and educative role. Clearly the LEA Inspectorate can offer curriculum advice, and senior officers from both lead departments fulfil the line management function, but what is needed additionally is a structure which addresses personal and professional issues. Problem areas such as leadership styles and personality clashes need to be discussed freely and confidentially. Time needs to be taken to give staff positive feedback, information on training, and careers advice. Supervision and support sessions need to be regular and uninterrupted. Ideas and problems that come up in supervision need to be appropriately fed back to management meetings and/or staff meetings. Staff have a right to this kind of support and it becomes a mechanism of quality control because it involves target-setting, goals and reviews. Staff may also need specialist support or outside consultants for particular pieces of work.

We have also adopted the social work model of taking time out for team-building and we spend two days each year away on a university campus with a trainer who has worked with us for four years. This is an important annual event and very hard work; the residential component was requested by staff so that they could combine self-development and team-building with a relaxing evening away from family and other pressures! Last year senior staff spent a weekend away on a management training weekend which proved to be very challenging and the management consultant was invited back to work with the staff team to great effect. Staff have made

ıat this should also be an annual event roughly at the begin-
school year and this has considerably enhanced our review

ıear that staff spend a lot of time in meetings discussing what
they do! At Pen Green we have adopted a community development model
of working with parents and children which involves planning, taking action
and reflection at all stages and which aims at empowering not deskilling.
To work in this way we need

> to be prepared to work with contradictions and confusions. It is not a
> field for people who like to be clear-cut, precise and polished . . . it is
> a field for compromise, negotiation, flexibility, sharing and a balance
> of conflicting interests.
>
> (Jordan, 1987, p. 36)

To achieve this we also need to work closely with other professional colleagues from other disciplines, so that we can develop a common philosophy and provide an effective service. To make this possible we share much
of our in-house training with colleagues from health and social services,
and with parent volunteers. (We pay for supply cover so that the playgroup
staff can attend training sessions and meetings.) We try to avoid stereotyping and 'blaming' other agencies and we have gained an understanding
of each other's management structures and the constraints that other
agency workers experience through a programme of working lunches,
reviews and seminars.

WHO BENEFITS?

Working as a team is a process not a technique. It is rooted in an ideology of empowerment, encouraging adults (whether parents or staff) to take
control of their own lives and giving children permission to do the same.

Working as we do with parents and staff implies a different way of working with children and they are the beneficiaries both directly and indirectly.
Instead of a fragmented service where children can be developmentally
assessed twice in one day by different (well-meaning) professionals, where
children's health, educational and social/welfare needs are kept separate,
professionals and parents plan and work co-operatively. Instead of twenty
different workers being 'involved' in the case of abused or neglected children and few making any impact, families can seek support from one or
two people they self select and they can get it within their own community. In this way they are not pathologized. Instead of a perceived
dichotomy between the needs of parents and the needs of children, where
both end up fighting for recognition, there is an acceptance that they are
equally important.

HOW DO WE KNOW WE HAVE
ACHIEVED A QUALITY SERVICE?

I have outlined the forums we have set up for parents to express their views, and our own staff meetings and group work reviews give us a great deal of critical information on the service we provide. Parents evaluate all the groups they attend and staff who are well trained and properly supervised have learned how to take criticism and constantly review their own practice. Part of our initial vision was to provide a high quality and developmentally appropriate curriculum to all the children who come into the centre. Parents help us to evaluate how successfully we have achieved this goal.

Quality in the curriculum means parents and staff need to work together

Nursery staff spend many hours each week planning the nursery activities and assessing children's development. We believe it is critical that what we do is shared with parents and that parents have a great deal of the information that informs that process. Parents have always been encouraged to get involved in curriculum development, either through attendance at staff meetings, courses where parent volunteers and parent supply staff participate or through study groups. Several years ago staff were introduced to the concept of 'schemas' (Athey, 1990 and Chapters 5 and 6 in this book) and have spent a great deal of their in-service training on increasing their understanding of the patterns in children's play. We had always based our curriculum on observations of children's interests and preoccupations but with the help of Chris Athey and Tina Bruce we developed an intellectual framework and a helpful language to describe what we saw. Parents were involved in 'schema' training, and 'schema spotting' from the start, and were equally fascinated with the way we could all now reconcile bits of children's behaviour that had seemed random, or even counter-productive, with a cognitive structure. We were all equally impressed with how persistently children returned to *their* primary concerns (at home and at nursery) despite well-meaning staff trying to encourage them into more 'teacher-led' activities. Staff and parents both gained from making videos at home and in the nursery and looking in some detail at their own children's behaviour. Staff and parents then analysed their observations with the help of our very supportive early years consultant, Tina Bruce, who has worked with us since 1989. We feel that we have created a most successful pedagogue/practitioner partnership. Parents began to record observations on children at home and these observations were shared with staff and became the basis for planning for children in the nursery. Parents were encouraged to make audio tapes of their observations if they weren't confident writing things down (Arnold, 1996).

Now all new parents are encouraged to make observations after the initial home visit and are introduced to our ideas about curriculum development. The children's open files, which always contained records of work, home visits, and staff observations, have been transformed into rather splendid folders emblazoned with 'A record of my achievement'. These folders contain material from home and nursery. In our experience all parents, even where there has been child neglect or child abuse, care passionately about their children's development and are keen to collaborate.

This curriculum programme has moved a stage further with the advent of the National Curriculum and the important task of establishing nursery children's right to a curriculum that is not 'pre' anything but has intrinsic value. Nursery staff were reluctant to become familiar with unwieldy National Curriculum documents but when these were made more accessible, took pleasure in mastering the language of attainment targets and levels of achievement. Our new assessment 'pack' links National Curriculum objectives with our nursery objectives as simply as possible. Interestingly when this was shared with parents it was an after-school-club parent volunteer who expressed anxieties about the dangers of an over-rigid curriculum being imposed on young children. The same parent expressed concerns about other parents feeling the need to push children too hard. We concluded that for staff and parents simply having all the information in an accessible form was empowering. Perhaps most important for parents was the fact that staff recognized their enormous contribution to their own child's development and their key role in their children's learning. Most important for staff was the salutary reminder that parents gave us, that children only have 'one shot' at being three and four. We may need to protect their right to an education which meets both their cognitive and their affective needs.

WHAT ABOUT THE FUTURE?

We have survived vandalism and fires, cuts in services and enormous changes in legislation by constantly going back to the community users and asking what is most important to them; and by asking ourselves, 'is what we are doing "good enough"?'

We had a two-day closure and review of services one year when staff offered all-day crèche facilities so that as wide a representation as possible of our 300 plus users could come in at different times. The aim was to discuss what we could hold on to with a cut in staffing and what had to go. All the sessions were very well attended. We recorded all the passionate arguments that were made by parents, each fighting to maintain the corner of the service that was most relevant to them! Some were concerned with maintaining maximum flexibility in the nursery, others with retaining after-school provision for five- to eleven-year-olds or groups for parents. Symbolically, at the end of each session, parents and staff were given gas-filled balloons on which they wrote messages. Some gave the balloons to staff to keep, some sent them off with angry or poignant messages. This review marked an ending but was also a celebration of the future. It was also enormously helpful for our staff learning curve. The temptation for staff had been to try to be paternalistic and protect parents and children from the reality of the cuts and this was not helpful. Parents who use a service, value it and feel some ownership of it will probably want to fight for it when times are hard. With the kind of framework I have described it is possible for staff, parents and children to take risks and to take responsibility for services. This chapter started with a quotation from Lena Dominelli about powerless groups challenging their position in society. Parents (principally women) and children are, I believe, under-valued and often feel powerless. Working collectively there is nothing that they cannot achieve.

FURTHER READING AND TOPICS FOR DICUSSION

Vision and values

Does your centre or school have a clear vision and explicitly stated values? If so, who was involved in writing them? Did all the stakeholders' views get heard? How often do you go back to your vision and values and review and revise what you wrote? How do you evaluate your achievements?

Roles and relationships

How do you feel about the 80:20 theory, i.e. do 20 per cent of the staff do 80 per cent of the work most of the time?

What motivates you and the other members of your team? What are the intrinsic rewards and the extrinsic rewards for the important job that you are doing? Does every member of staff receive support and supervision and have a training profile?

Further reading

Leadership in Early Childhood (Rodd, 1994).

The Nursery Teacher in Action (Lally, 1991).

'Evaluaton and regulation: a question of empowerment' (Dahlberg and Asen, 1994).

Parents and Teachers Together (Stacey, 1991).

11

WORKING WITH PARENTS

John Rennie

This chapter will argue that working with parents should be an integral part of early years provision. It will present a rationale of why this should be; suggest a basis for sound practice; examine programmes at particular stages of a child's development; describe some programmes in action; identify actual and desired outcomes; take a brief look at possible future developments; and offer a mission statement for all those working with children in their early years.

WHY INVOLVE PARENTS?

Amongst professionals and others working with children in their early years, there is now an overwhelming acceptance of the value – to children, to parents and to the workers – of involving parents in work with children. (Whether this translates into an equally strong programme of parental involvement is discussed later in this chapter.) Such broad acceptance, though welcome, has been a long time coming. Even after the Plowden Report (DES, 1967) and the ensuing Community Development Project

(CDP) in the late 1960s and early 1970s, the case for parental involvement had to be argued energetically, not least because of the lack of both supportive evidence and political awareness of the effectiveness of such involvement. At that time, the argument was decidedly one-dimensional. It was founded on the obvious truth that parents are the child's first, and continuing, educators. From this, using only the flimsy evidence available – despite the powerful polemical 'evidence' from the CDPs – the rather plaintive cry was, 'You know it makes sense'. However appealing, this did not cut much ice with workers in the field. What were much more effective in bringing about change were the practical and innovative programmes at grass-roots level which were founded and supported by a few enlightened LEAs and foundations in the UK. These were inspired often by international experience filtering back here from the USA (the 'Head Start' programme), UNICEF's Third World efforts and the community-based projects so ambitiously mounted by organizations such as the Bernard Van Leer Foundation of the Netherlands in many countries worldwide.

Now, the situation in the UK is transformed in terms of availability of evidence, legal entitlements of parents and solid practice on the ground. Through a succession of Acts of Parliament (the Education Acts of 1980, 1981, 1986 and 1988) far-reaching legislation has been introduced. In addition, the Parents Charter has served to summarize these requirements and even to extend them to some extent. The legislation of the last decade was completed in 1990 by the 'Reporting of Individual Pupil Achievement' regulations. In total, all this has strengthened the rights of parents to:

- express a preference as to which school their children shall attend;

- receive information about the school;

- receive information about their children's work and progress (including an annual written report and specific information about achievements at the key stages);

- participate in the management of their children's school by becoming elected parent governors and through discussion of the governors' report at their annual meeting;

- be involved, where appropriate, in the assessment and review of special needs provision.

Though the Children Act 1989 sought to create a balance in the responsibility for a child's welfare between the state (the community), the parent and, for the first time, the child, it did nevertheless delineate parental responsibility more clearly. Stemming from the Children Act, the then DFE produced a Code of Practice on Special Educational Needs (SEN) which clearly identified parental rights in provision for their own children with such needs (see Chapter 8). Accordingly, LEAs are charged with being proactive in involving parents in determining such provision and the best practice is now very enlightened.

Faced with such a barrage of legislation, many workers have been sometimes disconcerted by the new roles demanded of them, particularly teachers, with the huge pressures brought by the introduction of the National Curriculum on top of other major educational changes. Nevertheless, the legislation is now in place and since nearly all of the proposals which finally reached the statute book had bi-partisan support, it seems likely that the future will bring only minor modification rather than yet more major legislation.

The *evidence* for parental involvement has been even more prolific, though disparate. It has long been well recognized that it is parents who provide the fundamental teaching for children of those crucial first skills – eating, walking, talking, toilet-use, washing – but still the depth of that home learning is often unrecognized. Whereas much of this parent teaching is, if not planned and structured, at least conscious and deliberate, much more is passed on to children by example and attitude, consciously or otherwise. Bernstein first claimed the existence of different 'codes' of language which follow from such examples. Tizard and Hughes (1984) have shown clearly how language development is tied to much everyday experience in the home. Mayall (1986) has presented a similar case in the health field. Nevertheless, it seems likely that equally fundamental developments are 'taught' in this haphazard, unplanned and uncoordinated way at home: aspects such as values, expressing (or not) emotion, love and tenderness, or responding to relationships. Empirical evidence is harder to come by in such areas though an early childhood worker who genuinely involves parents can readily make the connection between the child and the parent.

Evidence for the benefits of parental involvement on children's attainment is more readily available. In the USA, the National Council for Citizens in Education has assiduously compiled three bibliographies over the years drawing together very many examples which prove the case. First, *The Evidence Grows* (1981), then *The Evidence Continues to Grow* (1989) and finally *The family is critical to student achievement* (1994). The three books together provide outline documentation of scores of projects across the USA where detailed education has proved the benefits to children's learning and attainment of the involvement of parents in education. Examples are drawn from right across the country including projects with ethnic minorities, indigenous groups, all social and cultural groups, in urban and rural areas and in combinations of all these. Edited by Henderson and

Berla, the books constitute a prodigious case.

In the UK, Woodhead (1985) reviewed a variety of early years pro-grammes in the USA to assess their implications for the field in the UK. His work accords strongly with Henderson's evidence and he shows that parental involvement improved children's performance, led to higher teacher expectations, increased children's motivation and increased par-ents' confidence and aspirations. Also in the UK, *Raising Standards* (Widlake and McLeod, 1984) compared 1,000 disadvantaged pupils who had participated in a parental involvement programme in one city with 1,000 middle-class children from the same city and 1,000 matched children from a nearby city, on a range of criteria, particularly reading attainment and attitudes to reading. On all criteria, the children who had been in the programme scored at least as well as the middle-class children and on all criteria, on average, were more than two years ahead of the matched group – startling statistics indeed. Had similar results been obtained from the introduction of a new reading scheme, the resultant clamour from teach-ers for such golden resources can be readily imagined!

THE BASIS FOR SOUND PRACTICE

Perhaps inevitably, much of the early work in parental involvement, par-ticularly the great expansion of such work which followed the publication of the Plowden Report, was aimed primarily at disadvantaged parents. This was not surprising for two reasons. First, 'disadvantaged' had a relatively clear definition at that time. Indeed, the Inner London Education Authority (ILEA) devised six indices of disadvantage against which to measure the sum of disadvantage in any given school: factors such as lack of basic amenities in homes, overcrowding, take-up of free school meals, etc. Such schools could readily be shown to be 'failing' in comparison with schools in more advantaged areas. Thus, action was targeted on these 'pri-ority' areas of greatest need. Second, 'compensatory' education – a notion arriving in the UK from the USA in the mid-1960s, propagated, *inter alia*, by a liberal educator, Harry H. Passow, proved attractive to many teach-ers. This despite the fact that it was predicated on the notion of 'deficit' in families. Compensatory education and the priority areas fitted well together.

It was an approach doomed to failure yet, paradoxically, to endure. It was doomed because it involved labelling parents who, no matter how badly off they were, resented the label every bit as much as new citizens to the UK resented the label 'immigrant' and for equally valid reasons. They felt patronized and they often were patronized since the teachers, too, fell into the labelling trap. Perhaps more importantly, the labelling encouraged lower expectations and the dulling effect of that on achievement is well documented.

The reason such work endured into the 1980s and, to a lesser extent, into the 1990s, is partly due, no doubt, to the powerful stimulus such work received at its inception. It might also be due to the palpable growth both in poverty and in the gap between rich and poor in the 1980s, which, together, highlight disparities and support labelling. It was certainly not because of a lack of better practical, proven exemplars elsewhere. Eric Midwinter's seminal and powerful work in the Liverpool Educational Priority Area (EPA) was grounded in quite a different philosophy (Midwinter, 1972). He showed that the community in such areas could be a rich source of interest within the curriculum and that parents from the most disadvantaged homes had the talent and commitment to play vital roles in the education of their children – at home and at school, and best of all in partnership with teachers. Thus was the immutable triangle of parent, teacher, child established.

Midwinter's work, and his many books, inspired other pioneers in places such as Coventry, Southampton, Hackney, Walsall, Leicestershire and elsewhere. From this growing movement sprang the widespread belief, amongst community educators in particular, of the strength and value of parent–teacher partnership. From this, in turn, has grown the even more fruitful notion of Parents as Co-educators, but more of that later.

Community educators believe that partnership – and the synergy which stems from it – is the chief building block in all work in education, health and community development. In working with parents, it is the keystone. It begins by teachers recognizing their need to build their own confidence in working with parents, something for which they have not been trained since initial teacher training has not yet caught up with good practice in the field. They must then recognize, too, that parents are in the same boat either through being excluded for so long or from the failure they might have experienced at their own schools. Next, teachers and parents must recognize their own strengths. Teachers know how to work with groups, to organize learning materials, to create a learning environment. They need to use those skills to help bring the far greater knowledge parents have of their own children to bear and to encourage the parents to use such knowledge and experience, as well as other skills which collectively parents are bound to have, with their children at home.

Such a process must, of course, be rooted in mutual respect between teacher and parent. Each must recognize the strengths of the other, and be tolerant of perceived weaknesses. A simple example is to describe the difference between the deficit model and the partnership model in a group focusing on the parenting role. In the former, the teacher assumes that the parents know little about parenting – and explains it to them. In the latter, the teacher assumes that parents have a range of knowledge and experience and therefore uses a more Socratic approach – asking questions (What would you do? How do you cope with that?) and drawing from the group disparate responses. These form the basis of discussion, possibly leading to a consensus or perhaps to the realization that there might be several 'right' answers. This is an active role for both teachers and parents in which all concerned have an opportunity to air their views and to learn from each other.

Such an approach is all the more important when the parents have additional specific experience with their own children; for example, where the families come from ethnic minorities or the children have special educational needs. No good teacher would discount the validity and strength of different cultural values and mores which inevitably show through the children in class. When working with such parents, it needs to be recognized that the parents have an additional cultural understanding of their children's environment and that the range of 'right' answers might become even wider. The same will apply where parents have children who are disabled or have exceptional ability.

In advocating this non-didactic and inclusive style of work, it has to be admitted that the role of the teacher or worker is more challenging and demanding than the one she or he has probably been trained to do. A young teacher, for example, having recently completed her training, might well feel that the National Curriculum is the core of her work and that it must be 'delivered', a term which has become common currency but which heavily implies the passing down of knowledge rather than the drawing out of knowledge. The fact that the National Curriculum will be all the more effectively taught if the parents understand the aims and are involved in the 'delivery' might be less obvious to this teacher. It is clear that in-service training and support in developing the skills to involve parents is, therefore, essential – yet this is so frequently not available to too many teachers.

Equally, the parents come to this new style of working with the support, perhaps, of only other parents who might be just as uncertain. Then, as Braun (1992) points out, '. . . in many settings, parents come to the partnership relatively powerless (especially) where the child has a place because of a referral or because of . . . social disadvantage (e.g. single parent, low income, inadequate housing)'. In such cases, if parents are not to withdraw through feeling a lack of control or even participation in control, teachers and workers need to value overtly the special experiences which the parents bring to the situation.

In a climate where parents see their entitlements being granted through legislation and see nurseries and schools elsewhere becoming welcoming to parents, their antipathy will emerge if they do not receive a similar welcome. Happily, where teachers and workers have excluded parents previously, once they begin to involve them, the experience is frequently a liberating, uplifting one where the teachers' enhanced role can be so much more rewarding.

AGES AND STAGES

Paradoxically, some of the most effective work with families with young children takes place in secondary schools (those with a community remit), community centres, community education and/or adult education centres. Of course, much of this work is either aimed directly at teaching parenting skills, or, more effectively, stems naturally from work with groups of adults, almost always all women in the early stages, drawn together as evident affinity groups. Such groups include women living in the same neighbourhood, or having preschool-aged children in common, or people who have joined a club or an evening or daytime class for a specific activity. As with groups of parents invited to join groups in their children's nursery or infant/junior school, the common bond is a valuable foundation for real mutual respect and an overt recognition by workers and group members of the strengths of each other's knowledge and experience. Ironically, some of the most effective learning takes place as work develops quite naturally, away from the original purpose for coming together. Successful women's groups have grown from invitations to attend regular coffee mornings; purposeful family health groups have grown from parents coming to hear about children's reading; parenting groups have developed from parent and toddler groups in nurseries and schools.

Affinity groups of this kind have become all the more important now that we live in a society where the traditional family support structures of close-knit neighbourhoods with nearby extended families have long since disappeared. Whether the mother is a lone parent living in a high-rise flat or a stay-at-home mother with a partner out at work, the affinity group offers a real opportunity to share learning with others with similar needs.

Once the child joins a nursery or preschool group, and even more so when he starts school, the affinities of the parents overlap most obviously. They have children of the same age; they live in the same catchment area; their children are being educated or cared for by the same worker or teacher; frequently, they have other affinities such as housing, income or class. This confluence of affinity and need demands to be met with an openness and welcome from the workers and teachers in nurseries and schools because it is nothing less, to steal a phase from the National Curriculum, than a 'key stage' in the child's development – indeed it is *the* key stage.

School-Effectiveness has become an international movement in the last ten years or so. This movement has recognized that the search for the most significant factors which characterize 'good' or 'successful' schools is central to the battle to develop effective schools. Research has been undertaken to identify these factors in many countries and one factor which consistently emerges is 'good home–school relations'. Indeed, one Australian author (Townsend, 1994) claims that effective schools and community schools are synonymous. CEDC's pack *Parents as Co-educators* (1993) says that good home–school relations means that a school:

- *Communicates* basic information to parents effectively, and ensures ... opportunities to ... discuss matters (relating) to their own children and families;

- is *accessible*, offering parents opportunities to make contact, to visit and to raise concerns;

- *capitalizes on parental influence* by ... encouraging ways in which parents can support their children's learning;

- provides ... *a sense of identity, shared purpose and belonging* through encouraging parents to become involved in the life and work of the school.

Many schools have, these days, accepted such principles though not enough have yet recognized the necessity to make this a whole-school approach, every bit as vital as whole-school approaches to language or maths, for instance. There are still too many schools which, having opted to develop their parental links, leave it all to a designated teacher, thus inadvertently ghettoizing the work and ensuring that it is perceived by teachers and parents as low-status, peripheral activity. Equally essential from the school's point of view is the need to recognize that this whole-school approach is a long-term task, with its own stages of development, all of which need reflection and planning on the basis of carefully monitored outcomes. The next section will look at these programme stages and offer practical examples from successful practice.

ACTING IN CONCERT

Several writers have argued for academically defined sequential stages for parental involvement. In reality, however, given the vagaries and disparities of availability of resources, personalities, agencies, key workers and parents, local policy changes and, not least, sheer opportunity, such carefully structured planning is neither practicable nor even desirable. What is offered below is no more than a practical set of guidelines, based on actual experience and useful only as a flexible tool to assist planning and reflection. Given those provisions, the stages might approximate to the following:

- *Confidence-building* – for both teachers/workers and parents.

- *Awareness-raising and starting participation* – leading to teachers working directly with parents in school and parents with children at home.

- *Real involvement* – where parents understand the role of the school, the curriculum and their part in it, at home and school, and participate fully.

- *Parent–teacher partnership* – genuine joint work, in the classroom, in the parents' room, at home. Parents participating in planning and in making materials and supporting teachers in the 'delivery'.

- *Parents as co-educators* – partnership extending to parents having a real role alongside teachers in the delivery of the curriculum with teachers in charge in school and parents at home.

Currently, in our schools, the range of work in this field is as wide as it ever was. It is often said that some schools used to have notices saying 'No parents beyond this point'. Sadly, in 1996 a few schools retain such notices. Others have dispensed with the notices and yet retained the attitudes behind them. Such schools are diminishing in number but they often exist amidst schools where real partnership is in operation. Pragmatically, it must be recognized that there will always be great diversity in the level of commitment to this work. Not all schools will attain the 'co-educators' status but targets need, at least, to be seen by all.

SUCCESSFUL PRACTICE

Confidence-building is the foundation of all work with families. It has been likened to a gardener 'double digging' to prepare the ground for seeding. This is a fine metaphor but one which is too one-sided. The confidence of both teachers and parents needs to be built. Consequently, all the activities at this stage need to be non-threatening to both sides. It is no use opening the doors for the first time and expecting families to participate, say, in a maths workshop. Parents have been excluded from the education process for too long. Much more fruitful are simple and friendly invitations for parents to call in for something social, or at least convivial, where they will be called on to *do* no more than observe or chat to other parents. Teachers and workers, too, will not be faced with heavy preparation nor tricky presentations of their work. Simple ways forward are:

- morning coffee with an exhibition of children's work;

- a school assembly with parents sitting observing at the back;

- an open afternoon to see an exhibition, or a carol service or a special event;

- a cup of tea in the last half hour of the day, when parents are coming to collect children anyway, with a few minutes to give information;

- a parents' newsletter.

A hundred other ways are equally valid, many of them spelled out by Pugh *et al.* (1987), Pugh and De'Ath (1989) and *Parents as Co-educators* (CEDC, 1993).

Awareness raising and starting participation demands more orientation to the caring and educational purposes of the nursery or school but is so much easier when the foundations of confidence have been laid. Many schools now have a parents room which is a clear signal to all parents that they have a place, literally as well as a metaphorically, in the school. It is almost a litmus paper test of the real attitude of headteachers, especially if they say they have no room for a parents room. In new schools, making the medical room dual use will fit the bill. In old schools, the conversion of a cloakroom or other space is frequently possible. But the parents room is not merely symbolic. It can become a real springboard for parental involvement and an occasional refuge where the parents make the rules, being careful that no small clique takes it over as a power-base.

This stage will be a good time to create a more varied and challenging set of opportunities such as:

- DIY evenings where parents have a relaxed evening trying out a circuit of things the children do in nursery and school each day;

- a parent and toddler club;

- parents' quiz evenings;

- parent netball-teams or choirs;

- parents helping plan and present the assembly;

- a toy library;

- a uniform and sports gear swap-shop;

- parents invited on outings;

- parents assisting with school Christmas parties, organizing jumble sales, fund raising, etc.

So far, these activities will have ensured that parents and teachers know each other better and become relaxed about doing things in school together. Now begins the process which will challenge parents and teachers alike but which will begin to make a measurable difference to children's learning and achievement. Real involvement requires the actual day-to-day participation by parents in the life and work of the nursery or school, during the day and at home. It requires parents, aided by workers and teachers who are themselves treading new ground, to learn new skills and to have the confidence to put them into action. Such a programme of involvement might include some of the following:

- Parents planning their own programme of activity in the parents room with some of it concentrating on helping the school and their own children, some on things of benefit to themselves (e.g. a hairdressing session, a bulk-buy club, a social outing);

- five-session workshops for parents on reading or maths to help them help children at home;

- parents learning how to listen to reading and doing this occasionally in the classroom;

- parents taking assembly one day each week;

- parents managing the toy library and swap-shop;

- special groups for parents on parenting or relationships or money management;

- one or two parents undertaking surveys of all parents to identify skills to add to the activities of the school or parents room.

Once this kind of activity is an everyday occurrence in the school, it is merely a step towards partnership. By now, mutual respect will be well established. Many teachers and parents will be on first-name terms, used to planning together and working together. Partnership requires all these things and it is more difficult to indicate the areas of partnership which will develop since it depends so much upon the ambitions and aspirations of all the partners. However, a few which have happened in some places include:

- Teams in the classroom. Here, the teacher prepares roles for a team of three, four or five helpers – parents who will spend a half day working with her as the leader of a team of adults in the classroom.

- Two or three parents managing a rota of other parents coming in to use their special talents with children in the classroom, with teachers, or with parents in the parents room.

- Parents devising and producing materials for their own and the teachers' use in the teaching of maths and reading with guidance from teachers.

- Further education lecturers providing award-bearing courses for parents in parents room.

- A parents' sub-committee of the governing body to advise on the views of parents on policy matters.

- Home-learning packs for use by parents at home, prepared by teachers and parents, with guidance on use available from teachers.

- Structured programmes of paired reading done by parents in the classroom and at home.

Very few places have gone through all the stages and used all the strategies described here. To reach this stage requires complete commitment. However, in many places, particularly schools, many of the strategies have been practised and some few places have begun to take steps towards the ultimate aim of parents as co-educators. A few examples will provide the flavour of such ambitious programmes.

- In Coventry, parents have been trained as 'link workers' – para-professionals who work in the community with parents and others to help provide additional services. These include second language groups and early childhood provision.

- In Leeds, a scheme known as 'Read It', devised by staff at the City's Education 2000 base, signed up nearly 3,000 parents in the first few weeks of a programme to involve parents in the structured support, at home, of their children's reading.

- In Manchester, parents can now receive accreditation through the Open College Network for their work in supporting their children's learning.

- In Warwickshire, the Parent Partnership Scheme works directly with parents of children with special educational needs to help them understand their children's education and be better supported in their concerns. The emphasis is on providing parental support through personal visits, liaison with statutory and voluntary agencies and establishing parent groups in schools. These groups enable parents to discuss issues of mutual concern, together and with relevant professionals, thus enabling them to join in support for their own children.

- In Coventry, for no less than twenty-three years, parents staffing annexes to a nursery centre, supported by peripatetic professionals, have been producing comparable outcomes to those achieved by nurseries staffed by fully-qualified nursery staff.

- In Corby, Pen Green Family Centre has pioneered parent participation in the full range of its work with children for many years and is seen as an unqualified success (see Chapter 10).

Together, these examples show the depth of achievement which can accrue from a full-scale partnership.

OUTCOMES

A number of the studies referred to earlier in this chapter have offered concrete evidence of the benefits of working with families, particularly in relation to children's improved performance in school. What follows is a range of possible outcomes – all noted in various studies, but few of which can ever be guaranteed. Certainly, they are all aimed at, and they are all potential outcomes of any well-planned and well-executed programme of work with families. Doubtless, some programmes will claim to achieve all these outcomes, but most will make more modest claims. Looking at the outcomes from the point of view of the key participants, they seem to fall into four separate but overlapping groups.

Outcomes for *children* have been much the most well researched. First, the confidence children gain from seeing their own parents in nursery or centre or school is palpable. Once the parents are seen by their children to be at ease in the situation, that confidence grows even more. Even for those children whose parents are not able to be present, it appears to be encouraging and comforting to them to see greater numbers of adults round them. Second, the children will begin to receive much more constructive support for their learning at home. The vast majority of parents are very interested in their child's learning. Without professional backing, though, they might well be offering inappropriate support at home, which is eventually counter-productive. When parents and teachers are working together, the home support is likely to chime well with the work in school and the child receives a consistent and constructive message.

Third, when parent and child are working happily together – at home or in nursery or school – the benefits to their relationship are obvious. Conversely, when the messages from home and school are not in harmony, the child is uncertain and anxious and relationships suffer all round. Fourth, the learning pay-off is very high. The mass of evidence is huge and irrefutable – so much so that it is now possible to claim that teachers and workers who do not involve parents are acting unprofessionally.

For *teachers*, the benefits are just as great. First, very high numbers of teachers report a feeling of confidence stemming from the fact that they know parents are on their side and trust them. The same is true of workers in nurseries and family centres. Second, teachers greatly appreciate direct help in school. The workload of teachers has increased dramatically and the tensions in modern society are greater than ever. In nursery or school, a shared workload and a collaborative effort, with the certainty of back-up when the child goes home, are inevitably going to be of benefit to the teacher.

Third, when home and school are working together harmoniously, both children and parents will have a more positive attitude towards school. All teachers know the benefits which accrue from that. Fourth, even more importantly, the teacher has the gratification of seeing children having greater success in their learning – and that is probably the most powerful motivating factor for teachers.

Finally, in addition to warm feelings of support and success, the actual role and status of the preschool worker or teacher are enhanced. Parents who observe at first hand the sheer scale of keeping thirty preschoolers constructively occupied are invariably impressed. The teacher's stock rises. Instead of parents sitting at home, perhaps jumping to the wrong conclusions and, at best, complaining of a lack of information or clarity, they are alongside the staff, seeing things happen at first hand and recognizing the value. Also, a teacher who is working with a class of children and has five extra adults in the room is under stress. But when she sees herself as manager of a six-adult team, all with defined roles, her own role is enhanced and is thus more effective.

Perhaps the greatest beneficiaries are the *parents*. First, most parents coming into school or nursery for the first few times lack confidence. Whether this is because it is a long time since they were in such a place, or because of a feeling of failure from those days, or for other reasons, this regularly seems to be the case. As they begin to realize the value of what they are seeing, as well as the possibility of a role for themselves and a consequent gain for their children, confidence rises rapidly. Second, the opportunity to work with their children in a way which they themselves recognize as constructive and effective brings them even closer to their children.

Third, and for many parents this will be the greatest pay-off, they have the pleasure of seeing their children's educational performance improve. Nothing succeeds like success. Fourth, and related to it, the parents have the immense gratification of knowing that they have made a real contribution to their child's improvement.

Fifth, and perhaps most interestingly, very many parents who become involved with their children's learning find their own interest in learning being rekindled. Not surprisingly, maybe, many of the parents who decide to enter further or adult education as a result of their work with their children are often parents with few or no qualifications of note – they suddenly begin to recognize their own worth. Claims have been made that this raised confidence and new interest in learning both bring a new impetus to the child's learning, in turn. Many teachers feel that this is the case but there is, as yet, no hard evidence to support such a belief.

Finally, and powerfully, parents begin to feel a sense of ownership of the education process. They are no longer the innocent bystanders or, at best, the passive supporters of the school. They are key players in the learning process. That is a great gift to present to any parent.

Children, parents and teachers, then, are the key beneficiaries of family involvement programmes. However, the *community* itself also benefits. The nursery centre or school becomes a natural focus for the community. Social, cultural, welfare and educational provision begins to be mixed. Families see such places as a first port of call in times of need. Pen Green Centre in Corby, Brownsover First School in Rugby, and Hazel Primary School in Leicester are outstanding examples of what the benefits can be at each stage.

In such communities, there is less likelihood of vandalism (as the Sports Council proved with their work in Walsall) and there is better collaboration between the voluntary and statutory agencies. Best of all, it is the basis for the learning community which educators have long advocated and which politicians are now recognizing as vital for community well-being, socially and economically.

MISSION STATEMENT

It seems that, in this country, we have adopted the notion of a mission statement from the USA but there are those who still argue that a statement of aims and objectives remains the more appropriate way of indicating purpose. However, the mission statement has particular virtues. It talks of outcomes and attitudes as much as aims; it is more readily written jargon-free; it is an overt and positive declaration of intent. It is closer to the charter concept without being so one-sided as charters often are.

The only way to produce a mission statement with a chance of success is to involve all the workers and/or teachers in a process to develop one. It is little use a manager or head deciding unilaterally, or solely in collaboration with senior staff, the wording of a mission statement. This must stem directly from the actual work on the ground of all the staff seeking to achieve the mission. Staff will not make such an achievement unless they have a sense of ownership of the statement. And they will not have that sense of ownership unless they have been involved in drawing up the statement. What is offered here, therefore, is not a model for all early years establishments. Rather, it is a basic framework to act as a set of guidelines for individual playgroups, nurseries, family centres, schools and others to devise their own specific statement. It is often useful to spell out the values of the place and then to identify the practices which should automatically follow from it. The outcome might look something like:

A Mission Statement for Goodchild Nursery School

The staff of this nursery believe that:

- All children here deserve our best efforts at all times.

- The parents of our children, as their first and continuing carers and educators, are our partners.

- Best progress will be made when children can see parents and staff working happily in partnership.

We therefore aim:

- To provide a warm, secure and caring environment for all our children.

- To recognize that all our children are individuals with their own different needs.

- To welcome parents to partner us in meeting those needs in the most effective way.

- To provide a stimulating learning process for all our children.

- To assist parents to continue this process at home.

- To celebrate the successes of all the children, parents and teachers.

- To invite and welcome constructive criticism, help, advice and suggestions.

- To continue to look for even more effective ways to improve our service to families.

LOOKING TO THE FUTURE

One of the most disconcerting developments in the last twenty years has been the speed with which the rate of social and political change has begun to catch up with the rate of technological change. Apparent solutions to social issues, often radical in concept, fall over themselves in competing for attention. Politicians from across the political spectrum surprise each other by finding agreement on one new idea or another. In attempting to predict the future, therefore, a crystal ball is of little use – we know that change will be constant. However, most future change is still rooted, at least, in the present. The half-dozen or so future developments suggested here are, therefore, more than a wish-list. They are simply extrapolations on what is already happening now, somewhere.

The idea of school as a *natural focus for the community* is hardly new. From Henry Morris onwards, it has found many advocates like Michael Young, Harry Ree and Eric Midwinter. Having had a brief spell of popularity in the 1960s and early 1970s, it is now returning – albeit in a new guise and in much more penurious circumstances. Now, there is a new champion of the cause – Amitai Etzioni, the American sociologist and philosopher. He sees schools as instruments to shore up the moral foundations of society in a communitarian movement which is 'part change of heart, part renewal of social bonds, part reform of public life' (Etzioni, 1995). He has left it to others to put the flesh on those particular bones.

Remarkably, it was the UK's Department of Health which in 1995, as part of its response to the International Year of the Family, gave out a range of small grants to identify and describe 'family-friendly' organizations such as shopping malls, colleges – and schools. Etzioni's school, like Henry Morris's (who believed that even the architecture should be conducive to the wider use of the school building) would surely be family-friendly.

It would be accessible, metaphorically and physically, warm and welcoming to adults as well as children. Our current vogue of having much wider representation on governing bodies – an excellent idea inadequately supported – could, with goodwill, thrive and become a model of democratic partnership. In such a situation, it would not be necessary to have a four-week 'Ready for School' group for each year's new entry. Children would have grown to the age of entry partly in the school – indeed the age of entry in reality would be pre-natal. Parent and child would be as at home in the school as they are now in a village hall's parent and toddler club.

In the USA, Joy Dryfoos (1995) has called for more radical change in actual provision. She advocates so-called 'full-service schools'. She points out that 'The cumulative effects of poverty have created social environments that challenge educators, community leaders, and practitioners of health, mental health, and social services to invent new kinds of institutional responses'. She sees, and logically explains, the need for schools to provide a range of other services, primarily health, as a natural extension of their 'site-based' provision (the USA version of local management of schools). Her persuasive case is built not on theory but on the solid practice of, for instance, school-based health clinics which have evolved in many high schools across the USA and the more recent proliferation in elementary schools. Typically, they are outreach from a health authority, hospital or community health centre, under the auspices of medical practitioners. By 1993, 574 such clinics were in existence with the numbers growing apace. Dryfoos reports that the first question usually asked about school-based services is 'Where do parents fit in?'

Dryfoos does not stop at health services on school sites. She also makes a convincing case for mentoring, Family Resource Centres, parenting programmes, after-school centres and other provision familiar to the community school movement in the UK. Unlike more polemical commentators, from both left and right, Dryfoos costs out her programmes – which she is able to do because her case is founded on actual practice – and shows where the money can come from. She is as much about efficient services, more appropriate delivery and more effective inter-agency collaboration as she is about innovation. Our rulers have looked across the Atlantic for some very hard-nosed 'solutions' in recent years. Here is a vision which ought to have wider appeal.

A third and perhaps more obvious future development lies in the growth and more creative use of *new technology*. John Abbot, the restless and occasionally discomfiting founder of Education 2000, was the first educator in the UK to mount a thorough programme of computer-aided learning in this country, in Letchworth. His ideas were too frequently seen as mere technology schemes. Fortunately, the leading practitioner of Education 2000, Judith Robinson, leader of Leeds 2000, has shown how effective Abbot's ideas can be when linked with the community. In Leeds, imaginative programmes have linked parents, pupils, schools and technology. 'Read It', referred to earlier, is but one example.

What is often forgotten in talking about computers is that the five-year-old playing computer games in 1990 is already about to start secondary school. In ten years from now, 2006, there will be a generation of young adults, many of them already parents, who will not only be at ease with computers but will have been so from birth. They will be the first generation of adults born into the computer age or, rather, the PC age. As McLuhan (1962) pointed out, they accepted the computer as part of their natural environment. Additionally, the vast majority will be using computers not only at home but in work, education and training. Many of them will be more proficient with computers than the teachers of their children. Computers already are no longer for boffins only, of course. By 2006, they will be a regular, familiar, family tool. As such, any parental involvement programme which includes the computer not merely as a focus but as a normal part of the programme will be welcomed by parents. Better to start such programmes at once.

In Trinidad and Tobago, the *Life Centres* run by Servol have attracted worldwide attention (Pantin, 1979). Gerry Pantin, a Catholic priest in Trinidad's Laventille district at the time, was the brilliantly creative mind behind Servol's foundation. Having begun as a small organization to help very disadvantaged young people to find an aim in life, Servol's Life Centres now cover most communities in Trinidad and provide a huge range of services. They might well be called 'full service centres', echoing Dryfoos, since they provide outstanding early childhood provision, parenting programmes, pre-natal classes, relationship counselling, family support, anti-violence programmes, even community cafeteria meals. But do they have any relevance for the UK?

It would be quite inappropriate, of course, for UK organizations to ape a culturally based, bottom-up body such as Servol. In any case, Pantin's whole philosophy is one of 'respectful intervention' – listening to what the community wants and helping them provide it. That stance is entirely appropriate, in all circumstances. However, having learned that lesson, there is still mileage in learning from Servol's successful practice – adopting and adapting and ensuring that new developments are community-friendly. Not the least important lesson from Servol is that such methodologies are cost-effective *and* relatively low-cost.

A fifth future growth point might well be in the *preschool field*. This is not the place to comment on recent central government initiatives but it is clear that the quarter of a century which has passed since the then-DES White Paper, *A Framework for Expansion*, has provided little resolution of a range of issues around preschool provision. The Halsey Report (DES, 1972), written when government financing of services was relatively unquestioned – it was, after all, Margaret Thatcher who ordered the White Paper – advocated a range of provision, particularly the 'hybrid' education and care model. Since then, the playgroup movement has grown tremendously, and new notions such as vouchers, workplace nurseries, nursery annexes have had their moments, some more enduring than others.

It seems highly improbable, now, that early years provision will ever grow as a unified service, something which could only come about in the unlikely event of large-scale central funding becoming available. Much more likely is a continuation of the current broad range of provision. It does seem possible, too, that it will be parent pressure which will ensure that there will, in fact, be real growth. It is fairly plain to see that all the resources to create the additional early childhood opportunities that we need as a society are already in place. Nor does it need the most fertile imagination to recognize that there are attractive, feasible ways of harnessing those resources through community partnerships with strong parental involvement, to provide a more coherent and relevant service. It only needs the political will to launch the process – and the first party to provide it will find they have a real vote-winner on their hands.

Finally, the *communitarian movement* itself is a possible growth point. Etzioni speaks of the 'social webs' which communities provide in neighbourhoods, at work, in clubs and associations, binding individuals into caring groups who help maintain a civic, social and moral order. He points out that to make their contributions, the communities themselves need to be shored up. More controversially, he states 'This requires a new respect for the role that institutions, such as local schools, have in sustaining communities'. That role will be enhanced and all the more viable when parents are involved in real partnership as co-educators.

PART 3
TRAINING

12

TRAINING TO WORK IN
THE EARLY YEARS

Denise Hevey and Audrey Curtis

INTRODUCTION

This chapter is divided into three parts. Part one considers recent developments in vocational training which affect people working at what have traditionally been regarded as sub-professional levels in all types of early years services. Part two focuses on the history of, and current issues in, the training of early years teachers – one of the three professional groups that have a major role in early years services. Part three draws on both of these accounts to focus on the debate over what should constitute the ideal form of training and qualifications for 'professionals' in the early years field. Although parts one and two reveal very different approaches, both agree that training for work in the early years is at a crossroads. Decisions and events in the next few years are likely to have a profound effect on the nature of the early years professional or professionals for many years to come.

RECENT DEVELOPMENTS IN TRAINING
FOR EARLY YEARS WORKERS

Most people will be aware of the three main professional groups traditionally involved with young children and their families – teachers, health
visitors and social workers. What often comes as a surprise is the fact that
the majority of day care and preschool education services throughout the
UK are not staffed by these groups of professionals but by a largely unqualified army of more than 200,000 child care and education workers. In
England and Wales alone there are roughly 100,000 self-employed childminders and at least 50,000 playgroup leaders and assistants in some 20,000
playgroups (PLA, 1995). Workers with young children and their families
are also found in day nurseries, nursery and primary schools, crèches, parent and toddler groups, family centres, parent support and home visiting
schemes, toy libraries, playbuses and many other types of provision.

The vast majority (97 per cent) of these people who work with young
children are women, most with family responsibilities of their own (Hevey
and Windle, 1990). Many work part time, some as unpaid volunteers. Wages
are low and turnover rates are high. According to a report by the European
Childcare Network (European Commission, 1990), nannies earn just over
half the average pay of women workers and childminders less than half.
The only education and training opportunities open to the majority are
part-time, low-cost and not formally assessed or accredited. These vary
from as little as one evening a week for six weeks (the typical length of a
childminder's pre-registration course) to one day a week for a year (the
Diploma of the Preschool Learning Alliance). A recent survey of 419 day
care providers in England and Wales revealed that the commonest qualification for heads of nurseries and nursery staff was the NNEB while playgroup workers had most frequently attended courses run by the Preschool
Learning Alliance (or Mydiad Ysgolian Meithrin in Wales). Unfortunately,
'the great majority of childminders had no relevant qualifications' (p. 6),
however loosely interpreted, and neither did a third of playgroup workers
or a fifth of private day nursery staff (Moss *et al.*, 1995).

There has never been a statutory training or qualification requirement
for employment in or provision of early years services. The Children Act
1989 for the first time empowers local authorities to provide but it does
not require them to do so and guidance accompanying the Act (DH, 1991)
merely suggests the personal qualities and experience that might be looked
for in early years personnel. One is forced to conclude that this lack of
concern over training and qualifications for what are in reality highly
responsible roles is underpinned by something more fundamental than free
market philosophy. Rather it reflects confused and outmoded public attitudes which commonly regard the care of young children as an extension

of the mothering role and assume it all comes naturally to women. Such attitudes in turn reinforce the low status of early years work, helping to keep pay low and turnover high.

Similar attitudes were reported in the National Child Care Staffing Study carried out in America in 1988:

> As a nation we are reluctant to acknowledge child care settings as a work environment for adults, let alone commit resources to improving them. Even though many Americans recognize that child care teachers are underpaid, outdated attitudes about women's work and the family obscure our view of teachers' economic needs and the demands of their work. If a job in child care is seen as an extension of women's familial role of rearing children, professional preparation and adequate resource compensation seem unnecessary.
>
> (Whitebook, 1990, p. 3)

The reference here to 'child care teachers' does not equate with the UK notion of a qualified teacher. In fact, only 31 per cent of the 'child care teachers' in charge of classes and centres had a degree or equivalent qualification and only 65 per cent had any training in child development. Nevertheless, the survey found that formal education qualifications combined with relevant training were key predictors of high quality care.

THE ADVENT OF NATIONAL VOCATIONAL QUALIFICATIONS

In 1986, concerned by discontent on the part of employers and unfavourable international comparisons of the level of qualifications in the UK workforce, the government established the National Council for Vocational Qualifications with a remit to reform and rationalize the whole confusing picture of vocational qualifications into a single comprehensive, progressive framework. The new National Vocational Qualifications (NVQs) and their Scottish counterparts (SVQs) were to provide a guarantee of competence to do a job through being based on nationally agreed occupational standards and being assessed primarily in the workplace.

Each NVQ (or SVQ) is made up of modules or 'units of competence' which have meaning and value in employment and which allow for credit towards a full award to be built up on a unit by unit basis over an extended period of time. There are no formal academic entry requirements and no one is forced to take a particular course or to complete 'time-serving' periods in order to gain access to assessment. Ideally, candidates should be able to put themselves forward for assessment when they are ready, regardless of how long or short a time it has taken them to become competent or what mode of study or preparation they have followed. Overall, this represented a radical shift away from traditional qualifications geared to the needs of young people in full-time education and training and based on specification of syllabus 'inputs' in terms of the knowledge and skills that all students must cover in a given period, regardless of their maturity and previous experience. Instead the focus was shifted to achieving 'outcomes' in the workplace in terms of the functions a competent worker should be able to carry out and the knowledge that they draw on in order to perform competently in different circumstances.

The NCVQ/SCOTVEC system provides a framework for all vocational and professional qualifications with five levels of achievement. Broadly speaking Level One reflects the most basic competences carried out under constant supervision; Level Three denotes competence in a broad range of activities, many of which are complex, and considerable individual responsibility and autonomy; Level Five corresponds to the competence expected of a senior professional and includes the application of fundamental principles and complex techniques, plus analysis, diagnosis, planning, evaluation, and managerial responsibilities of a strategic nature.

DEVELOPING NVQS IN CHILD CARE AND EDUCATION

By the end of 1994 NVQs (and SVQs) had been accredited to cover more than 80 per cent of occupations in the UK with outstanding work continuing mainly at higher professional levels and in more specialist occupations. It was as part of these wider national reforms that occupational standards for work with young children and their families were developed by the 'Working with Under Sevens Project' based at the National Children's Bureau between 1989 and 1991 (Hevey, 1991a). More than 3,000 practitioners and managers from across the spectrum of child care and education settings and from all parts of the UK were involved or consulted at some stage in the development of the standards. This helped to ensure their acceptability and to determine that the key values and principles which early years workers hold dear were fully integrated into the standards. These include a commitment to both 'care' and 'education' functions in all work with young children; the importance of anti-discriminatory practice and of parent involvement; child-centredness and the need to value and meet the needs of each child as an individual.

The first NVQs and SVQs in Child Care and Education at Levels Two and Three were accredited by the NCVQ and SCOTVEC at the end of 1991 and formally launched in February 1992. Transferability is enhanced through designation of a common core of units at each level of the qualifications covering the primary functions of promoting the welfare, learning and development of young children within a safe, secure and stimulating environment. A limited number of 'endorsements' (combinations of option units) then allow for a degree of specialization to suit different roles and settings such as 'Family Day Care', 'Preschool Provision' and 'Special Needs'. In addition, the structure of the qualifications is designed to encourage progression through the inclusion of some units, or modified versions of units, in the core of the qualification at both levels.

Both the standards and qualifications have been well received and roundly endorsed by organizations such as the Local Government Management Board (Messenger and Curtis, 1991) and even those trade unions and professional associations who had at first been sceptical. The potential of the new qualifications was seen in terms of:

- improved access to nationally recognized, work-related qualifications for thousands of women;

- comparability with other skilled occupations leading to increased status and recognition for child care work;

- improved standards of child care and education based on nationally agreed criteria for worker performance;

- a framework for progression within the work role or into higher education and professional training;

- enhanced transferability of workers across a wide variety of child care and education settings and into related occupations based on common competences;

- a mechanism for specifying quality of provision through graded levels of qualification as well as numbers of staff.

The report of the Rumbold Committee stated:

> We welcome the work of the National Council for Vocational Qualifications (NCVQ) towards establishing agreed standards for child care workers, including those in education settings. We believe that, *given adequate resourcing*, it could bring about significant rationalization of patterns of training. It should also improve the status of early years workers through recognition of the complex range and high level of the skills involved and by opening up prospects for further training.
>
> (DES, 1990a, para. 176, p. 24, our emphasis)

The Equal Opportunities Commission stated in their discussion paper and action plan, *The Key to Real Choice*:

> The need in the UK for a professional career structure for child care

workers is acute. Work now being done in preparation for National and Scottish Vocational Qualifications in child care may represent an important first step, but will need to be *systematically resourced* and implemented.

(EOC, 1990, para. 2.2.4, p. 4, our emphasis)

IMPLEMENTING NVQs IN CHILD CARE AND EDUCATION

By the end of 1994 over 300 assessment centres had been approved to offer NVQs and SVQs in Child Care and Education, many taking the recommended 'best practice' form of consortia involving education, social services and the private and voluntary sectors. However, despite evidence of considerable interest and demand, implementation to date is proving to be much slower than had been hoped. Three years after the qualifications were launched only 856 candidates in England and Wales had achieved Level Two awards and a further 243 had been awarded Level Three certificates (NCVQ, 1995a). Although some time lag between introduction and candidate success is to be expected because of the need to create a new assessment infrastructure and the demanding nature of the assessment process, the primary reason for lack of take-up is quite simply lack of resources.

> The new model of education and training (or learning) assumes that companies and other employing organizations will become major providers of learning opportunities.
>
> (Jessup, 1991, p. 95)

As the above quotation makes clear the NVQ/SVQ system, in line with wider government policy on vocational education and training, assumes that training will be funded by employers and that assessment of competence will take place largely in the workplace through extension of the roles of existing line managers and supervisors. This also conveniently hides the increased costs of individual competence-based assessment when compared with mass administration of the simple written tests which are the basis of most traditional qualifications. Early years services quite simply breach these assumptions. A high proportion of early years workers are self-employed, most of the rest work in community groups or nurseries, which by their very nature are small scale and are 'employed' by organizations which are too small to provide their own in-house training or assessment programmes. Early years workers tend to have a high degree of autonomy and responsibility in their work roles and roughly three-quarters of the workforce are not regularly supervised (Hevey and Windle,

1990). Even when a potential work-based supervisor/assessor is present, on-going child care responsibilities within small-scale settings may make it unrealistic for him/her to carry out detailed assessments of candidates.

The only practical option for implementation of NVQs and SVQs in child care and education in most cases is through shared training arrangements and the employment of peripatetic assessors who can visit and assess candidates in their individual workplaces. But this requires the setting up of entirely new training and assessment infrastructures (Wedge, 1991) with considerable resource implications (Ross, 1990). Unlike other sectors of industry, there simply is no place to hide the costs and low pay means that early years workers cannot generally afford to finance themselves.

Promoting implementation of NVQs is a key aspect of the government's strategy for achieving National Education and Training Targets (NACETT, 1995) and the network of local Training and Enterprise Councils (TECs) is the main mechanism used for targeting resources. In January 1994 VOL-CUF (now called the National Early Years Network) published the results of a survey of all 82 TECs in England and Wales concerning assistance available to support implementation of NVQs in Child Care and Education. The results were a complete mishmash with every TEC operating a different policy. Some gave no help at all, twenty-two offered some assistance in training assessors but only seven TECs said they were able to support candidates financially.

One is forced to conclude that the arrival of NVQs/SVQs to date has succeeded in raising expectations only to leave many potential candidates in the early years world frustrated and disappointed that they cannot get access to the qualifications they need and want. Yet the potential for improvement in standards of child care and education is already starting to be borne out in practice.

> The general opinion is that these qualifications do reflect the skills and knowledge necessary for child care workers . . .The actual system of assessment in the workplace appears to be causing no problems. Permission is always sought from parents and carers, and a full explanation given to colleagues before observations begin. It is here that we have noticed an obvious consequence of NVQ implementation. All our candidates have reported that they have had to look rigorously at their working practice to ensure that they meet the NVQ performance criteria. In many cases, this has led to a noticeable improvement and updating of practice. If this continues to be the case, then NVQ will definitely be a good idea for child care workers and, more importantly, the children and families they care for and educate.
>
> (Davies, 1995, p. 12)

The introduction of Modern Apprenticeships (DTI, 1994) with NVQ Three outcomes as the minimum target, could be one way of assisting NVQ implementation amongst young people, but many experienced practitioners in the early years field are sceptical of this method of training believing maturity is an important quality for full-time work with young children and that most 16–19-year-olds are better off on full-time education and training courses with limited work experience.

GENERAL NATIONAL VOCATIONAL QUALIFICATIONS (GNVQS)

NVQs (and SVQs) were designed to provide a new work-based route to qualifications and primarily aimed at those already in employment. It was not surprising, therefore, to find that colleges and other training institutions found that 16–19-year-olds could not cram in enough work experience to fulfil all the NVQ or SVQ requirements whilst on full-time education and training courses. They were also unsuitable in other ways. Young people need time to explore a variety of possible job roles before making a commitment, to extend their general education keeping options for progression to higher education open and to develop the core or generic skills such as communication and working with others which older, more experienced workers often take for granted. It was to meet this perceived need that General National Vocational Qualifications were developed for five occupational areas and launched on a pilot basis in September 1992. GNVQs and GSVQs are meant to provide a broad-based preparation for work in a broad occupational sector like Health and Care (which includes child care). Like NVQs and SVQs they have adopted a modular structure with units composed of outcome statements and elaborated through specific performance criteria, though, more like National Curriculum Targets, these are statements of attainment rather than statements of competence. Unlike NVQs and SVQs, GNVQs have externally set tests at the end of each unit and are designed to have exact academic equivalences. Intermediate Level GNVQ is pitched at five good GCSEs and Advanced GNVQ is designated equivalent to two A levels (NCVQ, 1995b). (N.B.: GSVQs build on the pre-existing SCOTVEC module system and are designed to articulate with the Scottish education system and 'highers'.)

GNVQs are proving extremely popular with 164,000 students already enrolled in over 2,000 schools and colleges nationwide. A mapping exercise is currently being carried out in conjunction with the Occupational Standards Council for the Care Sector to identify progression routes from the GNVQ in Health and Care and to establish what modifications may be needed in order to promote access to professional training in nursing, social work and teaching and to encourage direct recruitment into employment. Many of the young people following GNVQ courses express the wish to 'work with children' but it is questionable how well the current GNVQ in Health and Care prepares them for this role since it includes relatively limited options in child care and very little at all about education services. Whilst the GNVQ provides a good general background, young people entering employment will still require top-up training and a significant amount of work experience to achieve the appropriate NVQ standards in Child Care and Education at Level Two or Three.

COMPLETING THE FRAMEWORK

Many people have suggested that the best analogy for the NCVQ/SCOTVEC framework is that of a multi-dimensional climbing frame rather than a single ladder of qualifications. Like a climbing frame there are several different ways of getting on and it is possible to move sideways as well as up. Increasing use of common units in, for example, management or training or administration mean that transferability of qualifications and hence career change is made easier. A good climbing frame might be expected to have several different peaks rather than a single pinnacle. So it should be possible for early years workers with NVQ level three to branch out in order to become, for example, a registration and inspection officer, a centre manager, a community organizer, an adult educator/trainer or a qualified teacher. As yet these options are not open, partly because the NCVQ climbing frame is not complete and partly because of barriers such as the requirements for subject specialism in teacher training described in the second part of this chapter.

The Local Government Management Board is currently supporting a feasibility study into the components needed to complete the framework in the early years field. This should include an additional 'endorsement' for work in primary education at NVQ level three and the development of new occupational standards at NVQ level four. The next major issue will then be how any new multi-disciplinary qualification in child care and education at Level Four might interface with existing professional qualifications. Exploring the interfaces could only be done effectively if the relevant single-discipline professions were also described in competence terms. It may be surprising to note just how much progress has already been made in this direction. Occupational standards for social workers in their first year of qualification are being drafted. Teacher training requirements have already been modified towards outcome statements, albeit not expressed in the same manner as competence outcomes within NVQs or SVQs. Work is in progress to develop national occupational standards for health promotion professionals and the Royal College of Nursing has joined the Occupational Standards Council for Care. Many nurses are already involved with NVQs/SVQs in their capacity as assessors for the Care awards at levels two and three and fears about undermining the professional status for which they have fought so hard would appear to be diminishing.

Despite initial scepticism from the professions, many are now coming to accept competence-based qualifications and the option of work-based routes as the shape of things to come and are now actively engaged in discussions with NCVQ and SCOTVEC. One should not assume that the adjustments are all to be made on the part of existing professional groups and that the benefits in terms of access and improved training opportunities will only flow from them down to vocational levels. Modules from the flexible, multi-disciplinary training schemes which will be needed for early years workers at the proposed NVQ/SVQ level four could also be highly attractive to traditionally trained teachers in, for example, introducing them to management or to adult education and training or to community work and so on. Not only is there growing interest in the idea that NVQs and SVQs, supported by open and flexible learning, could eventually provide an alternative work-based route to a range of professional qualifications (Hevey, 1994) but some professions are starting to consider how NVQ/SVQ unit accreditation could also become the basis for Continuing Professional Development schemes (Randall, 1995).

DEVELOPMENTS IN PROFESSIONAL TRAINING FOR EARLY YEARS TEACHERS

Since the nineteenth century there has been organized training of teachers in this country, set up originally by the voluntary bodies. In 1814 the British Society produced an outline for teacher training in primary schools which remained the model for courses until the early 1970s. It consisted of an academic entry qualification, a concurrent course of general education and professional training, a final examination and a probationary period of teaching, the whole culminating in the award of a teacher's certificate.

In 1960 all teacher training courses were extended from two to three years. Hitherto only the Froebel courses had offered courses of that length. This, and a sharp increase in the birth rate, led to a vast expansion in the number of teachers in training from 18,000 in 1958 to 114,000 by 1969. The next two decades were to see a drastic decline in the numbers. These rapid changes in student numbers, plus the introduction of the B.Ed degree in the mid-1960s and its subsequent extension to a four-year course granting graduate status to all members of the teaching profession, was to have far-reaching effects upon the training of teachers and on early years courses in particular. The effect of the introduction of a three-year B.Ed degree has yet to be seen.

By the mid-1960s there were no longer courses specifically for those wishing to work with the three–five age range in nursery school or class. All early years students followed a course of training which covered the age ranges three–seven years or three–eight years.

The rapid increase in student numbers followed by an even more rapid decrease led to dramatic changes within teacher training institutions. Colleges were encouraged to broaden their teaching and offered degree courses in the arts and the sciences as well as their traditional education areas. The James Report (HMSO, 1972) had recommended the ending of monotechnics and with this came the greater differentiation associated with present-day Institutes of Higher Education. In spite of their efforts, many colleges found themselves either over-staffed or with staff inappropriately qualified. However, excellent redundancy terms under the Crombie conditions encouraged many teacher trainers to apply for early retirement and among them were some of our finest trainers of early childhood educators. They were individuals who had been recruited into the colleges in the days when experience was considered more important than academic qualifications. Such tutors found themselves being overshadowed by young new entrants into teacher training, who had not necessarily been classroom teachers but who had the necessary academic status. This was to have an important effect upon early years training in the late 1970s and 1980s.

Colleges having shed staff with early years expertise were forced either to run their training courses for the infant and nursery years with inappropriately trained staff, or to close their nursery courses. As a result teachers professionally trained to work with young children were in short supply.

The shortage of early years teachers was further exacerbated by the introduction of the regulations laid down by the Council for the Accreditation of Teacher Education (CATE). The CATE requirement most likely to affect the number of courses offered for the training of early years teachers was the one which stated that all staff working on professional courses with students in initial training should have recent and relevant experience of the age range that they were teaching. Very properly, CATE rejected courses where the school experience of the lecturers was inappropriate and this led to a further decrease in the number of courses covering the three–five age range.

Circular 24/89 (Initial Teacher Training: Approval of Courses) laid down that all teachers following a B.Ed course must have a subject specialism which accounts for 50 per cent of their study time as well as a specific number of hours for each of the foundation subjects of the National Curriculum (science, mathematics and English).

During the government consultation period many early childhood specialists argued that an area of study like 'language and literacy' or 'aesthetic and creative' studies could be made rigorous enough to meet the regulations and yet would be more relevant to the needs of early years teachers (those preparing to work with three- to eight-year-olds). The government would not accept these arguments. Teachers preparing to work in the early years of schooling must have a subject discipline in the same way as those preparing to work with an older age range.

In November 1993 the introduction of new criteria for the initial training of primary school teachers, superseding Circular 24/89, laid down competencies and criteria which have to be met by all training institutions by September 1996. This Circular (DFE 14/93) also paved the way for the use of accreditation of prior learning to widen access across the curriculum and proposed consultation on new courses to prepare classroom assistants to support the teaching and learning of basic skills. This led to the introduction of the Specialist Teacher Assistant, a scheme which was piloted initially for a year in twenty-six further and higher educational institutions from September 1994. An extended pilot was introduced in September 1995. The course aims to develop teaching and learning skills in mathematics and English for classroom assistants working with Key Stage 1 children.

The Articled Teacher scheme was to be discontinued, but the Licensed Teacher scheme stayed. In September 1994 the Teacher Training Agency (TTA) was set up to replace CATE. Its remit was to promote teaching, raise standards in the profession and accredit initial training courses.

All these changes for promoting a more rigorous approach to the training of teachers are of importance but many early childhood educators query whether this instrumental approach to training is appropriate for those working with younger children.

There is no doubt that the introduction of the Circulars DFE 24/89 and 14/93 and the changing needs of the schools and early childhood centres have presented a problem to those educating the early childhood educators. The recent introduction of a voucher system for the education of four-year-olds and the 'desirable outcomes' (SCAA, 1995) pose other issues. How can teachers be prepared for the challenging work of the next century, when the needs of young children and their families may not be the same as they are today? Should there be a separate course for teachers working with the under fives or should we be advocating a situation as in Scotland where teachers working in the nurseries are expected to do a further course of training after gaining their qualifications in primary education?

THE EUROPEAN DIMENSION

Before we look at this crucial issue let us consider another factor which may well affect the training of early childhood workers and teachers in particular, that is the situation relating to our membership of the European Union.

Although education is not seen as an integral part of the Treaty of Rome, there were modifications during 1991 which will most probably have a bearing upon the training of teachers in the early years. The Directive which allowed equivalence in the recognition of qualifications has meant that teachers from European countries can be employed within the English education sector; so far this has been predominantly with statutory school aged children. There are, however, difficulties in accepting that there is equivalence with respect to the teaching of nursery school aged children since only in a few countries do teachers have the same level of training as we do in the UK. Furthermore, although the teachers may have the same length of training, in very few countries are they paid at the same level and in even fewer countries are teachers qualified to teach through the age range from three to eleven thus helping to ensure continuity and progression in children's education.

One of the strengths of our current teacher training programmes is that teachers are able to understand the development of children from three to eleven years or three to nine years and do not see starting statutory schooling as a cut-off point in this process. For example, although it is not standard practice in this country to teach children to read in the nursery school or class, in Europe generally, this is frowned upon and is seen as a threat to natural development before the age of five. Consensus in the UK would suggest that the interest in print shown by many children as a result of the programmes offered should be, and is, encouraged and developed. Therefore if the teacher has had no training in this aspect of education it could be very difficult for her to help the child appropriately.

In many parts of the EU there is a clearly defined distinction between care before six/seven years and education after. This militates against the concept of continuity and progression, which is one of the strengths of our system, made possible by the nature of our training.

Although government responsibility for young children is spilt between the Department of Health and the Department for Education and Employment, there is general agreement amongst professionals that there should be a greater educational input into all preschool institutions. As a result many local authorities are linking care and education in a positive way, or indeed placing total responsibility with the education committees (see Chapter 1).

The Rumbold Report (DES, 1990a) urged that there should be better quality in all early childhood provision. Before discussing further what constitutes a good early years training course to ensure this quality, it is important to consider what are the attributes we would like an early years teacher to possess.

WHAT MAKES A GOOD EARLY YEARS TEACHER?

Definitions of 'quality teaching' like those of 'good practice' are hard to find as most authors tend to be unwilling to commit themselves to state exactly what constitutes a 'good early years teacher'. However, it is essential to attempt this before considering how best to design the ideal training programme.

First of all, s/he is a professional, 'that is to say, professionals are persons who are able to carry out a complex and socially valued role for which defined expertise is required'. It is only teachers who are competent and qualified and mature who can be allowed 'the widest measure of professional autonomy' (Ward, 1986, p. 9).

Watts (1987) also had some appropriate comments to make on the topic of professionalism stating that

> whatever the future shape and nature of early childhood services, kindergarten teachers and other staff will continue to serve their clients well if they exemplify in their attitudes and behaviours the hallmarks of professionalism especially:
>
> - specific expertise and a specialized knowledge base;
>
> - commitment to continuing enquiry to advance the knowledge base;
>
> - altruism, service to a public good and assumptions of responsibility for their own continuing professional development.
>
> (Watts, 1987, p. 12)

Ebbeck, speaking at the OMEP World Congress in London in 1989, insisted that the hallmarks of professionalism are very important if we are to improve the status of early childhood educators.

WHAT SKILLS AND COMPETENCIES DOES AN EARLY YEARS TEACHER REQUIRE?

The DFE outlined the competencies expected of newly qualified primary teachers in Circular 14/93. In considering the knowledge and skills required the Circular places emphasis upon competence in the areas of curricular content, planning and assessment and an understanding of teaching strategies. But are these sufficient for the teacher working with children between the ages of three and seven/eight years?

Analysis of the role of the early years teacher, particularly those working within the three to five age range, leads to the conclusion that it is doubtful whether these competencies are sufficient.

The qualities required seem to fall naturally into three areas which can be developed with sensitive training.

Personal /social skills

S/he should be:

- A well-adjusted person with a positive self-image.

- A well-educated person with wide interests in the arts and an awareness of the physical world.

- Aware of and sensitive to the needs of others at all levels, regardless of cultural and social patterns.

- Committed, non-judgemental.

- Interested in and respectful of the autonomy of the child.

- Of an enquiring mind and alert to the need for further personal professional development.

- Be able to *communicate* by all possible means with colleagues, parents, other agencies and above all children, irrespective of their culture, religion or gender.

Professional skills

S/he should have:

- A sound knowledge of child development and educational theory.

- Ability to develop strategies to transmit knowledge to others.

- A deep understanding of the subjects in the early years curriculum and the value of play.

- A knowledge of and respect for cultural and social similarities and differences.

- Observational skills and ability to assess and evaluate not only the programmes they offer and the children's progress, but also themselves.

- A knowledge of the laws relating to families.

- A knowledge of policies and their underlying philosophy.
- Ability to act as an advocate for children.

Practical skills

S/he should be able to:

- Plan programmes which ensure both continuity and progression.
- Understand the point of view of others in order to manage the delivery of the programme in various settings with a range of people both professional and non-professional.
- Encourage the team of workers to adopt common strategies, which will allow the aims of the preschool to be met.
- Encourage the personal development of team members.

To summarize the adult's role I think we can do no better than quote Parry and Archer (1974, p. 139) who wrote:

> A teacher of young children obviously needs to possess certain qualities if she is to face well her responsibilities which are complex in nature and highly demanding of excellence of many kinds. She needs to be someone who is essentially human; someone who likes people, especially children, and is not only full of warmth and goodwill towards them but determined to do right by them. To achieve such ends she needs to be perceptive, sensitive, sympathetic and imaginative. She needs to be highly educated personally and professionally in those areas of knowledge, understanding and skill which she will be conveying to children, albeit indirectly at their stage of development and in those spheres of learning which are essential to her understanding of children and adults and to her skill in dealing with them.

HOW DO WE TRAIN TEACHERS?

Are we meeting the training needs of these teachers whom we expect to function in a variety of preschool settings, not just traditional nursery schools and classes?

The existing teacher training programmes preparing students to work with the three- to eight-year-old age range, if they have good selection procedures, should be able to select students with satisfactory personal/social qualities. However, once we move into the areas of professional and practical skills it does not appear that we are offering an appropriate curriculum to achieve the high level of professionalism expected.

Many of the attributes and skills listed are covered in the current syllabi in training institutions but the introduction in many places of a three-year B.Ed degree, with its emphasis upon six subjects in the primary curriculum, will make it almost impossible to devote the amount of time to the study of child development and observational skills so vital to our understanding of the growth and development of young children. Few would argue against the need to reform the initial teacher training programmes and to introduce a more rigorous regime, but current research into the way young children's thinking develops should have resulted in a greater, not a lesser study of child development. It is unbelievable that in political circles there are many who consider child development an unnecessary study for primary teachers.

Just as schools are undergoing change so are many of the early childhood establishments where young teachers are finding work. The traditional role of the teacher in her own closed domain has to be abandoned in these settings as there is much greater emphasis upon team work and co-operation. Students fortunate enough to have been trained in the institutes specializing in this age range will find it easier to cope but even then it is unlikely, with the pressures of the rest of the course, that they will have a real understanding of the needs of workers in many of the family and community centres where teachers are now employed. In these settings where the emphasis is often upon the child *and* the family, teachers need not only management and leadership skills but also the skills to work with parents and professionals from other disciplines. Such a training is not developed within the current initial training programmes.

WHAT SHOULD BE DONE?

Many early childhood educators are highly critical of the existing models of training, and there has been an attempt in recent years to institute changes. These changes seem even more necessary since the introduction of the new guidelines on the initial training of primary school teachers (DFE 14/93) which offer a 'school-based apprenticeship' with study in the subject areas of the National Curriculum.

Many would also agree that we need to create broader-based early years professionals whose training enables them to embrace the multi-disciplinary roles demanded by developments in service provision and the requirements of the Children Act 1989. So what are the options for change?

One way would be to improve and extend the existing early years initial training to broaden the knowledge base and include a variety of placements, not just in nursery and primary schools but in placements like family centres, combined centres, family support schemes and small-scale community-based provision. This would give the early years teachers the necessary knowledge, experience and competencies to be able to function effectively in any type of setting. However, in an already overcrowded initial teacher training programme this would seem impossible, particularly if the three-year B.Ed programme is adopted for those training for the four to seven age range.

A second option, with some parallels to the Scottish model of training for nursery teachers, would be to require a multi-disciplinary post-qualifying diploma in addition to initial professional training for all those working in the early years field. Such diplomas have already been pioneered successfully for many years by the Roehampton Institute. This would have the advantage of acceptability in posing the least threat to existing professional boundaries but it has two distinct disadvantages. First, it would leave a gap in the NCVQ ladder at level five which would provide a barrier to access to those emerging through the multi-disciplinary vocational route. Second, it is highly unlikely that funding would be available. On the other hand, it could be argued that if the early years teachers had only completed a three-year degree course then such a qualification should be seen as the equivalent of a PGCE.

Some institutions are attempting to tackle the necessary broad-based multi-disciplinary components at the other end of training and have developed a new type of BA (Early Years). These courses offer modules for all types of early childhood professionals. Although these multi-disciplinary degrees do not provide professional training in teaching, it is intended that when followed by a conventional PGCE it will provide graduates with qualified teacher status. Similarly, early years BA graduates could build on their studies with a Diploma in Social Work to give qualified social worker status. At the time of writing, students following this option may find it difficult to meet the TTA requirements for subject specialism. However, this option has distinct attractions because of the potential for articulation with the NVQ/SVQ system. With the resolution of issues concerned with academic equivalence and credit rating of higher level NVQs and SVQs on the not too distant horizon (HEQC, 1995) it should be feasible for those achieving the proposed multi-disciplinary NVQ/SVQ level four in Child Care and Education to be accredited for their prior learning and so gain substantial exemptions from an Early Years BA. Conversely, the taught modules of an Early Years BA might provide most of the underpinning knowledge requirements for candidates working towards their NVQ or SVQ level four in the workplace.

The Early Childhood Education Forum, which comprises representatives from the leading organizations in early childhood education and care, is constantly reviewing the issue. All members agree that collaboration and co-operation with regard to the three strands of health, care and education are essential. However, to create an entirely new profession of 'educators' would lead to a head-on confrontation with existing professional interests and inevitable protectionisms and it might mean depriving the worker of participation in a wider well-established professional body – be it of social workers or teachers or nurses – with all the advantages that flow from that.

The new group of professionals would not need the criteria for teacher status which would enable them to teach any age group, resulting in early years staff being cut off from the mainstream of education and a downward drift of salaries back to what is normally associated with child care rather than teaching. There is already a very real concern that the three-year B.Ed could result in a two-tier teaching profession, and a further change could be even more detrimental to the already poor image held by the public of early childhood workers.

CONCLUSION

Since the first edition of this book was published a number of changes have taken place which affect training to work in the early years.

- NVQs and SVQs in Child Care and Education have come on stream at Levels two and three and there is some evidence that their implementation is having a significant effect in raising standards in the workplace. However, implementation is being severely restricted through lack of resources in a field which is characterized by low pay and low qualification rates.

- Higher education and the professional bodies are starting to take NVQs/SVQs seriously and are actively engaged in their development at higher levels. The feasibility of an NVQ/SVQ level four for senior early years workers is being actively explored.

- The DFE introduced training for Specialist Teacher Assistants (STAs) to work alongside early years teachers in infant classrooms, but without any reference to the emerging NVQ/SVQ framework. These STAs will make a particular study of the teaching of English and mathematics at Key Stage 1 in order to provide more effective support to busy teachers but concerns inevitably exist that 'support' could turn to 'replace'.

- Teacher training is changing in a number of ways. New entrants now face the prospect of a shortened training with more time spent in schools, a tighter focus on the six subject areas of the National

Curriculum and even less time to learn about how young children learn or to see them in the context of their families and community.

- The anouncement of nursery vouchers means that the already bouyant demand for nursery places is bound to increase further. But there is still a distinct shortage of properly trained and qualified early years teachers and a dearth of specialist training courses in the early years age range.

We are still at a crossroads as far as training for work in the early years is concerned. Both further and higher education must meet the challenge to produce the sorts of high quality, flexible education and training opportunities in partnership with the workplace, which will equip child care and education workers at all levels with the knowledge, skills and competences they need to face ever-changing and demanding roles.

Suggestions for discussion

1. There is a tension between existing notions of what a professional is and what this implicitly implies about other types of workers. Are others by definition non-professional or even unprofessional? Is the downside of traditional professionalism exclusiveness and élitism? Can the advent of National (and Scottish) Vocational Qualifications bring a new style of professionalism to all child care and education workers?

2. This chapter raises issues about the extent to which a traditional, single-discipline based training, such as in education, is adequate to meet the demands of changing services in the child care and education field. Is it feasible to extend or adapt existing forms of traditional professional training to suit new styles of working or is a more radical solution needed? Would a multi-disciplinary approach really offer greater flexibility and transferability for a new generation of early years professionals or would they lose out through not sharing a sense of professional identity with an established group?

3. The authors write from a perspective which regards work with young children and their families as different and distinct from other types of work. This begs the question of how special are the early years anyway? Should the continuity that most are looking for run across age groups within the remit of a single professsion such as teaching (or social work or health visiting) or is it more important to have the basis in the training system of continuity across services and agencies within the early years age band?

Further reading

'Still in a muddle about early years training?' (Hevey, 1995).

'Higher level vocational qualifications – possibilities and opportunities' (Harrison, 1995).

REFERENCES

Abbott, L. and Rodger, R. (eds.) (1994) *Quality Education in the Early Years*. Buckingham: Open University Press.

Ainsworth, M., Blehar, M., Walters, E. and Wall, S. (1990) *Patterns of Attachment*, Hillsdale, New Jersey: Erlbaum.

Alderson, P. (1993) *Children's Consent to Surgery*, Milton Keynes: Open University Press.

Alexander, R. (1988) Garden or jungle? Teacher development and informal primary education, in A. Blyth (ed.) *Informal Primary Education Today*, Lewes: Falmer.

Allen, N. (1992) *Making Sense of the Children Act*, 2nd edition, Harlow: Longman.

Andersson, B. E. (1990) Intellectual and socio-emotional competence in Swedish school children related to early child care. Paper presented at the fourth European Conference on Developmental Psychology, Stirling, Scotland.

Armstrong, D. (1995) *Power and Partnership in Education*, London: Routledge.

Arnold, C. (1996) Unpublished MA thesis, Leicester University.

Association of Metropolitan Authorities (1991) *Children First*, London: AMA.

Athey, C. (1990) *Extending Thought in Young Children: A Parent–Teacher Partnership*, London: Paul Chapman.

Audit Commission (1994) *Seen but not Heard: Co-ordinating Community Child Health and Social Services for Children in Need*, London: HMSO.

Audit Commission (1996) *Counting to Five*, London: Audit Commission.

Bain, A. and Barnett, L. (1980) *The Design of a Day Care System in a Nursery*

Setting for Children Under Five, London: Tavistock Institute of Human Relations.

Ball, C. (1994) *Start Right: The Importance of Early Learning*, London: Royal Society of Arts.

Ball, M. and Stone, J. (1991) *Setting Up an Early Years Forum: a Step by Step Guide*, London: VOLCUF.

Barrett, G. (1986) *Starting School: an Evaluation of the Experience*, London: AMMA.

Barrs, M. *et al.* (1988) *ILEA: The Primary Language Record*, now available from Centre for Language in Primary Education, London.

Bartholomew, L. and Bruce, T. (1993) *Getting to Know You – a Guide to Record-Keeping in Early Childhood Education and Care*, London: Hodder & Stoughton.

BBC (1994) *Leaving Baby*, Panorama, 1st August 1994, BBC1.

Bellman, M. and Cash, J. (1987) *The Schedule of Growing Skills in Practice*, Windsor: NFER-Nelson.

Belsky, J. (1988) The 'effects' of infant day care reconsidered, *Early Childhood Research Quarterly*, Vol. 3, pp. 235–72.

Bennett, N., Desforges, C., Cockburn, A. and Wilkinson, E. (1984) *The Quality of Pupil Learning Experiences*, London: Lawrence Erlbaum.

BIC (1991) *Employers and Childcare*, Internal Note, London, March.

Birmingham Social Services (1996) *The Wraparound Project Final Report*, Birmingham City Council.

Blenkin, G. and Yue, N. (1994) Profiling early years practitioners: some first impressions from a national survey, *Early Years*, Vol. 15, no. 1, p. 13–22.

Bloom, B. S. (1964) *Stability and Change in Human Characteristics*, New York: Wiley.

Bower, T. G. R. (1977) *A Primer of Infant Development*, San Francisco: Freeman.

Bowlby, J. (1953) *Child Care and the Growth of Love*, London: Pelican.

Bradshaw, J. (1990) *Child Poverty and Deprivation in the UK*, London: National Children's Bureau.

Braun, D. (1987) *Spon Gate Mums' Group*, Coventry: Community Education Development Centre.

Braun, D. (1990) *Shared Care at Hillfields Nursery Centre*, Coventry: Community Education Development Centre.

Braun, D. (1992) Working with parent, in G. Pugh (ed.) (1992) *Contemporary Issues in the Early Years*, first edition, London: Paul Chapman.

Brown, B. (1990) *All Our Children*, London: BBC Education.

Brown, S. and Cleave, S. (1991) *Four-year-olds in School: Quality Matters*, Slough: NFER.

Browne, J. (1979) *Teachers of Teachers*, Sevenoaks: Hodder & Stoughton.

Bruce, T. (1987) *Early Childhood Education*, Sevenoaks: Hodder & Stoughton

Bruce, T. (1991) *Time to Play in Early Childhood Education*, Sevenoaks: Hodder & Stoughton.

Bull, J., Cameron, C., Candappa, M., Moss, P., Owen, C. and Statham, J. (1994) *Implementing the Children Act for Children under Eight*, London: HMSO.

Burchell, B., Mortimore, J. and Tizard, B. (1981) *Involving Parents in Nursery and Infant Schools*, Grant McIntyre.

Burgess, R. G., Hughes, C. and Moxon, S. (1991) A curriculum for the under fives?

Paper delivered at the Conference on Defining and Assessing Quality in the Education of Children from Four to Seven Years, University of Leuven, Belgium, 25–27 September.

Calder, P. (1990) The training of nursery workers: the need for a new approach, *Children & Society*, Vol. 4, no. 3, pp. 251–60.

Cameron, C. and Statham, J. (1994) Young children in rural areas: implementation of the Children Act, *Children & Society*, Vol. 8, no.1.

Cameron, R. J. and Sturge-Moore, L. (1990) *Ordinary Everyday Families: Under Fives Project*, MENCAP London Division, 115 Golden Lane, London EC1Y 0TJ.

Campbell, R. J. *et al.* (1990) *Assessing Three- to Eight-Year-Olds,* Slough: NFER.

Care Sector Consortium (1991) *National Occupational Standards for Work with Young Children and their Families*, available from National Children's Bureau, London.

Carpenter, B. (ed.) (1994) *Early Intervention: Where Are We Now*, Westminster College, Oxford.

Central Advisory Council for Education (1967) *Children and Their Primary Schools (Plowden Report)*, London: HMSO.

Children's Rights Development Unit (1994) *UK Agenda for Children*, London: CRDU.

Children's Rights Office (1995) *Building Small Democracies: the Implications of the UN Convention on the Rights of the Child for Respecting Children's Rights in the Family*, CRO.

Choices in Childcare (1995) *The 1995 Directory: Children's Information Services,* Choices in Childcare.

Clark, M. (1988) *Children under Five: Educational Research and Evidence*, London: Gordon & Breach.

Clarke-Stewart, A. (1991) Day care in the USA, in P. Moss and E. Melhuish (eds.) *Current Issues in Day Care for Young Children*, HMSO.

Cleave, S. and Brown, S. (1989) *Four Year Olds in School: Meeting their Needs*, Windsor: NFER.

Cloke and Davies (eds.) (1995) *Participation and Empowerment in Child Protection*, London: Pitman.

CNAF (1980) Consacre aux jeunes parents et la garde de leurs enfants, *Revue Informations Sociales*, 3/1980, Paris: CNAF.

Cole, M. (ed.) (1989) *Education for Equality: Some Guidelines for Good Practice*, London: Routledge.

Commission for Racial Equality (1991) *From Cradle to School: A Practical Guide to Race Equality and Child Care*, third edition, London: Commission for Racial Equality.

Committee on Child Health Services (1976) *Fit for the Future* (the Court Report) London: HMSO.

Community Education Development Centre (1993) *Parents as Co-educators*, Coventry: CEDC.

Concluding observations of the Committee on the Rights of the Child: United Kingdom of Great Britain and Northern Ireland (1995) CRC/C/15/Add.34, Geneva: United Nations.

Council on Interracial Books for Children (1980) *Ten Quick Ways to Evaluate*

Children's Books for Racism and Sexism, Council on Interracial Books for Children, 1841 Broadway, New York 10023.

Cowley, E. (1995) *Managing to Change*, London: National Children's Bureau.

Cowley, E. and Rouse Selleck, D. (1995) Play and learning, in Cowley op. cit.

Cowley, L. comp. (1991) *Young Children in Group Day Care: Guidelines for Good Practice*, London: National Children's Bureau.

Cranstoun, Y., McMahon, L. and Wood, D. (1980) *Working with Under Fives*, Grant McIntyre.

Curtis, A. (1986) *A Curriculum for the Pre-School Child: Learning to Learn*, Windsor: NFER-Nelson.

Curtis, A. (1991) *Early Childhood Explained: a Review of Provision in England and Wales*, OMEP (UK).

Dahlberg, G. and Asen, G. (1994) Evaluation and regulation: a question of empowerment, in Moss and Pence op. cit.

Daly, B. (1994) Portage and home visiting, in P. Mittler, and H. Mittler (eds.) *Innovations in Family Support for People with Learning Disabilities*, Chorley.

David, T. (1990) *Under Five – Under-educated?* Milton Keynes: Open University Press.

David, T. (ed.) (1993) *Educating Our Youngest Children: European Perspectives*, London: Paul Chapman.

Davies, A. (1995) Running assessment centres, *Coordinate*, Vol. 48, VOLCUF.

Davis, J. and Brember, I. (1991) The effects of gender and attendance period on children's adjustment to nursery classes, *British Educational Research Journal*, Vol. 17, no. 1.

Department for Education (1994) *Code of Practice on the Identification and Assessment of Special Educational Needs*, London: DFE/HMSO.

Department of Education and Employment (1995) *Key Stages 1 & 2 of the National Curriculum*, London: HMSO.

Department of Education and Science (1967) *Children and their Primary Schools* (the Plowden Report), London: HMSO.

Department of Education and Science (1972) *Education Priority Vol. 1, Problems and Policies* (The Halsey Report), London: HMSO.

Department of Education and Science (1978) *Report of the Committee of Inquiry into the Education of Handicapped Children and Young People* (the Warnock Report), London: HMSO.

Department of Education and Science (1985a) *Curriculum Matters 2*, London: HMSO.

Department of Education and Science (1985b) *Better Schools*, Cmnd 9469, London: HMSO.

Department of Education and Science (1989a) *Aspects of Primary Education: the Education of Children Under Five,* London: HMSO.

Department of Education and Science (1989b) *Assessments and Statements of Special Educational Needs: Procedures Within the Education, Health and Social Services*, Circular 22/89, London: HMSO.

Department of Education and Science (1989c) *Initial Teacher Training: Approval of Courses*, Circular 24/89, London: HMSO.

Department of Education and Science (1990a) *Starting with Quality: Report of the*

Committee of Inquiry into the Educational Experiences Offered to Three- and Four-Year-Olds (the Rumbold Report), London: HMSO.

Department of Education and Science (1990b) *Portage Projects: a Survey by HMI of Thirteen Projects Funded by Education Support Grants,* London: Department of Education and Science.

Department of Education and Science and Welsh Office (1989) *Science in the National Curriculum,* London: HMSO.

Department of Health (1989) Memorandum submitted by the Department of Health and Social Security, in House of Commons Education Select Committee, *Educational Provision for the Under Fives, Vol. II, Minutes of Evidence and Appendices,* London: HMSO.

Department of Health (1991) *The Children Act 1989 Guidance and Regulations, Volume 2: Family Support, Day Care and Educational Provision for Young Children,* London: HMSO.

Department of Health (1993) *The Children Act and Day Care for Young Children Registration* (LAC(93)1), London: Department of Health.

Department of Health and Social Security and Department of Education and Science (1976) *Co-ordination of Local Authority Services for Children Under Five* (LASSL (76)5) (S21 47 05), London: Department of Health and Social Security and Department of Education and Science.

Department of Health and Social Security and Department of Education and Science (1978) *Co-ordination of Services for Children Under Five* (LASSL (78)1) (HN(78)5), London: Department of Health and Social Security and Department of Education and Science.

Department of Trade and Industry (1994) *Competitiveness: Helping Business to Win,* Cm 2563, London: HMSO.

Derman-Sparks, D. (1989) *Anti-Bias Curriculum,* Washington DC: National Association for the Education of Young Children.

Dixon, B. (1989) *Playing them False: a Study of Children's Toys, Games and Puzzles,* Stoke-on-Trent: Trentham.

Dominelli, L. (1990) *Women and Community Action,* Birmingham: Venture Press.

Dowling, M. and Dauncey, E. (1984) *Teaching Three- to Nine-Year-Olds,* London: Ward Lock Educational.

Dowling, M. (1995) *Starting School at Four: a Joint Endeavour,* London: Paul Chapman.

Drummond, M. J. (1993) *Assessing Children's Learning,* London: David Fulton.

Drummond, M. J., Lally, M. and Pugh, G. (eds.) (1989) *Working with Children: Developing a Curriculum for the Early Years,* London: National Children's Bureau.

Drummond, M. J., Rouse, D. and Pugh, G. (1992) *Making Assessment Work: Values and Principles in Assessing Young Children's Learning,* London: NES Arnold/National Children's Bureau.

Dryfoos, J. G. (1995) *Full-Service Schools,* San Francisco, CA: Jossey Bass.

Duffy, B. and Griffin, S. (1995) *The Early Childhood Education Forum Vision Paper.*

Early Childhood Education Forum (forthcoming) *Quality in Diversity: Establishing an Agreed Framework for Early Learning in England and Wales for Children from 0-8 Years Old.*

Early Childhood Unit (1991) *Ensuring Standards in the Care of Young Children. Registering and Developing Quality Day Care* (a training pack for staff responsible for registration and inspection of childminding and day care under the Children Act 1989), London: National Children's Bureau.

Early Childhood Unit (1992) *The Future of Training in the Early Years: a Discussion Paper*, London: National Children's Bureau.

Early Years Curriculum Group (1989) *Early Childhood Education: the Early Years Curriculum and the National Curriculum*, Stoke-on-Trent: Trentham.

Early Years Curriculum Group (1992) *First Things First. Educating Young Children*, Oldham: Madeline Lindley.

Ebbeck, M. (1990) Preparing early childhood personnel to be pro-active policy working professionals, *Early Child Development and Care*, Vol. 58, pp. 87–96.

EC Childcare Network (1990) *Childcare in the European Communities 1985–1990 (Women of Europe Supplement No. 31)*, Brussels: European Commission Women's Information Service.

EC Childcare Network (1991) *Quality in Childcare Services*. Report of an EC Childcare Network Technical Seminar, Barcelona, May 1990, Brussels: European Commission Childcare Network.

EC Childcare Network (European Commission Network on Childcare and Other Measures to Reconcile Employment and Family Responsibilities) (1994) *Leave Arrangements for Workers with Children*, Brussels: European Commission Equal Opportunities Unit.

EC Childcare Network (European Commission Network on Childcare and Other Measures to Reconcile Employment and Family Responsibilites) (1995a) *Family Day Care in Europe*, Brussels: European Commission Equal Opportunities Unit.

EC Childcare Network (European Commission Network on Childcare and Other Measures to Reconcile Employment and Family Responsibilites) (1995b) *The Costs and Funding of Services for Young Children*, Brussels: European Commission Equal Opportunities Unit.

EC Childcare Network (European Commission Network on Childcare and Other Measures to Reconcile Employment and Family Responsibilities) (forthcoming) *Services for Young Children in the European Union 1990–1995*, Brussels: European Commission Equal Opportunities Unit.

Elfer, P. (ed.) (1995) *With Equal Concern . . .* Training materials to ensure day care and educational provision for young children takes positive account of the 'religious persuasion, racial origin and cultural and linguistic background of each child' (Children Act 1989), London: National Children's Bureau.

Elfer, P. (in press) Facilitating intimacy between young children and adults, *Early Years*.

Elfer, P. and Beasley, G. (1991) *Registration of Childminding and Day Care: Using the Law to Raise Standards*, London: HMSO.

Elfer, P. and McQuail, S. (1995) *Local Wishes and Expectations*, London: National Children's Bureau.

Elfer, P. and Selleck, D. (forthcoming) *Meeting the Learning Needs of Very Young Children in Early Childhood Centres,* London: National Children's Bureau.

Epstein, D. and Sealey, A. (1990) *Where it Really Matters*, Birmingham:

Development Education Centre.

Equal Opportunities Commission (1990) *The Key to Real Choice*, Manchester: Equal Opportunities Commission.

Etzioni, A. (1995) *The Spirit of Community*, London: Fontana.

European Commission (1988) *Childcare and Equality of Opportunity*, Brussels: European Commission.

European Commission (1990) *Childcare in the European Communities 1985-1990*, Brussels: European Commission.

Farquhar, S. E. (1990) Quality in early education and care: what do we mean?, *Early Child Development and Care*, Vol. 64, pp. 71-83.

Faulkner, D., Miell, D., Oates, J., Robinson, A., Sheldon, M. and Walsh, M. (1991) *Working with Under Fives*, Milton Keynes: Open University Press.

Fish, D. (1989) *Learning Through Practice in Initial Teacher Training*, London: Kogan Page.

Garner, P. and Sandow, S. (eds.) (1995) *Advocacy, Self-Advocacy and Special Needs*, London: David Fulton.

Gascoigne, E. (1995) *Working with Parents as Partners in SEN*, London: David Fulton.

Gillick v. West Norfolk and Wisbech AHA (1986) AC112.

Goldschmied, E. (1987) *Infants at Work*. (training video) Available from the Early Childhood Unit, National Children's Bureau.

Goldschmied, E. (1991) What to do with the under twos. Heuristic play. Infants learning, in Rouse (1991a) op. cit.

Goldschmied, E. and Hughes, A. (1994) *Heuristic Play with Objects* (training video), London: National Children's Bureau.

Goldschmied, E. and Jackson, S. (1994) *People Under Three*, London: Routledge.

Goldschmied, E. and Selleck, D. (1996) *Communication between Babies in their First Year* (video and training guide), London: National Children's Bureau.

Halsey Report (1972) *Education Priority Vol. 1, Problems and Policies*, London: DES.

Hanney, M. (1991) *Under Fives in Wales: a New Look at Service Provision*, Cardiff: National Children's Bureau.

Hanney, M. (1993) *Rural Child Care*, Highlight 124, London: National Children's Bureau.

Hannon, P., Weinberger, J. and Nutbrown, C. (1990) Ways of working with parents to promote early literacy development, *USDE Papers in Education*, 14, University of Sheffield Division of Education.

Hannon, P., Weinberger, J. and Nutbrown, C. (1991) A study of work with parents to promote early literacy development, *Research Papers in Education*, Vol. 6, no. 2, pp. 77–97.

Harrison, M. (1995) Higher level vocational qualifications – possibilities and opportunities, *Competence & Assessment*, Vol. 29, pp. 39–41.

Hart, R. (1992) *Children's Participation: from Tokenism to Citizenship*, Innocenti essays, Florence: UNICEF.

Health Advisory Service (1995) *Child and Adolescent Mental Healh Services – Together We Stand: the Commissioning, Role and Management of Child and Adolescent Mental Health Services*, London: HMSO.

Henderson and Berla (eds.) (1981) *The Evidence Grows*, USA: National Council for Citizens in Education.

Henderson and Berla (eds.) (1987) *The Evidence Continues to Grow*, USA: National Council for Citizens in Education.

Henderson and Berla (eds.) (1994) *A New Generation of Evidence*, USA: National Council for Citizens in Education.

Her Majesty's Inspectorate of Schools (1989) *The Education of Children Under Five*, London: HMSO.

Hevey, D. (1986) *The Continuing Under Fives Training Muddle*, London: VOLCUF.

Hevey, D. (1991a) *Final Report of the Working with Under Sevens Project*, presented to the Care Sector Consortium, National Children's Bureau.

Hevey, D. (1991b) Not child's play: developing occupational standards for workers with under sevens and their families, *Competence & Assessment*, Vol.15, pp. 11–14.

Hevey, D. (1994) NVQs at the leading edge, *Nursing Standard*, Vol. 8, p. 3.

Hevey, D. (1995) Still in a muddle about early years training?, *Coordinate*, Vol. 48, pp. 8–11.

Hevey, D. and Windle, K. (1990) Unpublished Report of Working with Under Sevens Project Occupational Mapping Survey.

Hewitt, S. (ed.) (1971) *The Training of Teachers*, London: ULP.

Higher Education Quality Council (1995) *Choosing to Change: Extending Access, Choice and Mobility in Higher Education* (the Robertson Report) Higher Education Quality Council.

High/Scope (1986) *Introduction to the High/Scope Preschool Curriculum: a Two-Day Workshop*, Ypsilanti, Michigan: High Scope Educational Research Foundation.

HMSO (1972) *Teacher Education and Teacher Training: a Report of a Committee of Enquiry under the Chairmanship of Lord James of Rusholme* (the James Report), London: HMSO.

HMSO (1976) Race Relations Act.

HMSO (1988) Education Reform Act.

HMSO (1989) The Children Act.

Holtermann, S. (1992) *Investing in Young Children: Costing an Education and Day Care Service*, London: National Children's Bureau.

Holtermann, S. (1995) *Investing in Young Children: Reassessing the Cost of an Education and Day Care Service*, London: National Children's Bureau.

Hopkins, D. (1985) *A Teacher's Guide to Classroom Research*, Buckingham: Open University Press.

Hopkins, J. (1988) Facilitating the development of intimacy between nurses and infants in day nurseries, *Early Childhood Development and Care*, Vol. 33, pp. 99–111.

Hornby, G. (1995) *Working with Parents of Children with Special Needs*, London: Cassell.

House of Commons (1987) *Special Educational Needs: Implementation of the Education Act 1981*, Education Science and Arts Committee, London: HMSO.

House of Commons (1989) *Educational Provision for the Under Fives*. First Report of the Education, Science and Arts Committee, session 1988–9, London: HMSO.

House of Commons Education Committee (1994) *Educational Provision for the*

Under Fives, London: HMSO.

Howes, C., Whitebook, M. and Phillips (1990) *Who Cares? Child Care Teachers and the Quality of Care in America*, executive summary of the National Child Care Staffing Study, Gordon & Breach.

Hurst, V. (1991) *Planning for Early Learning: Education in the First Five Years*, London: Paul Chapman.

Hutt, C. (1979) *Play in the Under Fives: Form, Development and Function*, New York: Brunner/Mazel.

Hutt, S.J., Tyler, S., Hutt, C. and Christopherson, H. (1989) *Play, Exploration and Learning*, London: Routledge.

Isaacs, S. (1930) *Intellectual Growth in Young Children*, London: Routledge & Kegan Paul.

Jeffs, T. (1995) Children's educational rights in a new ERA, in B. Franklin (ed.) *Handbook of Children's Rights: Comparative Policy and Practice*, London: Routledge.

Jessup, G. (1991) *Outcomes: NVQs and the Emerging Model of Education and Training*, Lewes: Falmer.

Jensen, J. (1993) Age integrated centres in Denmark, in EC Childcare Network *Annual Report 1992*, Brussels: European Commission Equal Opportunities Unit.

Jones, A. and Bilton, K. (1994) *The Future Shape of Children's Services*, London: National Children's Bureau.

Jordan, B. (1987) *Creative Social Work with Families*, Birmingham: BASW Publications.

Katz, L. (1987) *Burnout by Five*, Quoted in *The Times Educational Supplement*, 18 September 1987.

Kids Club Network (1989) *Guidelines of Good Practice for Out of School Care Schemes*, London: National Out of School Alliance (Now Kids Club Network).

Kirkwood, A. (1993) *The Leicestershire Inquiry*, Leicestershire County Council.

Korner, A. (1989) Infant stimulation: the pros and cons in historical perspective, *Zero to Three*, Vol. X, no. 2, pp. 11-17.

Kurtz, Z. and Woodruffe, C. (1989) *Working for Children? Children's Services and the NHS Review*, London: National Children's Bureau.

LAC, Department of Health (1993) *The Children Act and Day Care for Young Children Registration* (LAC [93] 1), London: DOH.

Labour Party (1994) *The Way Forward*, London.

Lally, M. (1991) *The Nursery Teacher in Action*, London: Paul Chapman.

Lane, J. (1990) Sticks and carrots: using the Race Relations Act to remove bad practice and the Children Act to promote good practice, *Local Government Policy Making*, Vol. 17, p. 3.

Lansdown, G. (1995) *Taking Part: the Case for Children's Participation*, IPPR.

Leach, P. (1994) *Children First*, Harmondsworth: Penguin.

Leadbetter, J. and Leadbetter, P. (1993) *Special Children: Meeting the Challenge in the Primary School*, London: Cassell.

Le Vine, R. A. (1989) Cultural environments in child development, in W. Damon (ed.) *Child Development Today and Tomorrow*, San Francisco: Jossey-Bass.

Levy, A. and Kahan, B. (1991) *The Pindown Experience and the Protection of*

Children: The Report of the Staffordshire Child Care Inquiry, Staffordshire County Council.

Lieberman, A. (1991) Attachment and exploration: the toddler's dilemma, *Zero to Three*, Vol. Xl, no. 3, pp. 6–10.

Lindon, J. (1996) *Growing Up: From Eight Years To Young Adulthood*, London: National Children's Bureau.

Local Goverment Management Board (1995) Unpublished draft survey of *Non-Teaching Staff in Primary and Nursery Schools*, Local Goverment Management Board.

Lubeck, S. (1986) *Sandbox Society*, Lewes: Falmer.

Maximé, J. (1986) Some psychological models of black self-concept, in S. Ahmed, J. Cheetham, and J. Small (eds.) *Social Work with Black Children and their Families*, London: Batsford.

Mayall, B. (1986) *Keeping Children Healthy*, London: Allen & Unwin.

McLean, S. V. (1991) *The Human Encounter*, Lewes: Falmer.

McQuail, S. and Pugh, G. (1995) *The Effective Organisation of Early Childhood Services*, London: National Children's Bureau.

Meadows, S. and Cashdan, A. (1988) *Helping Children Learn: Contributions to a Cognitive Curriculum*, London: David Fulton.

Melhuish, E. (1991) Research issues in day care, in P. Moss and E. Melhuish op. cit.

Melhuish, E. and Moss, P. (eds.) (1990) *Day Care for Young Children: International Perspectives*, London: Routledge.

Meltzer, H. (1994) *OPCS Survey of Day Care Services for Children*, London: Department of Health.

Menter, I. (1989) They're too young to notice: young children and racism, in G. Barrett (ed.) *Disaffection from School: the Early Years*, Lewes: Falmer.

Messenger, K. and Curtis, C. (eds.) (1991) *NVQ: the Workplace Revolution*, Luton: Local Government Management Board.

Midwinter, E. C. (1972) *Priority Education*, Harmondsworth: Penguin.

Milner, D. (1983) *Children and Race: Ten Years On*, London: Ward Lock Educational.

Möller, E. (1995) Information collected in Sweden on leave and child care services. Paper given at an EC Childcare Network seminar on 'Reconciling employment and caring for children: what information is needed for an effective policy', Brussels, October 13–14.

Moore, M. K. (1975) Object permanence and object identity. Paper presented at the conference of the Society for Research in Child Development, Denver, Colorado.

Moss, P. (1990) Work, family and the care of children: issues of equality and responsibility, *Children & Society*, Vol. 4, no. 2, pp. 145–66.

Moss, P. and Melhuish, E. (eds.) (1991) *Current Issues in Day Care for Young Children*, London: HMSO.

Moss, P., Owen, C., Statham, J., Bull, J. and Cameron, C. (1995) *Survey of Day Care Providers in England and Wales*, Thomas Coram Research Unit.

Moss, P. and Pence, A. (eds.) (1994) *Valuing Quality in Early Childhood Services. New Approaches to Defining Quality*, London: Paul Chapman.

Moss, P. and Penn, H. (1996) *Transforming Nursery Education*, London: Paul Chapman.

Moyles, J. (1989) *Just Playing? The Role and Status of Play in Early Childhood Education*, Milton Keynes: Open University Press.

National Advisory Council for Education and Training Targets (1995) *Report on Progress Towards the National Targets*, NACETT.

National Childminding Association (1991) *Setting the Standards*, National Childminding Association.

National Children's Bureau: Under Fives Unit (1990) *A Policy for Young Children: A Framework for Action*, London: National Children's Bureau.

National Children's Bureau: Early Childhood Unit (1991) *Ensuring Standards in the Care of Young Children, Registering and Developing Quality Day Care*, London: National Children's Bureau.

National Commission on Education (1993) *Learning to Succeed*, Heinemann.

National Commission on Education (1994) *The family is crirical to student attainment*.

National Consumer Council (1991) *Day Care Services for Under Fives: A Consumer View*, London: National Consumer Council.

National Council for Vocational Qualifications (1988) *Assessment in National Vocational Qualifications*, NCVQ Information Note No. 4, London: NCVQ.

National Council for Vocational Qualifications (1989) *The NVQ Criteria and Related Guidance*, London: NCVQ.

National Council for Vocational Qualifications (1994) *Annual Report*, London: NCVQ.

National Council for Vocational Qualifications (1995a) *NCVQ Monitor*, Spring issue, London: NCVQ.

National Council for Vocational Qualifications (1995b) *GNVQ Briefing: Information on the Form, Development and Implementation of GNVQs*, London: NCVQ.

National Curriculum Council (1989) *Special Educational Needs in the National Curriculum*, Curriculum Guidance 2, York: NCC.

National Early Years Network/Save the Children Fund (1995) *An Equal Future*, London.

National Foundation for Educational Research/Schools Curriculum Development Committee (1987) *Four-Year-Olds in School: Policy and Practice*, Windsor: NFER.

National Nursery Examination Board (1990) *The Diploma in Nursery Nursing*, NNEB.

Newell, P. (1991) *The UN Convention and Children's Rights in the UK*, London: National Children's Bureau.

Norwich, B. (1990) *Reappraising Special Needs Education*, London: Cassell.

Nutbrown, C. (1991) *Early Literacy Development and Work with Parents: Putting the Theory into Practice*, OMEP (UK).

Nutbrown, C. (1994) *Threads of Thinking – Young Children Learning and the Role of Early Education*, London: Paul Chapman.

OFSTED (1993a) *First Class: the Standards and Quality of Education in Reception Classes*, London: HMSO.

OFSTED (1993b) *Framework for Inspection*, London: HMSO.

Open University (forthcoming) *OU Course K504: Parents and Under Eights*, Health and Social Welfare Department, Open University, Milton Keynes.

Osborn, A. and Milbank, J. (1987) *The Effects of Early Education*, Oxford: Clarendon Press.

Pantin, G. (1979) *A Mole Cricket called Servol*, Pergamon & Vanheer.

Papousek, H. (1969) Individual variability in learned responses in human infants, in R. J. Robinson (ed.) *Brain and Early Behaviour*, London: Academic Press.

Parry, M. and Archer, H. (1974) *Pre-School Education*, London: Schools Council/Macmillan Educational.

Pascal, C. (1990) *Under Fives in Infant Classrooms*, Stoke-on-Trent: Trentham.

Piaget, J. (1951) *Play, Dreams and Imitation*, London: Routledge & Kegan Paul.

Preschool Learning Alliance (1995) *Numbers of Preschools and Numbers of Children*, factsheet, PLA.

Preschool Playgroups Association (1990a) *PPA Guidelines: Good Practice for Sessional Playgroups*, PPA.

Preschool Playgroups Association (1990b) *PPA Guidelines. Good Practice for Full Day Care Playgroups*, PPA.

Pringle, M. K. (1975) *The Needs of Children*, London: Hutchinson.

Prizant, B. and Wetherby, A. (1990) Assessing the communication of infants and toddlers: integrating a socio-emotional perspective, *Zero to Three*, Vol. Xl, no. 1, pp. 1–12.

Prosser, M. (1991) 'What makes me ME?' – children attempting to compile a model for self-assessment. Unpublished MA assignment, Cambridge Institute of Education.

Pugh, G. (1987) Early education and day care: in search of a policy, *Journal of Education Policy*, Vol. 2, no. 4, pp. 301–16.

Pugh, G. (1988) *Services for Under Fives: Developing a Co-ordinated Approach*, London: National Children's Bureau.

Pugh, G. (1989) Parents and professionals in preschool services: is partnership possible? in S. Wolfendale, (ed.) *Parental Involvement. Developing Networks between School, Home and Community*, London: Cassell.

Pugh, G. (1990) Developing a policy for early childhood education: challenges and constraints, *Early Child Development and Care*, Vol. 58, pp. 3–13.

Pugh, G. (1992) *An Equal Start for all our Children?* TES/Greenwich Lecture.

Pugh, G. and De'Ath, E. (1989) *Working Towards Partnership in the Early Years*, London: National Children's Bureau.

Pugh, G., Aplin, G,. De'Ath, E. and Moxon, M. (1987) *Partnership in Action: Working with Parents in Preschool Centres*, Vols. 1 and 2, London: National Children's Bureau.

Pugh, G. and McQuail, S. (1995) *The Effective Organization of Early Childhood Services: Summary and Strategic Framework*, London: National Children's Bureau.

Pugh, G. and Selleck, D. (1996) 'Listening to and communicating with young children' in Davie, R., Upton, G. and Varma, V. (eds.) *The Voice of the Child*, London, Falmer Press.

Randall, J. (1995) NVQs in higher education: a possible model, *Competence and*

Assessment, Vol. 29, pp. 10–15, Sheffield: Employment Department.

Rieser, R. and Mason, M. (1990) *Disability, Equality in the Classroom: a Human Rights Issue*, Inner London Education Authority.

Roaf, C. and Bines, H. (eds.) (1989) *Needs, Rights and Opportunities*, Lewes: Falmer.

Roberts, R. (1995) *Self-Esteem and Successful Early Learning*, London: Hodder & Stoughton.

Rodd, G. (1994) *Leadership in Early Childhood*, Milton Keynes: Open University Press.

Ross, D. (1990) *Costs of Implementing National Vocational Qualifications*, papers 1, 2 and 3, CCETSW/Local Government Training Board in conjunction with the ADSS North West Regional Training Unit.

Rouse, D. (ed.) (1991a) *Babies and Toddlers: Carers and Educators. Quality for Under Threes*, London: National Children's Bureau.

Rouse, D. (1991b) *An Italian Experience*. Unpublished. Available for reference at the Early Childhood Unit, National Children's Bureau.

Rouse Selleck, D. (1995) Play and learning, in Cowley op. cit.

Ruddick, S. (1989) *Maternal Thinking Towards a Politics of Peace*, New York: Ballantine.

SCAA (1995) *Preschool Education Consultation. Desirable Outcomes for Children's Learning and Guidance for Providers*, Draft Proposals, London: School Curriculum and Assessment Authority.

SCAA (1996) *Nursery Education: Desirable Outcomes for Children's Learning on Entering Compulsory Education,* London: School Curriculum and Assessment Authority.

Schaffer, H. and Emerson, P. (1964) The development of social attachments in infancy, *Child Development*, Vol. 29, p. 94.

Schools Council (1981) *The Practical Curriculum*, London: Schools Council.

Scott, G. (1989) *Families and Under Fives in Strathclyde*, Glasgow College and Strathclyde Regional Council.

SEAC (1990) *Records of Achievement in Primary Schools*.

Secretary of State for Education (1994) John Patten, address to North of England Conference, Chester, January 1994.

Sheffield LEA (1986) *Nursery Education Guidelines for Curriculum, Organization, Assessment*, City of Sheffield Education Department.

Sheffield LEA (1991a) *Observation, Record Keeping and Classroom Management.* Course materials, City of Sheffield Education Department.

Sheffield LEA (1991b) *Record-Keeping for Children Under Five in all Settings*, City of Sheffield Education Department.

Shorrocks, D. (1992) Evaluating Key Stage 1 assessments: the testing time of May 1991, *Early Years*, Vol. 13, no. 1, p. 16–20.

Siraj-Blatchford, I. (1990) A positive role, *Child Education*, November.

Siraj-Blatchford, I. (1994) *The Early Years: Laying the Foundations for Racial Equality*, Stoke-on-Trent: Trentham.

Siraj-Blatchford, J. and I. (eds.) (1995) *Educating the Whole Child: Cross-Curricular Skills, Themes and Dimension,* Buckingham: Open University Press.

Siraj-Blatchford, I. (1996) Challenging inequality and promoting respect, in C. Nutbrown, *Respectful Educators – Capable Learners*, London: Paul Chapman.

Smail, D. (1984) *Taking Care: an Alternative to Therapy*, London: Dent.

Smith, E. and Bennett, N. (1995) Play away, *Child Education*, Vol. 73, no. 3, p. 64–5.

Smith, P. K. (ed.) (1986) *Children's Play: Research, Development and Practical Applications*, New York: Gordon & Breach.

Stacey, M. (1991) *Parents and Teachers Together*, Milton Keynes: Open University Press.

Statham, J. (1991) *Under Fives in Sunderland: A Survey of Parents' Views of Preschool Provision*, London: National Children's Bureau.

Statham, J., Lloyd, E, and Moss, P. (1989) *Playgroups in Three Countries*. TCRU Working and Occasional Paper No. 8, London: Thomas Coram Research Unit.

Statham, J., Lloyd, E., Moss, P., Melhuish, E. and Owen, C. (1990) *Playgroups in a Changing World*, London: HMSO.

Stewart, J. and Walsh, K. (1989) *The Search for Quality*, Luton: Local Government Training Board.

Stroh, K. and Robinson, T. (1991) Developmental delay in young children, *Child Language Teaching and Therapy*, Vol. 7, no. 1, p. 7.

Sylva, K. (1994) The impact of early learning on children's later development, in C. Ball, *Start Right: The Importance of Early Learning*, London: Royal Society of Arts.

Sylva, K., Campbell, R. J., Coates, E., David, T., Fitzgerald, J., Goodyear, R., Jowett, M., Lewis, A. and Neil, S. St. J. (1990) *Assessing Three- to Eight-Year-Olds*, Windsor: NFER.

Sylva, K. and David, T. (1990) 'Quality' education in preschool provision, *Local Government Policy Making*, Vol. 17, no. 3, pp. 61–7.

Sylva, K. and Lunt, I. (1982) *Child Development: A First Course*, Oxford: Blackwell.

Sylva, K., Roy, C. and Painter, M. (1980) *Childwatching at Playgroup and Nursery School*, London: Grant McIntyre.

Sylva, K., Siraj-Blatchford, I. and Johnson, S. (1992) The effects of the National Curriculum on the pre-school, *International Journal of Early Childhood*, Vol. 24, no. 1. p. 41–51.

Thoburn, J. (1986) Quality control in child care, *British Journal of Social Work*, Vol. 16, no. 5, pp. 543–56.

Tizard, B. and Hughes, M. (1984) *Young Children Learning*, London: Fontana.

Tobin, J., Wu, D. and Davidson, D. (1989) *Preschool in Three Cultures: Japan, China and the United States*, Yale University Press.

Tomlinson, J. (1986) The co-ordinator of services for under fives, *TACTYC*, Vol. 7, no. 1, Autumn.

Tomlinson, J. (1991) Attitudes to children: are children valued?, *Early Years*, Vol. 11, no. 2.

Townsend, T. (1994) *Effective Schooling for the Community*, London: Routledge.

Trevarthen, C. (1992) An infant's motives for speaking and thinking in the culture, in A. H. Wold (ed.) *The Dialogical Alternative*, Oxford University Press.

Under Fives Unit (1990) *A Policy for Young Children: A Framework for Action*, London: National Children's Bureau.

Unicef (1989) *The Draft Convention on the Rights of the Child*.

Unicef-UK (1990) Convention on the Rights of the Child, 55 Lincoln's Inn Fields, London WC2 3NB.

United Nations (1995) *Concluding Observations of the Committee on the Rights of the Child: United Kingdom of Great Britain and Northern Ireland,* CRC/C15/Ad 34, Geneva.

Vernon, J. and Smith, C. (1994) *Day Nurseries at the Crossroads. Meeting the Challenge of Childcare in the 90s,* London: National Children's Bureau.

VOLCUF (1994) TECs and early years workers: getting help for NVQs, *Coordinate,* Vol. 39, VOLCUF.

Vygotsky, L. S. (1978) *Mind in Society: the Development of Higher Level Psychological Processes,* Harvard University Press.

Walker, R. (1985) *Doing Research,* London: Methuen.

Ward, E. (1986) Sound policies promote effective programmes for young children, in *Children are Worth the Effort: Today, Tomorrow and Beyond: a Memorial to Evangeline Ward 1920-85,* Canberra: Australian Early Childhood Association.

Watt, J. (1990) *Early Education: The Current Debate,* Edinburgh: Scottish Academic Press.

Watts, B. N. (1987) Changing families: changing children's services, *Australian Journal of Early Childhood Education,* Vol. 12, no. 3, pp. 4–12.

Webster, B. (1990) Reviewing services for under fives and their families in Gloucestershire, *Local Government Policy Making,* Vol. 17, no. 3.

Wedge, D. (1991) Building a consortium, in Messenger and Curtis op. cit.

Weinberger, J., Hannon, P. and Nutbrown, C. (1990) *Ways of Working with Parents to Promote Early Literacy Development.* USDE Papers in Education no. 14, University of Sheffield Division of Education.

Wells, G. (1985) *Language Development in the Preschool Years,* Cambridge University Press.

Whitebrook, M., Howes, C. and Phillips (1990) *Who Cares? Child Care Teachers and the Quality of Care in America.* Executive Summary of the National Child Care Staffing Study, Berkley, Child Care Employee Project.

Widlake, P. and McLeod, F. (1984) *Raising Standards,* Coventry: Community Education Development Centre.

Williams, P. (1995) *Making Sense of Quality: a Review of Approaches to Quality in Early Childhood Services,* London: Early Childhood Unit, National Children's Bureau.

Wolfendale, S. (1983) *Parental Participation in Children's Development and Education,* London: Gordon & Breach.

Wolfendale S. (1990) *All About Me,* Nottingham: NES Arnold.

Wolfendale, S. (1993a) Thirty years of change: children with special educational needs, in G. Pugh (ed.) *Thirty Years of Change for Children,* London: National Children's Bureau.

Wolfendale, S. (1993b) Involving parents in assessment, in S. Wolfendale (ed.) *Assessing Special Educational Needs,* London: Cassell.

Wolfendale S. (1993c) *Baseline Assessment, A Review of Current Practice, Issues and Strategies for Effective Implementation.* OMEP (UK)/Trentham.

Wolfendale, S. (1994) Policy and provision for children with special educational needs, in S. Riddell and S. Brown (eds.) *Special Educational Needs Policy in the 1990s –Warnock in the Market Place,* London: Routledge.

Wood, D., McMahon, L. and Cranstoun, Y. (1980) *Working with Under Fives,*

London: Grant McIntyre.

Woodhead, M. (1976) *Intervening in Disadvantage*, Windsor: NFER–Nelson.

Woodhead, M. (1985) Pre-school education has long-term effects: but can they be generalized?, *Oxford Review Education*, Vol. 11, no. 2, pp. 133–55.

Woodhead, M. (1991) Psychology and the cultural construction of children's needs, in M. Woodhead, M. Light and R. Carr (eds.) *Growing up in a Changing Society*, London: Routledge.

Working Group Against Racism in Children's Resources (1990) *Guidelines: For the Evaluation and Selection of Toys and Other Resources for Children*, Working Group Against Racism in Children's Resources, 460 Wandsworth Road, London SW8 3LX.

Zigler, E. F. (1987) Formal schooling for four-year-olds? No, *American Psychologist*, Vol. 42, no. 3, pp. 254–60.

AUTHOR INDEX

SUBJECT INDEX

(Entries marked * – further references can be found in the Author Index.)